COLLINS POCKET REFERENCE

QUOTATIONS

HarperCollins*Publishers*

HarperCollins Publishers
P.O. Box, Glasgow G4 0NB

First published 1995

Reprint 10 9 8 7 6 5 4 3 2 1 0

ISBN 0 00 765937 7

A catalogue record for this book is available
from the British Library

Printed in Germany by Elsnerdruck, Berlin

INTRODUCTION

Books of quotations answer two basic questions: 'Who said what?' and 'What was said by whom?' The uses to which they are put are many and various: readers', writers' and speakers' companion, crossword-solving aid, memory jogger, a diverting browse.

A pocket book of quotations must serve the same purpose as a comprehensive volume, however reduced. It should contain the quotations most people would reasonably expect to find (tranches of the Bible, Shakespeare, Johnson, Wilde, plus the famous one-offs – power corrupts, let them eat cake, etc.) with a sprinkling of not so well known and even fairly recent topical phrases.

For reasons of space, the following have been excluded: songs, hymns, nursery rhymes, ballads, proverbs, liturgies – with some exceptions.

Each generation has its head stuffed with different allusions to, memories of, history, politics, morality, literature, art, music, etc., but I hope the range of quotations selected is wide enough for most ages; that there will be recognition of old favourites and appreciation of the unfamiliar (as I found myself in the compiling); that, in short, the collection will be entertaining and useful.

Samuel Johnson claimed that the quotations in his *Dictionary* contributed 'to the stability or enlargement of the language.' Our daily discourse is certainly enriched, enlivened or enhanced by these 'disiecta membra', the gobbets of wit and wisdom, of the great and the good and the not so great and good of the last two-and-a-half thousand years. Quotations reinforce – and decorate. They may be detached feathers, but nobody minds you sticking them in your own cap. Someone has always said what you want to say so much better.

Thanks to Alan Durndell, Joe Fisher, Roddy Forsyth, Lorraine Harvey, Kevin McCarra, Leslie Verth, Mike Watson MP, Christina Whyte and Winifred Whyte for their assistance.

Hamish Whyte

HOW TO USE THIS BOOK

The quotations are arranged by authorship, in alphabetical order, with a brief biography for each author. Quotations from each author are numbered for purposes of the Index, as explained below. Information on the sources appears in square brackets after each quotation. Book and play titles are in italics; essays and poems in plain type within single quotes. If known, the date of publication is given. Prose sources may also give a volume (Roman numerals) and/or chapter number (Arabic) or title; a play will have act and scene numbers where known. 'Ib' (ibid) indicates that the quotation comes from the same source as the previous one.

The Index gives key words with an alphabetical listing of the quotations in which that word appears, the authorship and the number of the quotation under that author. In this way there is no need for page numbers, yet each quotation can be found quickly and easily.

Acton, First Baron (1834–1902)
English historian and moralist

1. Power tends to corrupt, and absolute power corrupts absolutely. Great men are almost always bad men ... There is no worse heresy than that the office sanctifies the holder of it. [Letter to Bishop Mandell Creighton, 1887]

Addison, Joseph (1672–1719)
English essayist, poet, playwright and statesman

1. A reader seldom peruses a book with pleasure until he knows whether the writer of it be a black man or a fair man, of a mild or choleric disposition, married or a bachelor. [*The Spectator*, March 1711, 1]

2. Thus I live in the world rather as a spectator of mankind, than as one of the species, by which means I have made myself a speculative statesman, soldier, merchant, and artisan, without ever meddling with any practical part in life. [Ib.]

3. Sir Roger told them, with the air of a man who would not give his judgement rashly, that much might be said on both sides. [*The Spectator*, July 1711, 122]

4. 'We are always doing,' says he, 'something for Posterity, but I would fain see Posterity do something for us. [*The Spectator*, August 1714, 583]

Aeschylus (525–456 BC)
Greek dramatist and poet

1. Zeus who leads mortals on the road to understanding, Zeus who has ordained that wisdom comes through suffering. [*Agamemnon*, 176]

Aesop (6th century BC)
Greek fabulist

1. The gods help those who help themselves. [*Fables*, 'Hercules and the Waggoner']

2. Don't count your chickens before they are hatched. [*Fables*, 'The Milkmaid and her Pail']

3. The boy cried 'Wolf, wolf!' and the villagers came out to help him. [*Fables*, 'The Shepherd Boy and the Wolf']

4. The lamb that belonged to the sheep whose skin the wolf was wearing began to follow the wolf in the sheep's clothing. [*Fables*, 'The Wolf in Sheep's Clothing']

Agate, James (1877–1947)
English dramatic critic and novelist

1. The English instinctively admire any man who has no talent and is modest about it. [Attr.]

Akins, Zoë (1886–1958)
American poet, dramatist and screenwriter

1. The Greeks Had a Word for It. [Title of play, 1930]

Alcott, Louisa May (1832–1888)
American writer and children's novelist

1. Housekeeping ain't no joke. [*Little Women*, Part I (1868)]

Alexander, Sir William, Earl of Stirling (c. 1567–1640)
Scottish poet, courtier and statesman

1. The weaker sex, to piety more prone. [*Doomsday* (1614), Hour V]

Ali, Muhamad (1942–)
American heavyweight boxer

1. Float like a butterfly, sting like a bee. [Catch phrase]

Allen, Woody (Allen Stewart Konigsberg) (1935–)
American film director, writer, actor and comedian

1. It's not that I'm afraid to die. I just don't want to be there when it happens. [*Without Feathers* (1976), 'Death (A Play)']

Ambrose, Saint (c. 340–397)
French-born Bishop of Milan, writer of music and hymns

1. *Si fueris Romae, Romano vivito more;*
Si fueris alibi, vivito sicut ibi.
If you are in Rome, live in the Roman fashion; if you are elsewhere, live as they do there. [In Jeremy Taylor, *Ductor Dubitantium* (1660)]

Andersen, Hans Christian (1805–1875)
Danish novelist, dramatist and children's writer

1. The Ugly Duckling. [Story title (c. 1843)]

2. 'But the Emperor has nothing on at all! ' cried a little child. [*The Emperor's New Clothes* (c. 1843)]

Anonymous

1. Can't act, can't sing, slightly bald. Can dance a little. [Comment by a Hollywood executive on Fred Astaire's first screen test]

2. If anything can go wrong, it will. ['Murphy's Law', probably dating from the US in the 1940s. A Captain E. Murphy of the California Northrop aviation firm may have formulated it]

3. They'll be dancing in the streets of Raith tonight. [Falsely attributed to both Kenneth Wollstenholme and David Coleman, this reference to Raith Rovers fans dancing in a non-existent Scottish town – the team plays in Kirkcaldy – almost certainly originated in a BBC radio broadcast from London in 1963, after Raith Rovers defeated Aberdeen in a Scottish Cup tie]

Arabian Nights
Collection of stories written in Arabic

1. Who will change old lamps for new ones? ... New lamps for old ones? [*The History of Aladdin*]

2. Open Sesame! [*The History of Ali Baba*]

Archimedes (c. 287–212 BC)
Greek mathematician, of Syracuse; physicist and inventor

1. *Eureka!*
   I've got it! [In Vitruvius Pollio, *De Architectura*]

Arendt, Hannah (1906–1975)
German-born American political theorist

1. [Of Eichmann]
   It was as though in those last minutes he was summing up the lessons that this long course in human wickedness had taught us – the lesson

of the fearsome, word-and-thought-defying banality of evil. [*Eichmann in Jerusalem: A Report on the Banality of Evil* (1963)]

Argenson, Marquis d' (1694–1757)
French politician and essayist

1. *Laisser-faire.*
No interference. [*Mémoires* (published posthumously)]

Ariosto, Ludovico (1474–1533)
Italian epic poet and comic dramatist

1. *Natura il fece, e poi roppe la stampa.*
Nature first made him, and then smashed the mould. [*Orlando furioso* (1516), X]

Aristophanes (c. 445–385 BC)
Greek comic dramatist and satirist

1. What do you think of 'Cloudcuckooland'? [*Birds*, 819]

2. Old age is a second childhood. [*Clouds*, 1417]

Aristotle (384–322 BC)
Greek philosopher; pupil of Plato and tutor of Alexander the Great

1. The whole is more than the sum of the parts. [*Metaphysics*]

2. One swallow does not make a summer, neither does one fine day; similarly one day or brief time of happiness does not make a person entirely happy. [*Nicomachean Ethics*, I]

3. What we have to learn to do, we learn by doing. [Ib.]

4. Man is by nature a political animal. [*Politics*, I]

5. Tragedy, then, is the imitation of an action that is serious, has magnitude, and is complete in itself ... through incidents arousing pity and fear it effects a catharsis of these and similar emotions. [*Poetics*, VI]

6. [Of the dramatic form of tragedy]
A whole is that which has a beginning, a middle, and an end. [Ib. VII]

Armstrong, Neil (1930–)
American astronaut; first man on the moon

1. [On stepping on to the moon]
   That's one small step for a man, one giant leap for mankind. [*New York Times*, 21 July 1969]

Armstrong, Sir Robert (1927–)
British public servant

1. [Replying to an allegation in court that a letter he had written on behalf of the British Government had contained a lie]
   It contains a misleading impression, not a lie. It was being economical with the truth. [*The Observer*, 23 November 1986, in Jeffrey Care (ed.), *Sayings of the Eighties* (1989)]

Arnold, Matthew (1822–1888)
English poet, critic, essayist and educationist

1. The Sea of Faith
   Was once, too, at the full, and round earth's shore
   Lay like the folds of a bright girdle furl'd.
   But now I only hear
   Its melancholy, long, withdrawing roar,
   Retreating, to the breath
   Of the night-wind, down the vast edges drear
   And naked shingles of the world.

   Ah, love, let us be true
   To one another! for the world, which seems
   To lie before us like a land of dreams,
   So various, so beautiful, so new,
   Hath really neither joy, nor love, nor light,
   Nor certitude, nor peace, nor help for pain;
   And we are here as on a darkling plain
   Swept with confused alarms of struggle and flight
   Where ignorant armies clash by night. ['Dover Beach' (1867)]

2. Culture being a pursuit of our total perfection by means of getting to know, on all the matters which most concern us, the best which has been thought and said in the world. [*Culture and Anarchy* (1869), Preface]

3. For this [Middle] class we have a designation which now has become

pretty well known, and which we may as well still keep for them, the designation of Philistines. [*Culture and Anarchy*]

Ascham, Roger (1515–1568)
English scholar, educationist and archer

1. There is no such whetstone, to sharpen a good wit and encourage a will to learning, as is praise. [*The Schoolmaster* (1570)]

Ashford, Daisy (1881–1972)
English child author

1. Oh I see said the earl but my own idear is that these things are as piffle before the wind. [*The Young Visiters* (1919), 5]

Atlas, Charles (Greek Mythology)
Titan compelled to support the sky on his shoulders as punishment for rebelling against Zeus

1. You too can have a body like mine! [Charles Atlas body-building courses]

Attlee, Clement (1883–1967)
English statesman, Labour politician and Prime Minister

1. Democracy means government by discussion but it is only effective if you can stop people talking. [Speech, June 1957]

Auden, W. H. (1907–1973)
English poet, essayist, critic, teacher and dramatist

1. Private faces in public places
   Are wiser and nicer
   Than public faces in private places. [*The Orators* (1932)]

2. Look, stranger, on this island now. [*Collected Poems*, 1933–1938, 'On This Island']

3. Lay your sleeping head, my love,
   Human on my faithless arm. [Ib. 'Lullaby']

4. This is the Night Mail crossing the Border,
   Bringing the cheque and the postal order. [Ib. 'Night Mail']

5. Read *The New Yorker*, trust in God;
And take short views. [*Collected Poems*, 1939–1947, 'Under Which Lyre']

6. A poet's hope: to be,
like some valley cheese,
local, but prized elsewhere. [*Collected Poems*, 1958–1971, 'Shorts II']

7. A shilling life will give you all the facts. ['Who's Who']

Augier, Emile (1820–1889)
French dramatist and poet; author of comedies of manners

1. *La nostalgie de la boue.*
Homesickness for the gutter. [*Le Mariage d'Olympe* (1855), I]

Augustine, Saint (354–430)
Numidian-born Christian theologian, philosopher and scholar

1. *Da mihi castitatem et continentiam, sed noli modo.*
Give me chastity and continence, but not yet. [*Confessions* (397–398), VIII]

Aurelius, Marcus (121–180)
Roman emperor and Stoic philosopher

1. Remember that no one loses any other life than this which he now lives, nor lives any other than this which he now loses. [*Meditations*, II, 14]

2. The universe is change; life is what thinking makes of it. [Ib. IV, 3]

Austen, Jane (1775–1817)
English novelist, noted for insightful portrayal of middle-class families

1. It is a truth universally acknowledged, that a single man in possession of a good fortune, must be in want of a wife. [*Pride and Prejudice* (1813), 1]

2. One half of the world cannot understand the pleasures of the other. [*Emma* (1816), 9]

3. [Of the Battle of Albuera in 1811]
How horrible it is to have so many people killed! – And what a

blessing that one cares for none of them! [Letter to Cassandra Austen, 1811]

Austin, Alfred (1835–1913)
English poet laureate and journalist

1. [On the illness of the Prince of Wales]
   Across the wires the electric message came:
   'He is no better, he is much the same. [Attr.]

Bacon, Francis (First Baron Verulam and Viscount St Albans) (1561–1626)
English philosopher, essayist, politician, lawyer and courtier

1. Knowledge itself is power. [*Meditationes Sacrae* (*Religious Meditations*, 1597), 'Of Heresies']

2. Mahomet made the people believe that he would call a hill to him, and from the top of it offer up his prayers for the observers of his law. The people assembled: Mahomet called the hill to come to him again and again; and when the hill stood still, he was never a whit abashed, but said, 'If the hill will not come to Mahomet, Mahomet will go to the hill. [*Essays* (1625), 'Of Boldness']

3. Riches are for spending. [Ib. 'Of Expense']

4. He that hath wife and children, hath given hostages to fortune; for they are impediments to great enterprises, either of virtue or mischief. [Ib. 'Of Marriage and Single Life']

5. The joys of parents are secret, and so are their griefs and fears. [Ib. 'Of Parents and Children']

6. Revenge is a kind of wild justice, which the more man's nature runs to, the more ought law to weed it out. [Ib. 'Of Revenge']

7. What is Truth? said jesting Pilate; and would not stay for an answer. [Ib. 'Of Truth']

8. All colours will agree in the dark. [Ib. 'Of Unity in Religion']

Bagehot, Walter (1826–1877)
English economist, political philosopher and journalist

1. A Parliament is nothing less than a big meeting of more or less idle people. [*The English Constitution* (1867), 'The House of Lords']

Ballads
N.B. Most ballads are of uncertain date and exist in many versions.

1. Yestreen the Queen had four Maries,
   The night she'll hae but three;
   There was Marie Seaton, and Marie Beaton
   And Mary Carmichael and me. ['The Queen's Maries']

2. The king sits in Dunfermline town,
   Drinking the blude-red wine;
   'Oh, where will I get a gude skipper
   To sail this ship of mine?'... ['Sir Patrick Spens']

3. 'Tom Pearse, Tom Pearse, lend me your grey mare,
   All along, down along, out along, lee.
   For I want for to go to Widdicombe Fair,
   Wi' Bill Brewer, Jan Stewer, Peter Gurney, Peter Davey, Dan'l
   Whiddon, Harry Hawk;
   Old Uncle Tom Cobbleigh and all.
   Old Uncle Tom Cobbleigh and all. ['Widdicombe Fair']

Bangs, Edward (fl. 1775)
American writer of songs

1. Yankee Doodle came to town
   Upon a little pony;
   He stuck a feather in his hat,
   And called it macaroni. ['Yankee Doodle']

Bankhead, Tallulah (1903–1968)
American actress

1. [To an admirer]
   I'll come and make love to you at five o'clock. If I'm late start without
   me. [In E. Morgan, *Somerset Maugham* (1980)]

2. I'm as pure as the driven slush. [*The Observer*, 'Sayings of the Week',
   1957]

Barbour, John (c. 1316–1395)
Earliest-known Scottish poet; churchman and scholar

1. A! fredome is a noble thing!
   Fredome mayss man to haiff liking;

Fredome all solace to man giffio:
He levys at ess that frely levys!... [*The Bruce* (1375), I]

Barnum, Phineas T. (1810–1891)
American showman and author

1. There's a sucker born every minute. [Attr.]

Barrie, Sir J. M. (1860–1937)
Scottish dramatist, novelist and journalist

1. I'm a second eleven sort of chap. [*The Admirable Crichton* (1902), III]

2. To die will be an awfully big adventure. [*Peter Pan* (1904), III]

3. Do you believe in fairies? ... If you believe, clap your hands! [Ib. IV]

4. There are few more impressive sights in the world than a Scotsman on the make. [*What Every Woman Knows* (1908), II]

Baruch, Bernard M. (1870–1965)
American financier, government adviser and author

1. Let us not be deceived – we are today in the midst of a cold war. [Speech, South Carolina, 1947]

Baudelaire, Charles (1821–1867)
French lyric poet, translator and critic

1. *La nature est un temple où de vivants piliers*
Laissent parfois sortir de confuses paroles;
L'homme y passe à travers des forêts de symboles
Qui l'observent avec des regards familiers.
Nature is a temple in which living columns sometimes utter confused words. Man walks through it among forests of symbols, which watch him with knowing eyes. [*Les Fleurs du Mal* (1857), 'Correspondances']

2. *Il faut épater le bourgeois.*
One must shock the bourgeois. [Attr.]

Bax, Sir Arnold (1883–1953)
English composer of romantic works

1. One should try everything once, except incest and folk-dancing. [*Farewell my Youth* (1943)]

Baxter, Stanley (1928–)
Scottish comic actor

1. Sausages is the boys. [McKellar Watt advertisement, 1960s]

Bayly, Thomas Haynes (1797–1839)
English song and ballad-writer, novelist and dramatist

1. Absence makes the heart grow fonder. ['Isle of Beauty', song, 1830]

Beaumont, Francis (1584–1616)
*English dramatist and poet; wrote plays in collaboration with John
Fletcher (1579–1625)*

1. You are no better than you should be. [*The Coxcomb* (produced 1612,
published 1647), IV]

2. I'll put a spoke among your wheels. [*The Mad Lover*, III]

3. Kiss till the cow comes home. [*The Scornful Lady* (produced 1610,
published 1616), II]

Beauvoir, Simone de (1908–1986)
*French novelist, autobiographer, feminist critic, teacher of philosophy
and companion of Sartre*

1. *On ne naît pas femme: on le devient.*
One is not born a woman: one becomes a woman. [*Le Deuxième Sexe
(The Second Sex*, 1949–1950)]

Beaverbrook, Lord (Max Aitken, First Baron Beaverbrook) (1879–1964)
*Canadian-born British newspaper proprietor; Conservative MP and
Minister; political writer*

1. [Of Lloyd George]
He did not care in which direction the car was travelling, so long as
he remained in the driver's seat. [*New Statesman*, 1963]

Beckett, Samuel (1906–1989)
*Irish dramatist of the Theatre of the Absurd, novelist and poet; Nobel
prize 1969*

1. *Estragon*: ... Let's go.
   Vladimir: We can't.
   Estragon: Why not?
   Vladimir: We're waiting for Godot. [*Waiting for Godot* (1955), I]

Becon, Thomas (1512–1567)
English Protestant divine; preacher, teacher and chaplain to Cranmer

1. For when the wine is in, the wit is out. [*Catechism* (1560)]

Bede, The Venerable (673–735)
English monk, historian and scholar; author of biblical commentaries and a treatise on physical science

1. When we compare the present life of man with that time of which we have no knowledge, it seems to me like the swift flight of a lone sparrow through the banqueting-hall where you sit in the winter months ... This sparrow flies swiftly in through one door of the hall, and out through another ... Similarly, man appears on earth for a little while, but we know nothing of what went on before this life, and what follows. [*Ecclesiastical History*, II]

Beerbohm, Sir Max (1872–1956)
English satirist, cartoonist, dramatic critic, essayist and parodist

1. Mankind is divisible into two great classes: hosts and guests. [Attr.]

Beethoven, Ludwig Van (1770–1827)
German composer of genius; bridged classical and Romantic periods

1. *Muss es sein? Es muss sein.*
   Must it be? It must be. [Epigraph to the final movement of his String Quartet in F Major, Op. 135, 1826]

Behan, Brendan (1923–1964)
Irish dramatist, novelist and Republican

1. Never throw stones at your mother,
   You'll be sorry for it when she's dead,
   Never throw stones at your mother,
   Throw bricks at your father instead. [*The Hostage* (1958), I]

2. I wish I'd been a mixed infant. [Ib. II]

3. Other people have a nationality. The Irish and the Jews have a psychosis. [*Richard's Cork Leg* (unfinished at Behan's death, completed by Alan Simpson and first staged in 1972), I]

Behn, Aphra (1640–1689)
English Restoration dramatist, novelist, poet, translator and spy; first Englishwoman to live by her pen

1. Love ceases to be a pleasure, when it ceases to be a secret. [*The Lover's Watch* (1686), 'Four o'clock. General Conversation']

2. Faith, Sir, we are here today and gone tomorrow. [*The Lucky Chance* (1687), IV]

Bell, Alexander Graham (1847–1922)
Scots-born American inventor of the telephone and educator of the deaf

1. Mr Watson, come here: I want you. [First words spoken on his telephone, 1876]

Belloc, Hilaire (Joseph Hilary Pierre Belloc) (1870–1953)
French-born English writer of light verse, essays, biographies and criticism; Liberal MP

1. I shoot the Hippopotamus
with bullets made of platinum,
Because if I use leaden ones
his hide is sure to flatten 'em. [*The Bad Child's Book of Beasts* (1896), 'The Hippopotamus']

2. And always keep a-hold of Nurse
For fear of finding something worse. [*Cautionary Tales* (1907), 'Jim']

3. When I am dead, I hope it may be said:
'His sins were scarlet, but his books were read. [*Sonnets and Verse* (1923), 'On His Books']

Benchley, Robert Charles (1889–1945)
American essayist, humorist and actor

1. I must get out of these wet clothes and into a dry martini. [Line delivered in film *The Major and the Minor*, 1942; scriptwriters Charles Brackett and Billy Wilder]

Benda, Julien (1867–1956)
French novelist and philosopher

1. *La Trahison des Clercs.*
The treachery of the intellectuals. [Title of book, 1927]

Bennett, Alan (1934–)
English stage, film and television dramatist; actor and diarist

1. You know life ... it's rather like opening a tin of sardines. We are all of us looking for the key. [*Beyond the Fringe* (1962)]

Benson, A. C. (1862–1925)
English scholar, essayist, literary critic and biographer

1. Land of Hope and Glory, Mother of the Free,
How shall we extol thee, who are born of thee?
Wider still and wider shall thy bounds be set;
God who made thee mighty, make thee mightier yet. [Song, 1902]

Bentley, Edmund Clerihew (1875–1956)
English journalist and epigrammatist

1. The art of Biography
Is different from Geography.
Geography is about Maps,
But Biography is about chaps...

2. Sir Christopher Wren
Said, 'I am going to dine with some men.
If anybody calls
Say I am designing St Paul's. [*Biography for Beginners* (1905)]

Bentley, Richard (1662–1742)
English classical scholar, chaplain and librarian

1. It is a pretty poem, Mr Pope, but you must not call it Homer. [In John Hawkins (ed.), *The Works of Samuel Johnson* (1787), IV, 'The Life of Pope']

Berlin, Irving (Israel Baline) (1888–1989)
Russian-born American writer of popular songs and Broadway musicals

1. I'm dreaming of a white Christmas. ['White Christmas', song, 1942; in film *Holiday Inn*]

Berlioz, Hector (1803–1869)
French Romantic composer; founder of modern orchestration

1. Time is a great teacher, but unfortunately it kills all its pupils. [Attr.]

Berners, Lord (1883–1950)
English composer of ballets, artist and novelist

1. [Of T. E. Lawrence]
   He's always backing into the limelight. [Attr.]

Betjeman, Sir John (1906–1984)
English poet laureate (1972), writer on architecture, and broadcaster

1. Come, friendly bombs, and fall on Slough
   It isn't fit for humans now,
   There isn't grass to graze a cow
   Swarm over, Death!... [*Continual Dew* (1937), 'Slough']

2. Miss J. Hunter Dunn, Miss J. Hunter Dunn,
   Furnish'd and burnish'd by Aldershot sun,
   What strenuous singles we played after tea
   We in the tournament – you against me! [*New Bats in Old Belfries*
   (1945), 'A Subaltern's Love Song']

Bevan, Aneurin (1897–1960)
Welsh Labour politician and minister; miner, unionist and orator

1. We know what happens to people who stay in the middle of the road.
   They get run over. [*The Observer*, 'Sayings of the Week', 1953]

2. I read the newspapers avidly. It is my one form of continuous fiction.
   [Ib. 1960]

Bevin, Ernest (1881–1951)
*English trade unionist and Labour politician; foreign secretary,
1945–51*

1. [On the Council of Europe]
   If you open that Pandora's Box you never know what Trojan 'orses
   will jump out. [In Sir Roderick Barclay, *Ernest Bevin and the Foreign
   Office* (1975)]

Bhagavadgita
Religious and philosophical Sanskrit poem

1. I am become death, the destroyer of worlds. [Quoted by J. Robert Oppenheimer on seeing the first nuclear explosion]

The Bible (King James Version)

Genesis

1. In the beginning God created the heaven and the earth.
   And the earth was without form, and void; and darkness was upon the face of the deep. And the Spirit of God moved upon the face of the waters.
   And God said, Let there be light: and there was light. [1:1–3]

2. And God said, Let us make man in our image, after our likeness. [1:26]

3. Be fruitful, and multiply, and replenish the earth, and subdue it. [1:28]

4. But of the tree of the knowledge of good and evil, thou shalt not eat of it: for in the day that thou eatest thereof thou shalt surely die. [2:17]

5. Am I my brother's keeper? [4:9]

6. And the Lord set a mark upon Cain. [4:15]

7. There went in two and two unto Noah into the ark, the male and the female. [7:9]

8. Behold, Esau my brother is a hairy man, and I am a smooth man. [27:11]

9. Now Israel loved Joseph more than all his children, because he was the son of his old age; and he made him a coat of many colours. [37:3]

10. Ye shall eat the fat of the land. [45:18]

Exodus

1. A land flowing with milk and honey; unto the place of the Canaanites, and the Hittites, and the Amorites, and the Perizzites, and the Hivites, and the Jebusites. [3:8]

2. Life for life,
   Eye for eye, tooth for tooth, hand for hand, foot for foot,

Burning for burning, wound for wound, stripe for stripe. [21:23–25]

Leviticus
1. Thou shalt love thy neighbour as thyself. [19:18]

Numbers
1. Be sure your sin will find you out. [32:23]

Deuteronomy
1. Man doth not live by bread only, but by every word that proceedeth out of the mouth of the Lord doth man live. [8: 3]

Joshua
1. Let them live; but let them be hewers of wood and drawers of water. [9:21]

Ruth
1. Intreat me not to leave thee, or to return from following after thee: for whither thou goest, I will go; and where thou lodgest, I will lodge: thy people shall be my people, and thy God my God:
   Where thou diest, will I die, and there will I be buried: the Lord do so to me, and more also, if ought but death part thee and me. [1:16–17]

II Samuel
1. Thy love to me was wonderful, passing the love of women. [1:26]

2. How are the mighty fallen, and the weapons of war perished! [1:27]

Esther
1. Let it be written among the laws of the Persians and the Medes, that it be not altered. [1:19]

Job
1. The Lord gave, and the Lord hath taken away; blessed be the name of the Lord. [1:21]

2. Man that is born of a woman is of few days, and full of trouble. [14:1]

Psalms
1. Out of the mouth of babes and sucklings hast thou ordained strength. [8:2]

2. The Lord is my shepherd; I shall not want.

He maketh me to lie down in green pastures: he leadeth me beside the still waters.

He restoreth my soul: he leadeth me in the paths of righteousness for his name's sake.

Yea, though I walk through the valley of the shadow of death, I will fear no evil: for thou art with me; thy rod and thy staff they comfort me.

Thou preparest a table before me in the presence of mine enemies: thou anointest my head with oil: my cup runneth over.

Surely goodness and mercy shall follow me all the days of my life: and I will dwell in the house of the Lord for ever. [23:1-6]

3. The days of our years are threescore years and ten; and if by reason of strength they be fourscore years, yet is their strength labour and sorrow. [90:10]

4. As for man, his days are as grass: as a flower of the field, so he flourisheth. [103:15]

5. The fear of the Lord is the beginning of wisdom. [111:10]

6. By the rivers of Babylon, there we sat down, yea, we wept, when we remembered Zion. [137:1]

Proverbs

1. As an ox goeth to the slaughter. [7:22]

2. He that spareth his rod hateth his son. [13:24]

3. Pride goeth before destruction, and an haughty spirit before a fall. [16:18]

4. Train up a child in the way he should go: and when he is old, he will not depart from it. [22:6]

5. As a dog returneth to his vomit, so a fool returneth to his folly. [26:11]

6. Where there is no vision, the people perish. [29:18]

7. Who can find a virtuous woman? for her price is far above rubies. [31:10]

Ecclesiastes

1. Vanity of vanities, saith the Preacher, vanity of vanities; all is vanity. [1:2]

2. To every thing there is a season, and a time to every purpose under the heaven:
   A time to be born, and a time to die; a time to plant, and a time to pluck up that which is planted;
   A time to kill, and a time to heal; a time to break down, and a time to build up;
   A time to weep, and a time to laugh; a time to mourn, and a time to dance;
   A time to cast away stones, and a time to gather stones together; a time to embrace, and a time to refrain from embracing;
   A time to get, and a time to lose; a time to keep, and a time to cast away;
   A time to rend, and a time to sew; a time to keep silence, and a time to speak;
   A time to love, and a time to hate; a time of war, and a time of peace. [3:1–8]

3. Cast thy bread upon the waters: for thou shalt find it after many days. [11:1]

4. Of making many books there is no end; and much study is a weariness of the flesh. [12:12]

Isaiah

1. Though your sins be as scarlet, they shall be as white as snow. [1:18]

2. They shall beat their swords into plowshares, and their spears into pruninghooks: nation shall not lift up sword against nation, neither shall they learn war any more. [2:4]

3. Whom shall I send, and who will go for us? Then said I, Here am I; send me. [6:8]

4. For unto us a child is born, unto us a son is given: and the government shall be upon his shoulder: and his name shall be called Wonderful, Counseller, The mighty God, The everlasting Father, The Prince of Peace. [9:6]

5. The wolf also shall dwell with the lamb, and the leopard shall lie down with the kid. [11:6]

6. Let us eat and drink; for to morrow we shall die. [22:13]

7. The voice of him that crieth in the wilderness, Prepare ye the way of the Lord, make straight in the desert a highway for our God. [40: 3–5]

Ezekiel

1. O ye dry bones, hear the word of the Lord. [37:4]

Daniel

1. Thou art weighed in the balances, and art found wanting. [5:27]

Hosea

1. They have sown the wind, and they shall reap the whirlwind. [8:7]

Apocrypha

1. He that toucheth pitch shall be defiled therewith. [Ecclesiasticus, 13:1]

2. Let us now praise famous men, and our fathers that begat us. [Ecclesiasticus, 44:1]

Matthew

1. They presented unto him gifts; gold, and frankincense, and myrrh. [2:11]

2. Fishers of men. [4:19]

3. Blessed are the poor in spirit: for theirs is the kingdom of heaven.
Blessed are they that mourn: for they shall be comforted.
Blessed are the meek: for they shall inherit the earth.
Blessed are they which do hunger and thirst after righteousness: for they shall be filled.
Blessed are the merciful: for they shall obtain mercy.
Blessed are the pure in heart: for they shall see God.
Blessed are the peacemakers: for they shall be called the children of God. [5:3–9]

4. Ye are the salt of the earth: but if the salt have lost his savour, wherewith shall it be salted? [5:13]

5. Love your enemies, bless them that curse you, do good to them that hate you, and pray for them which despitefully use you, and persecute you. [5:44]

6. He maketh his sun to rise on the evil and on the good, and sendeth rain on the just and on the unjust. [5:45]

7. Let not thy left hand know what thy right hand doeth. [6:3]

8. Lay not up for yourselves treasures upon earth, where moth and rust doth corrupt, and where thieves break through and steal:
But lay up for yourselves treasures in heaven. [6:19–20]

9. No man can serve two masters: ... Ye cannot serve God and mammon. [6:24]

10. Consider the lilies of the field, how they grow; they toil not, neither do they spin. [6:28]

11. Take therefore no thought for the morrow: for the morrow shall take thought for the things of itself. Sufficient unto the day is the evil thereof. [6:34]

12. Judge not, that ye be not judged. [7:1]

13. Neither cast ye your pearls before swine. [7:6]

14. Ask, and it shall be given you; seek, and ye shall find; knock, and it shall be opened unto you. [7:7]

15. By their fruits ye shall know them. [7:20]

16. Let the dead bury their dead. [8:22]

17. Come unto me, all ye that labour and are heavy laden, and I will give you rest. [11:28]

18. He that is not with me is against me. [12:30]

19. A prophet is not without honour, save in his own country, and in his own house. [13:57]

20. If the blind lead the blind, both shall fall into the ditch. [15:14]

21. Thou art Peter, and upon this rock I will build my church; and the gates of hell shall not prevail against it. [16:18]

22. Get thee behind me, Satan. [16:23]

23. What is a man profited, if he shall gain the whole world, and lose his own soul? [16:26]

24. For where two or three are gathered together in my name, there am I in the midst of them. [18:20]

25. With men this is impossible; but with God all things are possible. [19:26]

26. For many are called, but few are chosen. [22:14]

27. Render therefore unto Caesar the things which are Caesar's; and unto God the things that are God's. [22:21]

28. Ye blind guides, which strain at a gnat, and swallow a camel. [23:24]

29. Well done, thou good and faithful servant. [25:21]

30. I was a stranger, and ye took me in: Naked, and ye clothed me: I was sick, and ye visited me: I was in prison, and ye came unto me. [25:35 – 36]

31. The spirit indeed is willing, but the flesh is weak. [26:41]

32. All they that take the sword shall perish with the sword. [26:52]

Mark

1. My name is Legion: for we are many. [5:9]

2. Lord, I believe; help thou mine unbelief. [9:24]

3. Suffer the little children to come unto me, and forbid them not: for of such is the kingdom of God. [10:14]

4. It is easier for a camel to go through the eye of a needle, than for a rich man to enter into the kingdom of God. [10:25. Cf. Matthew, 19:24)]

Luke

1. Because there was no room for them in the inn. [2:7]

2. Behold, I bring you good tidings of great joy. [2:10]

3. Glory to God in the highest, and on earth peace, good will toward men. [2:14]

4. Physician, heal thyself. [4:23]

5. Love your enemies, do good to them which hate you. [6:27]

6. The labourer is worthy of his hire. [10:7]

7. Joy shall be in heaven over one sinner that repenteth, more than over ninety and nine just persons, which need no repentance. [15:7]

8. Bring hither the fatted calf, and kill it. [15:23]

9. Father, forgive them; for they know not what they do. [23:34]

John

1. In the beginning was the Word, and the Word was with God, and the Word was God. [1:1]

2. And the Word was made flesh, and dwelt among us. [1:14]

3. The wind bloweth where it listeth. [3:8]

4. God so loved the world, that he gave his only begotten Son, that whosoever believeth in him should not perish, but have everlasting life. [3:16]

5. Rise, take up thy bed, and walk. [5:8]

6. He that is without sin among you, let him first cast a stone at her. [8:7]

7. And ye shall know the truth, and the truth shall make you free. [8:32]

8. Jesus wept. [11:35]

9. In my Father's house are many mansions. [14:2]

10. I am the way, the truth, and the life: no man cometh unto the Father, but by me. [14:6]

11. Greater love hath no man than this, that a man lay down his life for his friends. [15:13]

12. Pilate saith unto him, What is truth? [18:38]

Acts of the Apostles

1. It is hard for thee to kick against the pricks. [9:5]

2. God is no respecter of persons. [10:34]

3. It is more blessed to give than to receive. [20:35]

4. A citizen of no mean city. [21:39]

Romans

1. The wages of sin is death. [6:23]

2. If God be for us, who can be against us? [8:31]

3. Rejoice with them that do rejoice, and weep with them that weep. [12:15]

4. Vengeance is mine; I will repay, saith the Lord. [12:19]

I Corinthians

1. Absent in body, but present in spirit. [5:3]

2. Though I speak with the tongues of men and of angels, and have not charity, I am become as sounding brass, or a tinkling cymbal.
...and though I have all faith, so that I could remove mountains, and have not charity, I am nothing.
And though I bestow all my goods to feed the poor, and though I give my body to be burned, and have not charity, it profiteth me nothing.
Charity suffereth long, and is kind; charity envieth not; charity vaunteth not itself, is not puffed up,
Doth not behave itself unseemly, seeketh not her own, is not easily provoked, thinketh no evil;
Rejoiceth not in iniquity, but rejoiceth in the truth; Beareth all things believeth all things, hopeth all things, endureth all things.
Charity never faileth: but whether there be prophecies, they shall fail; whether there be tongues, they shall cease; whether there be knowledge it shall vanish away. [13:1−8]

3. And now abideth faith, hope, charity, these three; but the greatest of these is charity. [13:13]

4. O death, where is thy sting? O grave, where is thy victory? [15:55]

II Corinthians

1. The letter killeth, but the spirit giveth life. [3:6]

2. There was given to me a thorn in the flesh, the messenger of Satan to buffet me. [12:7]

Philippians

1. The peace of God, which passeth all understanding. [4:7]

I Timothy

1. Old wives' fables. [4:7]

2. Drink no longer water, but use a little wine for thy stomach's sake and thine often infirmities. [5:23]

3. The love of money is the root of all evil. [6:10]

II Timothy

1. I have fought a good fight, I have finished my course, I have kept the faith. [4:7]

Titus

1. Unto the pure all things are pure. [1:15]

Hebrews

1. It is a fearful thing to fall into the hands of the living God. [10:31]

James

1. Faith without works is dead. [2:20]

2. Let your yea be yea; and your nay, nay. [5:12]

I John

1. Perfect love casteth out fear. [4:18]

Revelation

1. I am Alpha and Omega, the beginning and the ending, saith the Lord. [1:8]

2. Behold, I stand at the door, and knock. [3:20]

3. And I looked, and behold a pale horse: and his name that sat on him was Death. [6:8]

Bierce, Ambrose (1842–c.1914)
American short-story writer, essayist, journalist, versifier and soldier

1. *Egotist:* A person of low taste, more interested in himself than in me. [*The Cynic's Word Book* (1906); later republished as *The Devil's Dictionary*]

2. *Future:* That period of time in which our affairs prosper, our friends are true and our happiness is assured. [Ib.]

3. *Quoting:* The act of repeating erroneously the words of another. [Ib.]

4. *Patience:* A minor form of despair, disguised as a virtue. [Ib.]

Binyon, Laurence (1869–1943)
English war poet, art historian and critic

1. They shall grow not old, as we that are left grow old:
Age shall not weary them, nor the years condemn.
At the going down of the sun and in the morning
We will remember them. ['For the Fallen' (1914)]

Bion (fl. 280 BC)
Greek bucolic poet, of Smyrna

1. Though boys throw stones at frogs in sport, the frogs do not die in sport, but in earnest. [Quoted by Plutarch]

Bismarck, Prince Otto von (1815–1898)
German statesman; first Chancellor of the German Reich 1871–90

1. *Legt eine möglichst starke militärische Kraft, mit anderen Worten möglichst viel Blut und Eisen in die Hand des Königs von Preussen, dann wird er die Politik machen können, die Ihr wünscht; mit Reden und Schützenfesten und Liedern macht sie sich nicht, sie macht sich nur durch 'Blut und Eisen'!*
Put the strongest possible military power, in other words as much blood and iron as possible, in the hands of the King of Prussia, and then he will be able to carry out the policy you want; this cannot be achieved with speeches and shooting-matches and songs; it can only be achieved by 'blood and iron'! [Speech, Prussian House of Deputies, 1886]

2. *Die Politik ist die Lehre vom Möglichen.*
Politics is the art of the possible. [Remark to Meyer von Waldeck, editor of the St Petersburg Zeitung, 1863]

Blackstone, Sir William (1723–1780)
English judge, historian of English law and politician

1. It is better that ten guilty persons escape than one innocent suffer. [*Commentaries on the Laws of England* (1765–1769), IV]

Blake, Eubie (1883–1983)
American pianist and composer

1. [He died five days after his hundredth birthday]

If I'd known I was gonna live this long, I'd have taken better care of myself. [*The Observer*, 1983]

Blake, William (1757–1827)
English Romantic poet, engraver, painter and mystic

1. When the green woods laugh with the voice of joy. [*Songs of Innocence* (1789), 'Laughing Song']

2. Energy is Eternal Delight. [*The Marriage of Heaven and Hell* (c. 1790–93), 'The Voice of the Devil', Plate 4]

3. The cut worm forgives the plow. [Ib. 'Proverbs of Hell', Plate 7]

4. If the fool would persist in his folly he would become wise... [Ib. 'Proverbs of Hell', Plate 7]

5. Sooner murder an infant in its cradle than nurse unacted desires... [Ib. 'Proverbs of Hell', Plate 10]

6. If the doors of perception were cleansed every thing would appear to man as it is, infinite. [Ib. 'A Memorable Fancy', Plate 14]

7. For every thing that lives is Holy. [Ib. 'Chorus', Plate 27]

8. Tyger Tyger, burning bright
   In the forests of the night:
   What immortal hand or eye
   Could frame thy fearful symmetry?... [*Songs of Experience* (1794), 'The Tyger']

9. To see a World in a Grain of Sand
   And a Heaven in a Wild Flower
   Hold Infinity in the palm of your hand
   And Eternity in an hour.
   A Robin Red breast in a Cage
   Puts all Heaven in a Rage... ['Auguries of Innocence' (c. 1803), from 'The Pickering Manuscript']

10. And did those feet in ancient time
    Walk upon England's mountains green:
    And was the holy Lamb of God
    On England's pleasant pastures seen! [*Milton* (1804–1809), Preface]

Boccaccio, Giovanni (c.1313–1375)
Italian poet and celebrated writer of narrative fiction

1. Do as we say, and not as we do. [*Decameron* (1358), 3]

Boethius (c. 475–524)
Roman statesman, scholar and philosopher

1. *Quis legem dat amantibus? Major lex amor est sibi.*
   Who can give a law to lovers? Love is a greater law unto itself. [*De Consolatione Philosophiae* (c. 522–524), III]

Bogart, Humphrey (1899–1957)
American film actor

1. Play it, Sam. Play 'As Time Goes By'. [*Casablanca*, film, 1942; script by Julius and Philip Epstein and Howard Koch]

2. Here's lookin' at you, kid. [Ib.]

Bonhoeffer, Dietrich (1906–1945)
German Lutheran theologian; executed by the Nazis

1. *Der Mensch hat gelernt, in allen wichtigen Fragen mit sich selbst fertig zu werden ohne Zuhilfenahme der 'Arbeitshypothese: Gott.'*
   In all important questions, man has learned to cope without recourse to God as a working hypothesis. [*Widerstand und Ergebung: Briefe und Aufzeichnungen aus der Haft* (*Resistance and Surrender: Letters and Notes from Custody*, 1951), Letter to a friend, June 1944]

Borges, Jorge Luis (1899–1986)
Argentinian magic realist short-story writer; poet and librarian

1. [On the Falklands War of 1982]
   The Falklands thing was a fight between two bald men over a comb. [*Time*, 1983]

Bosquet, Pierre François Joseph (1810–1861)
French general

1. [Remark on witnessing the Charge of the Light Brigade, 1854]
   C'est magnifique mais ce n'est pas la guerre.
   It is magnificent, but it is not war. [Attr.]

Bossidy, John Collins (1860–1928)
American oculist

1. And this is good old Boston,
   The home of the bean and the cod,
   Where the Lowells talk only to Cabots,
   And the Cabots talk only to God. [Toast at Harvard dinner, 1910]

Bowen, Lord (1835–1894)
English judge and translator of Virgil

1. The rain it raineth on the just
   And also on the unjust fella:
   But chiefly on the just, because
   The unjust steals the just's umbrella. [In Walter Sichel, *Sands of Time* (1923)]

Bradford, John (c. 1510–1555)
English Protestant martyr; author of sermons and other religious works

1. [Remark on criminals going to the gallows]
   But for the grace of God there goes John Bradford. [Attr.]

Braxfield, Lord (1722–1799)
Scottish 'hanging' judge; notoriously harsh to political prisoners

1. [To an eloquent culprit at the bar]
   Ye're a vera clever chiel, man, but ye wad be nane the waur o' a hanging. [In Lockhart, *Life of Scott*]

2. [Gerald, a political prisoner, remarked that Christ had been a reformer]
   Muckle he made o' that; he was hanget [In Cockburn, *Memorials* (1856)]

Brecht, Bertolt (1898–1956)
German experimental dramatist and poet

1. *Erst kommt das Fressen, dann kommt die Moral.*
   Feeding your face comes first, then morality. [*Die Dreigroschenoper (The Threepenny Opera*, 1928), II.vi]

Bridie, James (Osborne Henry Mavor) (1888–1951)
Major Scottish dramatist, autobiographer, essayist and physician

1. Boredom is a sign of satisfied ignorance, blunted apprehension, crass

sympathies, dull understanding, feeble powers of attention and irreclaimable weakness of character. [*Mr Bolfry* (1943)]

Brillat-Savarin, Anthelme (1755–1826)
French jurist and gastronome

1. *La découverte d'un mets nouveau fait plus pour le bonheur du genre humain que la découverte d'une étoile.*
   The discovery of a new dish does more for the happiness of mankind than the discovery of a star. [*Physiologie du Goût* (1825)]

Bronowski, Jacob (1908–1974)
Polish-born British mathematician, writer and television presenter on the history of scientific achievement

1. Every animal leaves traces of what it was; man alone leaves traces of what he created. [*The Ascent of Man* (1973), 1]

Brontë, Anne (1820–1849)
English novelist and poet, sister of Charlotte and Emily

1. There is always a 'but' in this imperfect world. [*The Tenant of Wildfell Hall* (1848), 22]

Brontë, Charlotte (1816–1855)
English novelist; sister of Anne and Emily

1. [Of Mr Rochester]
   Reader, I married him. [*Jane Eyre* (1847), 38]

Brooke, Rupert (1887–1915)
English poet, known for his war poems and lighter verse

1. Stands the Church clock at ten to three?
   And is there honey still for tea? ['The Old Vicarage, Grantchester' (1912)]

2. If I should die, think only this of me:
   That there's some corner of a foreign field
   That is for ever England. ['The Soldier' (1914)]

Brougham, Lord Henry (1778–1868)
Scottish lawyer, politician, Lord Chancellor, abolitionist and journalist

1. The great Unwashed. [Attr.]

Brown Thomas (1663–1704)
English satirical poet, teacher, translator and pamphleteer

1. I do not love you, Dr Fell,
   But why I cannot tell;
   But this I know full well,
   I do not love you, Dr Fell. [*Works*(1719), Trans. of an Epigram of
   Martial]

Browne, Sir Thomas (1605–1682)
English physician, author and antiquary

1. We carry within us the wonders we seek without us: There is all Africa
   and her prodigies in us. [*Religio Medici* (1643)]

2. Charity begins at home, is the voice of the world. [Ib.]

3. What song the Sirens sang, or what name Achilles assumed when he
   hid himself among the women, though puzzling questions, are not
   beyond all conjecture. [*Hydriotaphia: Urn Burial* (1658)]

Browning, Elizabeth Barrett (1806–1861)
English poet, noted for her sonnets; wife of Robert Browning

1. For frequent tears have run
   The colours from my life. [*Sonnets from the Portuguese* (1850), 8]

2. How do I love thee? Let me count the ways, [Ib. 43]

Browning, Robert (1812–1889)
*English poet, noted for his dramatic monologues; husband of
Elizabeth Barrett Browning*

1. God's in his heaven,
   All's right with the world. [*Pippa Passes* (1841), I]

2. That's my last Duchess painted on the wall,
   Looking as if she were alive. I call
   That piece a wonder, now... ['My Last Duchess' (1842)]

3. Oh, to be in England
   Now that April's there, ['Home Thoughts, from Abroad' (1845)]

4. I sprang to the stirrup, and Joris, and he;
   I galloped, Dirck galloped, we galloped all three. ['How they brought
   the Good News from Ghent to Aix' (1845)]

5. Oh, the little more, and how much it is!
And the little less, and what worlds away! ['By the Fireside' (1855), 39]

Brummel, Beau (George Bryan Brummell) (1778–1840)
English dandy and wit; leader of Regency fashion

1. [Said of the Prince of Wales, 1813]
Who's your fat friend? [In Gronow, *Reminiscences* (1862)]

Buchan, John (First Baron Tweedsmuir) (1875–1940)
Prolific Scottish writer; novelist, editor, critic and journalist; lawyer, Conservative politician and Governor-General of Canada 1935–40

1. An atheist is a man who has no invisible means of support. [Attr.]

Buckingham, George Villiers, Second Duke of (1628–1687)
English courtier, member of the Cabal and comic dramatist

1. Ay, now the plot thickens very much upon us. [*The Rehearsal* (written 1663, performed c. 1671), III]

Buddha (Gautama Siddhartha) (c. 563–483 BC)
Indian religious teacher, the 'Enlightened'; founder of Buddhism

1. This Ayrian Eightfold Path, that is to say: Right view, right aim, right speech, right action, right living, right effort, right mindfulness, right contemplation. [In F.L. Woodward, *Some Sayings of the Buddha*]

Bulwer-Lytton, Edward George (First Baron Lytton) (1803–1873)
English novelist, dramatist, poet and politician

1. Beneath the rule of men entirely great
The pen is mightier than the sword. [*Richelieu* (1839)]

Bunyan, John (1628–1688)
English Nonconformist preacher, pastor and writer; imprisoned for his preaching

1. The name of the slough was Despond. [*The Pilgrim's Progress* (1678), I]

2. Hanging is too good for him, said Mr Cruelty. [Ib. I]

3. Who would true valour see,

Let him come hither;
One here will constant be,
Come wind, come weather.
There's no discouragement
Shall make him once relent
His first avow'd intent
To be a pilgrim. [Ib. II]

Burgon, John William (1813–1888)
English clergyman and Professor of Divinity

1. Match me such marvel save in Eastern clime,
   A rose-red city 'half as old as Time'! ['Petra' (1845)]

Burke, Edmund (1729–1797)
Irish-born British Whig statesman and political philosopher

1. Beauty in distress is much the most affecting beauty. [*A Philosophical Enquiry into the Origin of our Ideas of the Sublime and Beautiful* (1757), III, 9]

2. To complain of the age we live in, to murmur at the present possessors of power, to lament the past, to conceive extravagant hopes of the future, are the common dispositions of the greatest part of mankind. [*Thoughts on the Cause of the Present Discontents* (1770)]

3. Liberty, too, must be limited in order to be possessed. [*Letter to the Sheriffs of Bristol on the Affairs of America* (1777)]

4. A state without the means of some change is without the means of its conservation. [*Reflections on the Revolution in France and on the Proceedings in Certain Societies in London* (1790)]

5. Good order is the foundation of all good things. [Ib.]

6. You can never plan the future by the past. [*Letter to a Member of the National Assembly* (1791)]

7. In all forms of Government the people is the true legislator. [*Tracts on the Popery Laws* (1812), 3]

8. Slavery they can have anywhere. It is a weed that grows in every soil. [*Speech on Conciliation with America* (1775)]

9. The only thing necessary for the triumph of evil is for good men to do nothing. [Attr.]

Burns, Robert (1759–1796)
Scottish poet, songwriter and collector; Scotland's national bard

1. Man's inhumanity to man
   Makes countless thousands mourn!... ['Man was made to Mourn, a Dirge' (1784)]

2. The healsome parritch, chief o' Scotia's food...

   From scenes like these, old Scotia's grandeur springs
   That makes her lov'd at home, rever'd abroad:
   Princes and lords are but the breath of kings,
   'An honest man's the noblest work of God'. ['The Cotter's Saturday Night' (1785)]

3. Wee, sleekit, cowrin, tim'rous beastie,
   O, what a panic's in thy breastie! ['To a Mouse' (1785)]

4. Fair fa' your honest, sonsie face,
   Great chieftain o' the puddin-race! ['Address to a Haggis' (1786)]

5. Freedom and whisky gang thegither,
   Tak aff your dram! ['The Author's Earnest Cry and Prayer' (1786)]

6. But facts are chiels that winna ding,
   An' downa be disputed. ['A Dream' (1786)]

7. O wad some Power the giftie gie us
   To see oursels as ithers see us! ['To a Louse' (1786)]

8. Should auld acquaintance be forgot,
   And never brought to mind?...

   We'll tak' a cup o' kindness yet,
   For auld lang syne. ['Auld Lang Syne' (c. 1788)]

9. Hear, Land o' Cakes, and brither Scots...

   A chield's amang you takin notes,
   And faith he'll prent it. ['On the Late Captain Grose's Peregrinations Thro' Scotland' (1789)]

10. My heart's in the Highlands, my heart is not here,
    My heart's in the Highlands a-chasing the deer,

A-chasing the wild deer and following the roe—
My heart's in the Highlands, wherever I go!... ['My Heart's in the Highlands' (1790)]

11. The minister kiss't the fiddler's wife—
He could na preach for thinkin o't! ['My Love she's but a Lassie yet' (1790)]

12. Ae fond kiss, and then we sever!
Ae fareweel, and then forever!...

Had we never lov'd sae kindly,
Had we never lov'd sae blindly,
Never met — or never parted—
We had ne'er been broken-hearted. ['Ae Fond Kiss' (1791)]

13. Scots, wha hae wi' Wallace bled,
Scots, wham Bruce has aften led,
Welcome to your gory bed
Or to victorie! ['Scots, Wha Hae' (1793); also known as 'Robert Bruce's March to Bannockburn']

14. O, my luve's like a red, red, rose
That's newly sprung in June.
O, my luve's like the melodie,
That's sweetly play'd in tune. ['A Red Red Rose' (1794)]

15. The rank is but the guinea's stamp,
The man's the gowd for a' that...

For a' that, an' a' that,
It's comin yet for a' that,
That man to man the world o'er
Shall brithers be for a' that. ['A Man's a Man for a' that' (1795); also known by the title 'Is There for Honest Poverty']

16. The story of Wallace poured a Scottish prejudice in my veins which will boil along there till the flood-gates of life shut in eternal rest. [Letter to Dr John Moore, 1787]

17. To be overtopped in anything else, I can bear: but in the tests of generous love, I defy all mankind! [Letter to Clarinda (Mrs Agnes McLehose), 1788]

Burt, B. H. (1880–1950)
American songwriter

1. When you're all dressed up and no place to go. [Song title, 1913]

Burton, Robert (1577–1640)
English prose writer and clergyman

1. Tobacco, divine, rare, superexcellent tobacco, which goes far
   beyond all their panaceas, potable gold, and philosopher's stones, a
   sovereign remedy to all diseases ... But, as it is commonly abused by
   most men, which take it as tinkers do ale, 'tis a plague, a mischief,
   a violent purger of goods, lands, health, hellish, devilish, and damned
   tobacco, the ruin and overthrow of body and soul. [*Anatomy of
   Melancholy* (1621), II]

2. If there is a hell upon earth, it is to be found in a melancholy man's
   heart. [Ib. I]

Busenbaum, Hermann (1600–1668)
German Jesuit theologian

1. *Cui licitus est finis, etiam licent media.*
   Where the end is legitimate, the means are also legitimate, i.e. the
   end justifies the means. [*Medulla Theologiae Moralis* (1650)]

Butler, Samuel (1835–1902)
English novelist, painter, philosopher and scholar

1. I am the *enfant terrible* of literature and science. [*A Lecture on the Humour
   of Homer* (1892), 'Enfant Terrible': Myself']

2. The phrase 'unconscious humour' is the one contribution I have made
   to the current literature of the day. [Ib. 'Homo Unius Libri: Myself and
   "Unconscious Humour"']

3. A hen is only an egg's way of making another egg. [*Life and Habit*
   (1877)]

4. Parents are the last people on earth who ought to have children. [Attr.]

5. It was very good of God to let Carlyle and Mrs Carlyle marry one
   another and so make only two people miserable instead of four, besides
   being very amusing. [Letter to Miss Savage, 1884]

Byron, George Gordon, Lord (1788–1824)
English Romantic poet, satirist and traveller

1. 'Tis pleasant, sure, to see one's name in print;
   A Book's a Book, altho' there is nothing in't. [*English Bards and Scotch Reviewers* (1809), line 51]

2. The Assyrian came down like the wolf on the fold, ['The Destruction of Sennacherib' (1815)]

3. She walks in beauty, like the night
   Of cloudless climes and starry skies;
   And all that's best of dark and bright
   Meet in her aspect and her eyes:
   Thus mellow'd to that tender light
   Which heaven to gaudy day denies. ['She Walks in Beauty' (1815)]

4. There's not a joy the world can give like that it takes away. ['Stanzas for Music' (1815)]

5. So, we'll go no more a roving
   So late into the night
   Though the heart be still as loving,
   And the moon be still as bright... ['So, we'll go no more a roving' (1817)]

6. What men call gallantry, and gods adultery,
   Is much more common where the climate's sultry. [*Don Juan* (1819–1824), Canto I, 63]

7. Let us have wine and women, mirth and laughter,
   Sermons and soda-water the day after. [Ib. Canto II, 178]

8. Man, being reasonable, must get drunk;
   The best of life is but intoxication:
   Glory, the grape, love, gold, in these are sunk
   The hopes of all men, and of every nation. [Ib. Canto II, 179]

9. 'Tis strange – but true; for truth is always strange;
   Stranger than fiction. [Ib. Canto XIV, 101]

10. [Remark on the instantaneous success of *Childe Harold*]
    I awoke one morning and found myself famous. [In Thomas Moore, *Letters and Journals of Lord Byron* (1830), I]

Caesar, Caius Julius (c. 102–44 BC)
Roman statesman, historian and army commander; assassinated

1. *Gallia est omnis divisa in partes tres.*
   All Gaul is divided into three parts. [*De Bello Gallico*, I]

2. *Veni, vidi, vici.*
   I came, I saw, I conquered. [Letter, 47 BC]

3. [Remark on crossing the Rubicon]
   lacta alea est.
   The die is cast. [In Suetonius, *Lives of the Caesars*, 'Divus Julius']

4. *Et tu Brute?*
   You too, Brutus? [Last words]

Cage, John (1912–)
American experimental composer and writer

1. I have nothing to say, I am saying it, and that is poetry. ['Lecture on nothing', 1961]

Cagney, James (1904–1986)
American film actor, noted for roles as gangster

1. Look, Ma! Top of the world! [*White Heat*, film, 1949]

Campbell, Baron (1779–1861)
Scottish lawyer and politician; Lord Chancellor 1859

1. So essential did I consider an Index to be to every book, that I proposed to bring a Bill into parliament to deprive an author who publishes a book without an Index of the privilege of copyright; and, moreover, to subject him, for his offence, to a pecuniary penalty. [*Lives of the Chief Justices*]

Campbell, Mrs Patrick (1865–1940)
English actress; friend of George Bernard Shaw

1. I don't mind where people make love, so long as they don't do it in the street and frighten the horses. [Oral tradition]

Campbell, Roy 1901–1957
South African poet, translator of Spanish and journalist

1. You praise the firm restraint with which they write—

I'm with you there, of course:
They use the snaffle and the curb all right,
But where's the bloody horse? [*Adamastor* (1930), 'On Some South
African Novelists']

Campbell, Thomas (1777–1844)
Scottish poet, ballad-writer and journalist

1. 'Tis distance lends enchantment to the view,
And robes the mountain in its azure hue. [*Pleasures of Hope* (1799), 1]

2. Ye Mariners of England
That guard our native seas,
Whose flag has braved, a thousand years,
The battle and the breeze – ['Ye Mariners of England' (1801)]

3. O, I'm the chief of Ulva's isle,
And this Lord Ullin's daughter. ['Lord Ullin's Daughter' (1809)]

4. Now Barabbas was a publisher. [Attr. in Samuel Smiles, *A Publisher
and his Friends* (1891)]

Canetti, Elias (1905–1994)
*Bulgarian-born English novelist, dramatist and critic; Nobel prize
1981*

1. The great writers of aphorisms read as if they had all known each other
well. [*The Human Province* (1973)]

Carlyle Jane Welsh (1801–1866)
Scottish letter writer, literary hostess and poet; wife of Thomas Carlyle

1. [Referring to the death of Byron]
If they had said the sun and the moon was gone out of the heavens it
could not have struck me with the idea of a more awful and dreary
blank in the creation than the words: Byron is dead. [Letter to Thomas
Carlyle, 1824]

Carlyle, Thomas (1795–1881)
*Scottish historian, biographer, critic, essayist, teacher and translator;
husband of Jane Welsh Carlyle*

1. The barrenest of all mortals is the sentimentalist. [*Characteristics*]

2. He who first shortened the labour of copyists by device of *Movable Types* was disbanding hired armies, and cashiering most Kings and Senates, and creating a whole new democratic world: he had invented the art of printing. [*Sartor Resartus* (1834), I]

3. No man who has once heartily and wholly laughed can be altogether irreclaimably bad. [Ib. I]

4. The everlasting No. [Ib. II, chapter title]

5. The everlasting Yea. [Ib. 9, chapter title]

6. A whiff of grapeshot. [*History of the French Revolution* (1837), I]

7. [Of Robespierre]
The sea-green Incorruptible. [Ib. II]

8. The three great elements of modern civilization, Gunpowder, Printing, and the Protestant Religion. [*Critical and Miscellaneous Essays* (1838), 'State of German Literature']

9. The greatest of faults, I should say, is to be conscious of none. [*On Heroes, Hero-Worship and the Heroic* (1841), 'The Hero as Prophet']

10. Captains of industry. [*Past and Present* (1843), IV]

Carnegie, Andrew (1835–1919)
Scottish-born American philanthropist and ironmaster; benefactor of public libraries

1. Surplus wealth is a sacred trust which its possessor is bound to administer in his lifetime for the good of the community. [*The Gospel of Wealth*]

Carnegie, Dale (1888–1955)
American lecturer, teacher of public speaking and author

1. How to Win Friends and Influence People. [Title of book, 1936]

Carroll, Lewis (1832–1898)
English mathematician, deacon, children's novelist and photographer

1. 'What is the use of a book,' thought Alice, 'without pictures or conversations?' [*Alice in Wonderland* (1865), 1]

2. 'Curiouser and curiouser!' cried Alice. [Ib. 2]

3. 'You are old, Father William,' the young man said,

'And your hair has become very white;
And yet you incessantly stand on your head—
Do you think, at your age, it is right?' [Ib. 5]

4. [The Cheshire Cat]
This time it vanished quite slowly, beginning with the end of the tail, and ending with the grin, which remained some time after the rest of it had gone. [Ib. 6]

5. Then you should say what you mean,' the March Hare went on. 'I do,' Alice hastily replied; 'at least — at least I mean what I say — that's the same thing, you know.' [Ib. 7]

6. Twinkle, twinkle, little bat!
How I wonder what you're at!
Up above the world you fly,
Like a teatray in the sky. [Ib. 7]

7. Take care of the sense, and the sounds will take care of themselves. [Ib. 9]

8. The Drawling-master was an old conger-eel, that used to come once a week: *he* taught Drawling, Stretching, and Fainting in Coils. [Ib. 9]

9. Will you, won't you, will you, won't you, will you join the dance? [Ib. 10]

10. The Queen of Hearts, she made some tarts,
All on a summer day:
The Knave of Hearts, he stole those tarts,
And took them quite away! [Ib. 11]

11. 'Begin at the beginning,' the King said, gravely, 'and go on till you come to the end: then stop.' [Ib. 12]

12. 'Twas brillig, and the slithy toves
Did gyre and gimble in the wabe;
All mimsy were the borogoves,
And the mome raths outgrabe. [*Through the Looking-Glass* (1872), 1]

13. 'The time has come,' the Walrus said,
'To talk of many things:
Of shoes — and ships — and sealing wax — Of cabbages — and kings—
And why the sea is boiling hot
And whether pigs have wings.' [Ib. 4]

14. 'There's no use trying,' she said: 'one *can't* believe impossible things.' 'I dare say you haven't had much practice,' said the Queen. 'When I was your age, I always did it for half an hour a day. Why, sometimes I've believed as many as six impossible things before breakfast.' [Ib. 5]

15. You see it's like a portmanteau — there are two meanings packed up into one word. [Ib. 6]

16. The Lion looked at Alice wearily. 'Are you animal — or vegetable — or mineral?' he said, yawning at every other word. [Ib. 7]

17. For the Snark *was* a Boojum, you see. ['The Hunting of the Snark' (1876), 'The Vanishing']

Cary, Phoebe (1824–1871)
American poet

1. And though hard be the task,
   'Keep a stiff upper lip.' ['Keep a Stiff Upper Lip']

Catechism Shorter

1. Man's chief end is to glorify God, and to enjoy him forever. [Question 1]

Cato the Elder (234–149 BC)
Roman statesman, called 'the Censor'; writer and orator

1. *Delenda est Carthago.*
   Carthage must be destroyed. [In Pliny, *Natural History*]

Catullus, Caius Valerius (84–c. 54 BC)
Roman lyric poet, noted for his love poems

1. *Qui nunc it per iter tenebricosum
   Illuc, unde negant redire quemquam.*
   Now he goes along the darksome road, thither whence they say no one returns. [*Carmina*, 3]

2. *Vivamus, mea Lesbia, atque amemus.*
   My Lesbia, let us live and love. [Ib. 5]

3. *Miser Catulle, desinas ineptire,
   Et quod vides perisse perditum ducas.*

Poor Catullus, drop your sily fancies, and what you see is lost let it be lost. [Ib. 8]

4. *Sed mulier cupido quod dicit amanti,*
In vento et rapida scribere oportet aqua.
But what a woman says to her ardent lover should be written in wind and running water. [Ib. 70]

5. *Odi et amo: quare id factum, fortasse requiris.*
Nescio, sed fieri sentio et excrucior.
I hate and I love: why I do so you may indeed ask. I do not know, but I feel it happen and am in agony. [Ib. 85]

6. *Atque in perpetuum, frater, ave atque vale.*
And so, my brother, hail, and farewell evermore! [Ib. 101]

Cavell, Edith (1865–1915)
English nurse; executed by the Germans for helping Allied soldiers escape from Belgium

1. Standing, as I do, in the view of God and eternity I realize that patriotism is not enough. I must have no hatred or bitterness towards anyone. [Last words, reported in *The Times*, 1915]

Cervantes, Miguel de (1547–1616)
Spanish novelist and dramatist; author of the satirical romance Don Quixote, *thought to be the first modern novel*

1. Take care, your worship, those things over there are not giants but windmills. [*Don Quixote* (1605), I.8]

2. *La mejor salsa del mundo es el hambre.*
The best sauce in the world is hunger. [Ib. II.5]

Chalmers, Patrick Reginald (1872–1942)
British banker and writer on field sports

1. What's lost upon the roundabouts we pulls up on the swings! ['Green Days and Blue Days: Roundabouts and Swings']

Chamberlain, Neville (1869–1940)
English statesman and Conservative Prime Minister 1937–40; son of Joseph Chamberlain

1. I believe it is peace for our time ... peace with honour. [Speech after Munich Agreement, 1938]

Chamfort, Nicolas (1741–1794)
French writer, noted for his wit

1. *L'amour, tel qu'il existe dans la société, n'est que l'échange de deux fantaisies
   et le contact de deux épidermes.*
   Love, as it exists in society, is nothing but the exchange of two fantasies
   and the contact of two skins. [*Maximes et pensées* (1796), 6]

2. *Les pauvres sont les nègres de l'Europe.*
   The poor are the blacks of Europe. [Ib. 8]

Chandler, Raymond (1888–1959)
*American author of crime fiction; novelist, short-story and screen
writer*

1. Down these mean streets a man must go who is not himself mean;
   who is neither tarnished nor afraid. [*Atlantic Monthly* (1944), 'The
   Simple Art of Murder']

2. The demand was for constant action; if you stopped to think you were
   lost. When in doubt have a man come through a door with a gun in
   his hand. This could get to be pretty silly but somehow it didn't seem
   to matter. [Ib.]

Chaplin, Charlie (Sir Charles Chaplin) (1889–1977)
English comedian, film actor, director and satirist

1. All I need to make a comedy is a park, a policeman and a pretty girl
   [*My Autobiography* (1964)]

Chapman, George (c. 1559–c. 1634)
English poet, dramatist and translator of Greek and Latin

1. I am ashamed the law is such an ass. [*Revenge for Honour* (1654), III]

Chapman, Graham (1941–1989)
British comedian and scriptwriter

1. And now for something completely different. [Catch phrase
   popularized in *Monty Python's Flying Circus*, BBC TV programme,
   1969–1974; with John Cleese (1940–), Terry Gilliam (1940–),
   Eric Idle (1943–), Terry Jones (1942–) and Michael Palin (1943–)]

Charles II (1630–1685)
English King of Great Britain and Ireland from 1660; son of Charles I

1. [Comment on Rochester's epitaph on him]
   This is very true: for my words are my own and my actions are my ministers'. [In Thomas Hearne, *Remarks and Collections*]

2. He had been, he said, an unconscionable time dying; but he hoped that they would excuse it. [In Macaulay, *History of England* (1849)]

Charles V, Holy Roman Emperor (1500–1558)
Emperor 1519–56; King of Spain (as Charles I), 1516–1556

1. An iron hand in a velvet glove. [In Carlyle, *Latter-Day Pamphlets*]

Chateaubriand, François-René de (1768–1848)
French novelist, autobiographical writer and statesman

1. *L'écrivain original n'est pas celui qui n'imite personne, mais celui que personne ne peut imiter.*
   The original writer is not he who refrains from imitating others, but he who can be imitated by none. [*Génie de Christianisme* (1802), II.1]

Chaucer, Geoffrey (c. 1340–1400)
English poet, noted for his narrative skill and humour; public servant and courtier

1. Whan that Aprill with his shoures soote
   The droghte of March hath perced to the roote,
   And bathed every veyne in swich licour
   Of which vertu engendred is the flour. [*The Canterbury Tales*, General Prologue]

2. He nevere yet no vileynye ne sayde
   In al his lyf unto no maner wight.
   He was a verray, parfit gentil knyght. [Ib. General Prologue, The Knight]

3. He was as fressh as is the month of May. [Ib. General Prologue]

4. Nowher so bisy a man as he ther nas,
   And yet he seemed bisier than he was. [Ib. The Sergeant of the Lawe]

5. This world nis but a thurghfare ful of wo,
   And we ben pilgrimes, passinge to and fro;
   Deeth is an ende of every worldly sore. [Ib. The Knight's Tale]

6. The smylere with the knyf under the cloke. [Ib. The Knight's Tale]

7. To maken vertu of necessitee. [Ib. The Knight's Tale]

8. Mordre wol out, that se we day by day. [Ib. The Nuns' Priest's Tale]

9. Thou shalt make castles thanne in Spayne,
And dreme of joye, all but in vayne. [*The Romaunt of the Rose*]

Chekhov, Anton (1860–1904)
Russian short-story writer, realist dramatist and doctor

1. Man has been endowed with reason, with the power to create, so that he can add to what he's been given. But up to now he hasn't been a creator, only a destroyer. Forests keep disappearing, rivers dry up, wild life's become extinct, the climate's ruined and the land grows poorer and uglier every day. [*Uncle Vanya* (1897), I]

2. *Sonya*: I'm not beautiful.
Helen: You have lovely hair.
Sonya: No, when a woman isn't beautiful, people always say, 'You have lovely eyes, you have lovely hair. [Ib. III]

3. When a lot of remedies are suggested for a disease, that means it can't be cured. [*The Cherry Orchard* (1904), II]

Chesterfield, Philip Dormer Stanhope, Fourth Earl of (1694–1773)
English politician, statesman, letter writer and orator

1. The knowledge of the world is only to be acquired in the world, and not in a closet. [*Letters to his Son*, 1746]

2. An injury is much sooner forgotten than an insult. [Ib.]

3. Whatever is worth doing at all is worth doing well. [Ib.]

4. Advice is seldom welcome; and those who want it the most always like it the least. [Ib. 1748]

5. Religion is by no means a proper subject of conversation in a mixed company. [Letter to his Godson]

6. It is an undoubted truth, that the less one has to do, the less time one finds to do it in. One yawns, one procrastinates, one can do it when one will, and therefore one seldom does it at all. [Letter]

Chesterton, Gilbert Keith (1874–1936)
English novelist, poet, journalist, critic and essayist

1. The word 'orthodoxy' not only no longer means being right; it practically means being wrong. [*Heretics* (1905), 1]

2. A good novel tells us the truth about its hero; but a bad novel tells us the truth about its author. [Ib. 15]

3. The artistic temperament is a disease that afflicts amateurs. [Ib. 17]

4. The madman is not the man who has lost his reason. The madman is the man who has lost everything except his reason. [*Orthodoxy* (1908), 1]

5. If a thing is worth doing, it is worth doing badly. [*What's Wrong with the World* (1910), 'Folly and Female Education']

6. Before the Roman came to Rye or out to Severn strode,
The rolling English drunkard made the rolling English road. ['The Rolling English Road' (1914)]

7. [Telegram to wife (other venues have been suggested but this was the original)]
Am in Market Harborough. Where ought I to be ? [Quoted in M. Ward, *Return to Chesterton*]

Churchill, Lord Randolph (1849–1894)
English Conservative politician; Chancellor of the Exchequer 1886; father of Winston Churchill

1. Ulster will fight; Ulster will be right. [Public letter, 1886]

Churchill, Sir Winston (1874–1965)
English statesman; Conservative Prime Minister 1940–45, 1951–55; historian, army officer and biographer; Nobel prize for literature 1953

1. In war, resolution; in defeat, defiance; in victory, magnanimity; in peace, goodwill. [*The Second World War* (1948–54), I, Epigraph]

2. The maxim of the British people is 'Business as usual'. [Speech, 1914]

3. I would say to the House, as I have said to those who have joined this Government, 'I have nothing to offer but blood, toil, tears and sweat'. [Speech, House of Commons, 1940]

4. We shall not flag or fail. We shall fight in France, we shall fight on the seas and oceans, we shall fight with growing confidence and growing

strength in the air, we shall defend our island, whatever the cost may be, we shall fight on the beaches, we shall fight on the landing grounds, we shall fight in the fields and in the streets, we shall fight in the hills; we shall never surrender. [Speech, June, 1940]

5. Let us therefore brace ourselves to our duties, and so bear ourselves that, if the British Empire and its Commonwealth last for a thousand years, men will still say, 'This was their finest hour'. [Speech, June, 1940]

6. [On RAF pilots in the Battle of Britain]
Never in the field of human conflict was so much owed by so many to so few. [Speech, August 1940]

7. Give us the tools, and we will finish the job. [Broadcast, 1941]

8. To jaw-jaw is better than to war-war. [Speech, Washington, 1954]

9. [Marginal comment on a document]
This is the sort of English up with which I will not put. [In Ernest Gowers, *Plain Words* (1948)]

Cicero, Marcus Tullius (106–43 BC)
Roman orator, statesman, essayist and letter writer; murdered by agents of Mark Anthony

1. *Summum bonum.*
The greatest good. [*De Officiis*, I.5]

2. *Numquam se minus otiosum esse quam cum otiosus, nec minus solum quam solus esset*
Never less idle than when free from work, nor less alone than when completely alone. [Ib. III.1]

3. *Poetarum licentiae liberiora.*
The freedom of poetic licence. [*De Oratore*]

4. *O tempora! O mores!*
What an age! What customs! [*In Catilinam*, I.1]

5. *Cui bono?*
Who stands to gain? [*Pro Milone*, 12]

Clare, John (1793–1864)
English rural poet

1. I am – yet what I am, none cares or knows;
   My friends forsake me like a memory lost:
   I am the self-consumer of my woes. ['I Am' (1848)]

2. If life had a second edition, how I would correct the proofs. [Letter
   to a friend]

Clausewitz, Karl von (1780–1831)
German general and military philosopher

1. *Der Krieg ist nichts als eine Fortsetzung des politischen Verkehrs mit
   Einmischung anderer Mittel.*
   War is nothing but the continuation of politics by other means. [*Vom
   Kriege* (*On War*, 1832–34)]

Cobbett, William (1762–1835)
*English political journalist, reformer and politician; prose writer,
farmer and army officer*

1. [Of London]
   But what is to be the fate of the great wen of all? The monster, called
   ... 'the metropolis of the empire'? [*Political Register*, 1822, 'Rural Rides']

Colby, Frank Moore (1865–1925)
American editor, historian and economist

1. Men will confess to treason, murder, arson, false teeth, or a wig. How
   many of them will own up to a lack of humour? [*Essays*, I]

2. I have found some of the best reasons I ever had for remaining at the
   bottom simply by looking at the men at the top. [Ib. II]

Coleridge, Samuel Taylor (1772–1834)
*Leading English Romantic poet, philosopher and critic; father of
Hartley Coleridge*

1. It is an ancient Mariner,
   And he stoppeth one of three.
   'By thy long grey beard and glittering eye,
   Now wherefore stopp'st thou me? ['The Rime of the Ancient Mariner'
   (1798), 1]

2. As idle as a painted ship
Upon a painted ocean.

Water, water, every where,
And all the boards did shrink;
Water, water, every where
Nor any drop to drink. [Ib. 2]

3. Like one, that on a lonesome road
Doth walk in fear and dread,
And having once turned round walks on,
And turns no more his head;
Because he knows, a frightful fiend
Doth close behind him tread. [Ib. 6]

4. Swans sing before they die—'twere no bad thing
Should certain persons die before they sing. ['Epigram on a Volunteer
Singer']

5. In Xanadu did Kubla Khan
A stately pleasure-dome decree: ['Kubla Khan' (1816)]

6. That willing suspension of disbelief for the moment, which constitutes
poetic faith. [*Biographia Litereria* (1817), 14]

7. I wish our clever young poets would remember my homely definitions
of prose and poetry; that is prose = words in their best order; poetry
= the best words in the best order. [*Table-Talk* (1835), 12 July 1827]

8. What comes from the heart, goes to the heart. [Ib.]

Colton, Charles Caleb (c. 1780–1832)
English clergyman, poet, satirist, essayist and gambler

1. When you have nothing to say, say nothing. [*Lacon* (1820)]

2. Imitation is the sincerest form of flattery. [Ib.]

Confucius (c. 550–c. 478 BC)
*Chinese philosopher and teacher of ethics, on whose system of
morality Confucianism is based*

1. To be able to practise five things everywhere under heaven constitutes
perfect virtue ... gravity, generosity of soul, sincerity, earnestness, and
kindness. [*Analects*]

2. Everything has its beauty but not everyone sees it. [Ib.]

Congreve, William (1670–1729)
English dramatist, noted for his comedies of manners and witty dialogue

1. Eternity was in that moment. [*The Old Bachelor* (1693), IV.vii]

2. No mask like open truth to cover lies,
As to go naked is the best disguise. [*The Double Dealer* (1694), V.vi]

3. He that first cries out stop thief, is often he that has stolen the treasure. [*Love for Love* (1695), III.xiv]

4. Music has charms to soothe a savage breast. [*The Mourning Bride* (1697), I.i]

5. Heav'n has no rage, like love to hatred turn'd,
Nor Hell a fury, like a woman scorn'd. [Ib. III.viii]

Connell, James M. (1852–1929)
Irish socialist writer

1. Then raise the scarlet standard high!
Within its shade we'll live or die.
Tho' cowards flinch and traitors sneer,
We'll keep the red flag flying here. ['The Red Flag' (1889)]

Connolly, Cyril (1903–1974)
English literary editor, journalist, critic and author of prose and verse

1. The true index of a man's character is the health of his wife. [*Unquiet Grave*, pt.2]

Conrad, Joseph (1857–1924)
Polish-born British modernist novelist and short-story writer, sailor and explorer

1. The horror! The horror! [*Heart of Darkness* (1902), 3]

2. The terrorist and the policeman both come from the same basket. [*The Secret Agent* (1907), 4]

Conran, Shirley (1932–)
English journalist and novelist

1. Our motto: Life is too short to stuff a mushroom. [*Superwoman* (1975), Epigraph]

Constantine, Emperor (c. AD 288–337)
First Christian Roman emperor 306–337

1. *In hoc signo vinces.*
In this sign thou shalt conquer. [Attr. words of Constantine's vision, AD 312]

Cook, A. J. (1885–1931)
English miners' leader; prominent in General Strike of 1926

1. Not a minute on the day, not a penny off the pay. [Speech, 1926]

Coolidge, Calvin (1872–1933)
American statesman and lawyer; Republic President of the USA 1923–29

1. The business of America is business. [Speech, 1925]

Cousin, Victor (1792–1867)
French eclectic philosopher and educationist

1. *Il faut de le religion pour la religion, de la morale pour la morale, comme de l'art pour l'art...*
We must have religion for religion's sake, morality for morality's sake, as with art for art's sake... [Lecture, 1818]

Coward, Sir Noël (1899–1973)
English dramatist, noted for sophisticated comedies; actor, producer and composer

1. Extraordinary how potent cheap music is. [*Private Lives* (1930), I]

2. Mad dogs and Englishmen go out in the mid-day sun; ['Mad Dogs and Englishmen', 1931]

3. Don't put your daughter on the stage, Mrs Worthington. [Mrs Worthington, 1935]

4. Work is much more fun than fun. [*The Observer*, 'Sayings of the Week', 1963]

Cowper, William (1731–1800)
English poet; hymn and letter writer

1. The cups
   That cheer but not inebriate. ['The Winter Evening', *The Task*]

2. God moves in a mysterious way
   His wonders to perform;
   He plants his footsteps in the sea,
   And rides upon the storm. [*Olney Hymns* (1779), 35]

3. The poplars are felled, farewell to the shade,
   And the whispering sound of the cool colonnade! ['The Poplar Field'
   (1784)]

4. [On Johnson's inadequate treatment of *Paradise Lost*]
   Oh! I could thresh his old jacket till I made his pension jingle in his
   pockets. [*Letters and Prose Writings of William Cowper*, Letter to the Revd.
   W. Unwin, 1779]

Crabbe, George (1754–1832)
English narrative poet; clergyman, surgeon and botanist

1. The murmuring poor, who will not fast in peace. [*The Newspaper*
   (1785)]

2. Habit with him was all the test of truth,
   'It must be right: I've done it from my youth.' [*The Borough* (1810),
   'The Vicar']

3. 'The game,' he said, 'is never lost till won.' [*Tales of the Hall* (1819),
   'Gretna Green']

Crisp, Quentin (1908–)
English writer, publicist and model

1. There was no need to do any housework at all. After the first four
   years the dirt doesn't get any worse. [*The Naked Civil Servant* (1968)]

Croker, John Wilson (1780–1857)
Irish politician, dramatist, editor and essayist

1. A game which a sharper once played with a dupe, entitled, 'Heads I
   win, tails you lose.' [*Croker Papers*]

Crompton, Richmal (1890–1969)
English children's writer and teacher

1. Violet Elizabeth dried her tears. She saw that they were useless and she did not believe in wasting her effects. 'All right,' she said calmly, 'I'll thcream then. I'll thcream, an' thcream, an' thcream till I'm thick. [*Just William* (1925)]

Cromwell, Oliver (1599–1658)
English general and statesman; Puritan parliamentary army leader; Lord Protector 1653

1. I beseech you, in the bowels of Christ, think it possible you may be mistaken. [Letter to the General Assembly of the Church of Scotland, 1650]

2. You have sat too long here for any good you have been doing. Depart, I say, and let us have done with you. In the name of God, go! [Address to the Rump Parliament, 1653]

3. Mr. Lely, I desire you would use all your skill to paint my picture freely like me, and not flatter me at all; but remark all these roughnesses, pimples, warts, and everything as you see me, otherwise I will never pay a farthing for it. [In Horace Walpole, *Anecdotes of Painting in England* (1763)]

Crosland, T. W. H. (1868–1924)
English journalist and poet

1. The Unspeakable Scot. [Title of an essay]

cummings, e. e.(Edward Estlin) (1894–1962)
American lyric poet, noted for his experimental typography, and painter

1. a politician is an arse upon
   which everyone has sat except a man [*1 x 1* (1944), no. 10]

Dana, Charles Anderson (1819–1897)
American newspaper editor and reformer

1. When a dog bites a man that is not news, but when a man bites a dog that is news. [New York *Sun*, 1882]

Dante, Alighieri (1265–1321)
Renowned Italian poet and political philosopher

1. *Nel mezzo del cammin di nostra vita*
   Mi ritrovai per una selva oscura
   Che la diritta via era smarrita.
   Halfway through the journey of our life I found myself in a dark forest,
   bewildered, lost and forlorn. [*Divina Commedia* (1307), 'Inferno',
   Canto 1]

2. *PER ME SI VA NELLA CITTA' DOLENTE,*
   PER ME SI VA NELL'ETERNO DOLORE,
   PER ME SI VA TRA LA PERDUTA GENTE…
   LASCIATE OGNI SPERANZA VOI CH'ENTRATE!
   Through me one goes to the sorrowful city. Through me one goes to
   eternal suffering. Through me one goes among lost people … Abandon
   all hope, you who enter! [Ib. 'Inferno', Canto 3]

3. *L'amor che muove il sole e l'altre stelle.*
   True love that moves the sun and the universe. [Ib. 'Paradiso', Canto
   33]

Danton, Georges (1759–1794)
French revolutionary leader; Minister of Justice (1792–94); executed

1. [Remark to his executioner]
   Thou wilt show my head to the people: it is worth showing. [Attr.,
   1794]

Darwin, Charles (1809–1882)
*English naturalist, famous for his theory of evolution by natural
selection*

1. I have called this principle, by which each slight variation, if useful,
   is preserved, by the term of Natural Selection. [*The Origin of Species*
   (1859), 3]

2. The expression often used by Mr Herbert Spencer of the Survival
   of the Fittest is more accurate, and is sometimes equally
   convenient. [Ib. 3]

3. The highest possible stage in moral culture is when we recognize that
   we ought to control our thoughts. [*The Descent of Man* (1871), 4]

4. We must, however, acknowledge, as it seems to me, that man with all his noble qualities ... still bears in his bodily frame the indelible stamp of his lowly origin. [Ib. conclusion]

Davies, Scrope Berdmore (c.1783–1852)
English conversationalist

1. Babylon in all its desolation is a sight not so awful as that of the human mind in ruins. [Letter to Thomas Raikes, 1835]

Davies, William Henry (1871–1940)
Welsh poet, tramp and novelist

1. What is this life if, full of care,
   We have no time to stand and stare? [*Songs of Joy* (1911), 'Leisure']

Day, Clarence Shepard (1874–1935)
American essayist and humorist

1. 'If you don't go to other men's funerals,' he told Father stiffly, 'they won't go to yours.' [*Life with Father* (1935), 'Father plans']

Decatur, Stephen (1779–1820)
American naval commander

1. [Toast during a banquet to celebrate the victory over the 'barbary pirates' of Algeria, 1815]
   Our country! In her intercourse with foreign nations, may she always be in the right; but our country, right or wrong. [In Mackenzie, *Life of Decatur* (1846), 14]

Defoe, Daniel (c. 1661–1731)
English novelist, journalist, pamphleteer and political critic

1. He bid me observe it, and I should always find, that the calamities of life were shared among the upper and lower part of mankind; but that the middle station had the fewest disasters. [*The Life and Adventures of Robinson Crusoe* (1719), I]

2. I takes my man Friday with me. [Ib.]

3. From this amphibious, ill-born mob began
   That vain, ill-natur'd thing, an Englishman... [*The True-Born Englishman* (1701), I]

Dekker, Thomas (c. 1570–c. 1632)
English dramatist, and pamphleteer

1. Golden slumbers kiss your eyes,
   Smiles awake you when you rise:
   Sleep, pretty wantons, do not cry,
   And I will sing a lullaby:
   Rock them, rock them, lullaby. ['Patient Grissil' (1603), IV]

Delille, Abbé Jacques (1738–1813)
French poet and translator

1. *Le sort fait les parents, le choix fait les amis.*
   Relations are made by fate, friends by choice. [*Malheur et pitié* (1803), I]

De Mille, Cecil B. (1881–1959)
American film producer and director, known for his biblical epics

1. The public is always right. [In Colombo, *Wit and Wisdom of the Moviemakers*]

Demosthenes (c. 384–322 BC)
Athenian statesman and orator; opponent of Macedonian power

1. There is one safeguard, which is an advantage and security for all, but especially to democracies against despots. What is it? Distrust. [*Philippics*, II, section 24]

Dennis, John (1657–1734)
English critic and dramatist

1. A man who could make so vile a pun would not scruple to pick a pocket. [*The Gentleman's Magazine*, 1781]

De Quincey, Thomas (1785–1859)
English essayist and opium addict

1. Murder Considered as One of the Fine Arts. [Title of Essay, 1827]

2. It was a Sunday afternoon, wet and cheerless: and a duller spectacle this earth of ours has not to show than a rainy Sunday in London. [*Confessions of an English Opium Eater* (1822), II, 'The Pleasures of Opium']

Descartes, René (1596–1650)
French rationalist philosopher and mathematician; founder of modern philosophy

1. *Cogito, ergo sum.*
   I think, therefore I am. [*Discours de la Méthode* (1637)]

2. *Le bon sens est la chose du monde la mieux partagée, car chacun pense en être bien pourvu.*
   Common sense is the best distributed thing in the world, for we all think we possess a good share of it. [Ib.]

3. *La lecture de tous les bons livres est comme une conversation avec les plus honnêtes gens des siècles passés.*
   The reading of all good books is like a conversation with the finest men of past centuries. [Ib.]

Deschamps, Eustache (c. 1346–c. 1406)
French lyric poet, satirist and courtier

1. *Qui pendra la sonnette au chat?*
   Who will bell the cat? [Ballade: 'Le Chat et les souris' ('The Cat and the Mice')]

Destouches, Philippe Néricault (1680–1754)
French dramatist, author of moralizing comedies

1. *Les absents ont toujours tort.*
   The absent are always in the wrong. [*L'Obstacle Imprévu* (1717), I.vi]

Dickens, Charles (1812–1870)
English novelist, noted for his narrative, characterization and criticism of social evils

1. A smattering of everything, and a knowledge of nothing. [*Sketches by Boz* (1836), 'Sentiment']

2. 'Do you spell it with a "V" or a "W"?' inquired the judge. 'That depends upon the taste and fancy of the speller, my Lord,' replied Sam. [*The Pickwick Papers* (1837), 34]

3. Please, sir, I want some more. [*Oliver Twist* (1838), 2]

4. He was better known by the *sobriquet* of 'The artful Dodger'. [Ib. 8]

5. Language was not powerful enough to describe the infant phenomenon. [*Nicholas Nickleby* (1839), 23]

6. All is gas and gaiters! [Ib. 49]

7. It was a maxim with Foxey – our revered father, gentlemen – 'Always suspect everybody.' [*The Old Curiosity Shop* (1841), 66]

8. 'Bah!' said Scrooge, 'Humbug!' [*A Christmas Carol* (1843), Stave 1]

9. 'God bless us every one!' said Tiny Tim. [Ib. Stave 3]

10. 'I am a lone lorn creetur',' were Mrs Gummidge's words, ... 'and everythink goes contrairy with me.' [*David Copperfield* (1850), 3]

11. Barkis is willin'. [Ib. 5]

12. [Referring to Mr Micawber]
'In case anything turned up,' which was his favourite expression.
[Ib. 11]

13. Annual income twenty pounds, annual expenditure nineteen nineteen six, result happiness. Annual income twenty pounds, annual expenditure twenty pounds ought and six, result misery. [Ib. 12]

14. We are so very 'umble. [Ib. 17]

15. What a world of gammon and spinnage it is, though, ain't it! [Ib. 22]

16. Accidents will occur in the best-regulated families. [Ib. 28]

17. This is a London particular ... A fog, miss. [*Bleak House* (1853), 3]

18. The wind's in the east ... I am always conscious of an uncomfortable sensation now and then when the wind is blowing in the east. [Ib. 6]

19. Now, what I want is, Facts. Teach these boys and girls nothing but Facts. Facts alone are wanted in life. Plant nothing else, and root out everything else ... Stick to Facts, sir! [*Hard Times* (1854), I, 1]

20. It was the best of times, it was the worst of times, it was the age of wisdom, it was the age of foolishness, it was the epoch of belief, it was the epoch of incredulity, it was the season of Light, it was the season of Darkness, it was the spring of hope, it was the winter of despair, we had everything before us, we had nothing before us, we were all going direct to Heaven, we were all going direct the other way. [*A Tale of Two Cities* (1859), I, 1]

21. It is a far, far better thing that I do, than I have ever done; it is a far, far better rest that I go to than I have ever known. [Ib. III, 15]

22. The question about everything was, would it bring a blush into the cheek of a young person? [*Our Mutual Friend* (1865), I, 11]

23. He do the Police in different voices. [Ib. I, 16]

Dickinson, Emily (1830–1886)
American lyric poet, little known in her lifetime

1. Because I could not stop for Death—
He kindly stopped for me—
The Carriage held but just Ourselves—
And Immortality... ['Because I could not stop for Death' (c. 1863)]

2. What fortitude the Soul contains,
That it can so endure
The accent of a coming Foot—
The opening of a Door. ['Elysium is as far as to' (c. 1882)]

3. There is no Frigate like a Book
To take us Lands away ['There is no Frigate']

Diderot, Denis (1713–1784)
French philosopher of the Enlightenment; encyclopaedist, novelist, dramatist and satirist

1. Men will never be free until the last king is strangled with the entrails of the last priest. [*Dithyrambe sur la Fête des Rois*]

Diodorus Siculus (c. 1st century BC)
Sicilian-born Greek historian

1. [Inscription over library door in Alexandria]
Medicine for the soul. [*History*, I]

Diogenes (the Cynic) (c. 400–325 BC)
Greek ascetic philosopher

1. [*Kosmopolites*: origin of the word 'cosmopolitan']
I am a citizen of the world. [In Diogenes Laertius, *Lives of Eminent Philosophers*, 'Diogenes']

2. I do not know whether there are gods, but there ought to be. [In Tertullian, *Ad Nationes*]

Disraeli, Benjamin (First Earl of Beaconsfield) (1804–1881)
English statesman and novelist; Conservative Prime Minister 1868, 1874–80; son of Isaac DIsraeli

1. 'Two nations; between whom there is no intercourse and no sympathy; who are as ignorant of each other's habits, thoughts, and feelings, as if they were dwellers in different zones, or inhabitants of different planets; who are formed by a different breeding, are fed by a different food, are ordered by different manners, and are not governed by the same laws.'
'You speak of–' said Egremont, hesitatingly.
'THE RICH AND THE POOR.' [*Sybil* (1845), II, 5]

2. A Conservative government is an organized hypocrisy. [Speech, 1845]

3. Finality is not the language of politics. [Speech, 1859]

4. Is man an ape or an angel? Now I am on the side of the angels. [Speech, Meeting of Society for Increasing Endowments of Small Livings in the Diocese of Oxford, 1864]

5. An author who speaks about his own books is almost as bad as a mother who talks about her own children. [Speech at Banquet given in Glasgow on his installation as Lord Rector, 1873]

6. [His customary reply to those who sent him unsolicited manuscripts] Thank you for the manuscript; I shall lose no time in reading it. [Attr.]

7. There are three kinds of lies: lies, damned lies and statistics. [Attr.]

8. When I want to read a novel I write one. [Attr.]

Dodd, Ken (1931–)
English comedian, singer, entertainer and actor

1. [Commenting on Freud's theory that a good joke will lead to great relief and elation]
The trouble with Freud is that he never played the Glasgow Empire Saturday night after Rangers and Celtic had both lost. [TV interview, 1965]

Donne, John (1572–1631)
English metaphysical poet and divine

1. Just such disparity
   As is 'twixt air and Angels' purity,
   'Twixt women's love, and men's will ever be. ['Funeral Elegy' (1610)]

2. She, and comparisons are odious. [*Elegies* (c. 1595), 8, 'The Comparison']

3. Licence my roving hands, and let them go,
   Before, behind, between, above, below.
   O my America! my new-found-land,
   My kingdom, safeliest when with one man mann'd. [Ib. 19, 'To His Mistress Going to Bed']

4. Go, and catch a falling star,
   Get with child a mandrake root,
   Tell me, where all past years are,
   Or who cleft the Devil's foot... [*Songs and Sonnets* (1611), 'Song']

5. But I do nothing upon my self, and yet I am mine own *Executioner*. [*Devotions upon Emergent Occasions* (1624), 'Meditation', XII]

6. No man is an *Island*, entire of it self; every man is a piece of *Continent*, a part of the *main*; if a *clod* be washed away by the *sea*, *Europe* is the less, as well as if a *promontory* were, as well as if a *manor* of thy *friends* or of *thine own* were; any man's *death* diminishes *me*, because I am involved in *Mankind*; And therefore never send to know for whom the *bell* tolls; it tolls for *thee*. [Ib. XVII]

Dostoevsky, Fyodor (1821–1881)
Russian realist novelist, noted for his psychological insight

1. If you were to destroy in mankind the belief in immortality, not only love but every living force maintaining the life of the world would at once dry up. Moreover, nothing then would be immoral, everything would be lawful, even cannibalism. [*The Brothers Karamazov* (1879–1880), Part I, II, 6]

Douglas, Lord Alfred (1870–1945)
English poet; intimate of Oscar Wilde

1. I am the Love that dare not speak its name. ['Two Loves' (1896)]

Douglas, Archibald, Fifth Earl of Angus (c. 1449–1514)
Scottish courtier; Chancellor under Charles IV, 1493–98; father of
Gavin Douglas

1. [Said at a meeting of Scottish nobles, 1482, referring to his plan to
   capture Robert Cochrane]
   I shall bell the cat. [Attr.]

Douglas, Norman (1868–1952)
Austrian-born Scottish novelist, travel writer and essayist

1. Many a man who thinks to found a home discovers that he has merely
   opened a tavern for his friends. [*South Wind* (1917)]

Dowson, Ernest (1867–1900)
English decadent poet

1. They are not long, the days of wine and roses; ['Vitae Summa Brevis
   Spem Nos Vetat Incohare Longam' (1896)]

Doyle, Sir Arthur Conan (1859–1930)
Scottish novelist, short-story writer, doctor and war correspondent;
creator of the detective Sherlock Holmes

1. It has long been an axiom of mine that the little things are infinitely
   the most important. [*The Adventures of Sherlock Holmes* (1892), 'A Case
   of Identity']

2. It is quite a three-pipe problem, and I beg that you won't speak to
   me for fifty minutes. [Ib. 'The Red-Headed League']

3. [Dialogue between Watson and Holmes]
   'Excellent!' I cried.
   'Elementary,' said he. [*The Memoirs of Sherlock Holmes* (1894), 'The
   Crooked Man']

4. 'Is there any other point to which you would wish to draw my
   attention? ' 'To the curious incident of the dog in the night-time.' 'The
   dog did nothing in the night-time.' 'That was the curious incident,'
   remarked Sherlock Holmes. [Ib. 'Silver Blaze']

5. How often have I said to you that when you have eliminated the
   impossible, whatever remains, *however improbable*, must be the truth.
   [*The Sign of Four* (1890)]

6. It is my belief, Watson, founded upon my experience, that the lowest and vilest alleys of London do not present a more dreadful record of sin than does the smiling and beautiful countryside. [*The Adventures of Sherlock Holmes* (1892), 'Copper Beeches']

Drake, Sir Francis (c. 1540–1596)
English navigator, sailed round the world, 1577–80; known for his role in the defeat of the Spanish Armada

1. [Referring to the sighting of the Spanish Armada, during a game of bowls, 20 July 1588]
There is plenty of time to win this game, and to thrash the Spaniards too. [Attr. in *Dictionary of National Biography*]

Drayton, Michael (1563–1631)
English poet, noted for his odes, sonnets and pastoral verse

1. Since there's no help, come let us kiss and part,
Nay, I have done: you get no more of me,
And I am glad, yea glad with all my heart,
That thus so cleanly, I myself can free,
Shake hands for ever, cancel all our vows,
And when we meet at any time again,
Be it not seen in either of our brows,
That we one jot of former love retain; ['Idea', 61 (1619)]

Dryden, John (1631–1700)
English poet, noted as a satirist, heroic dramatist, critic and translator poet laureate 1668

1. Beware the fury of a patient man. [*Absalom and Achitophel* (1681), Part I, line 1005]

2. We must beat the iron while it is hot, but we may polish it at leisure [*Aeneis* (1697), Dedication]

3. None but the brave deserves the fair. ['Alexander's Feast' (1697), I]

4. Drinking is the soldier's pleasure;
Rich the treasure;
Sweet the pleasure;
Sweet is pleasure after pain. [Ib. III]

5. War, he sung, is toil and trouble;
Honour but an empty bubble.

Never ending, still beginning,
Fighting still, and still destroying,
If the world be worth thy winning,
Think, oh think, it worth enjoying. [Ib. V]

6. And, like another Helen, fired another Troy. [Ib. VI]

7. Whistling to keep myself from being afraid. [*Amphitryon* (1690), III.i]

8. I never saw any good that came of telling truth. [Ib. III.i]

9. Here lies my wife: here let her lie!
Now she's at rest, and so am I. ['Epitaph intended for his wife']

10. For present joys are more to flesh and blood
Than a dull prospect of a distant good. [*The Hind and the Panther*
(1687), Part III, line 364]

11. And love's the noblest frailty of the mind. [*The Indian Emperor* (1665),
II]

12. From harmony, from heavenly harmony
This universal frame began:
From harmony to harmony
Through all the compass of the notes it ran,
The diapason closing full in Man... ['A Song for St. Cecilia's Day'
(1687)]

13. [Of Chaucer]
Here is God's plenty. [*Fables Ancient and Modern* (1700), Preface]

Dubček, Alexander (1921–1992)
*Czechoslovak statesman; reforming Communist Party Secretary,
1968–69*

1. Socialism [or Communism] with a human face. [Translation of a report
in *Rudé právo*, 14 March 1968]

Dumas, Alexandre (Père) (1802–1870)
French romantic historical novelist and dramatist; cookery writer

1. *Cherchons la femme.*
Let us look for the woman. [*Les Mohicans de Paris*]

2. *Tous pour un, un pour tous.*
All for one, one for all. [*Les Trois Mousquetaires* (1844)]

Dumas, Alexandre (Fils) (1824–1895)
French dramatist, novelist and critic

1. All generalizations are dangerous, even this one. [Attr.]

Dunbar, William (c. 1460–c. 1525)
Scottish poet, noted for his versatility; satirist and courtier

1. Our plesance here is all vain glory,
   This fals world is but transitory,
   The flesh is bruckle, the Feynd is slee:
   Timor Mortis conturbat me . . . ['Lament for the Makaris' (1834 edition)]

2. London, thou art the flower of cities all!
   Gemme of all joy, jasper of jocunditie . . . ['London' (1834 edition)]

Dyer, Sir Edward (c. 1540–1607)
English poet; elegist and courtier

1. My mind to me a kingdom is,
   Such present joys therein I find,
   That it excels all other bliss
   That earth affords or grows by kind.
   Though much I want which most would have,
   Yet still my mind forbids to crave. ['In praise of a contented mind' (1588). Attr.]

Dylan, Bob (Robert Zimmerman) (1941–)
American singer and songwriter

1. How many roads must a man walk down
   Before you call him a man? . . .
   The answer, my friend, is blowin' in the wind,
   The answer is blowin' in the wind. ['Blowin' in the Wind', song, 1962]

Eden, Anthony (1897–1977)
English statesman; Conservative Prime Minister, 1955–1957

1. We are not at war with Egypt. We are in armed conflict. [Speech, 1956]

Edgeworth, Maria (1767–1849)
English-born Irish writer, noted for earliest 'regional novel'

1. Well! some people talk of morality, and some of religion, but give me a little snug property. [*The Absentee* (1812), 2]

Edison, Thomas Alva (1847–1931)
American inventor and industrialist

1. Genius is one per cent inspiration and ninety-nine per cent perspiration. [*Life*, 1932]

Edward VIII (later Duke of Windsor) (1894–1972)
King of Great Britain and Northern Ireland in 1936 (uncrowned); abdicated to marry an American divorcée; son of George V

1. I have found it impossible to carry the heavy burden of responsibility and to discharge my duties as King as I would wish to do without the help and support of the woman I love. [Radio broadcast after his abdication, 11 December 1936]

Edwards, Oliver (1711–1791)
English lawyer

1. I have tried too in my time to be a philosopher; but, I don't know how, cheerfulness was always breaking in. [In Boswell, *The Life of Samuel Johnson* (1791), 1778]

Ehrlichman, John D. (1925–)
American writer and business executive

1. [Of Patrick Gray, Acting Director of the CBI, who did not know his commission had been withdrawn]
Let him twist slowly, slowly in the wind. [Telephone remark to John Dean, 7/8 March 1973]

Einstein, Albert (1879–1955)
German-born American mathematical physicist (Nobel prize 1921)

1. Science without religion is lame, religion without science is blind. [*Science, Philosophy and Religion: a Symposium* (1941), 13]

2. [Of his part in the development of the atom bomb]
If only I had known, I should have become a watchmaker. [*New Statesman*, 1965]

Eliot, George (Mary Ann Evans) (1819–1880)
*English novelist, noted for her portrayal of provincial society; poet
and letter writer*

1. Animals are such agreeable friends – they ask no questions, they pass
   no criticisms. [*Scenes of Clerical Life* (1858), 'Mr. Gilfil's Love-Story', 7]

2. I've never any pity for conceited people, because I think they carry
   their comfort about with them. [*The Mill on the Floss* (1860), V, 4]

3. I should like to know what is the proper function of women, if it is
   not to make reasons for husbands to stay at home, and still stronger
   reasons for bachelors to go out. [Ib. VI, 6]

4. An election is coming. Universal peace is declared, and the foxes have
   a sincere interest in prolonging the lives of the poultry. [*Felix Holt*
   (1866), 5]

5. Our deeds still travel with us from afar,
   And what we have been makes us what we are. [*Middlemarch* (1872),
   70]

6. There is a great deal of unmapped country within us which would
   have to be taken into account in an explanation of our gusts and storms.
   [*Daniel Deronda* (1876), 24]

7. Debasing the moral currency. [*Theophrastus Such* (1879), title of essay]

Eliot, T. S. (1888–1965)
*American-born British poet, verse dramatist and critic; Nobel prize
for literature 1948*

1. In the room the women come and go
   Talking of Michelangelo.

   For I have known them all already, known them all—
   Have known the evenings, mornings, afternoons,
   I have measured out my life with coffee spoons...

   I grow old ... I grow old...
   I shall wear the bottoms of my trousers rolled. ['The Love Song of J.
   Alfred Prufrock' (1917)]

2. Signs are taken for wonders. ['Gerontion' (1920)]

3. Webster was much possessed by death

And saw the skull beneath the skin; ['Whispers of Immortality' (1920)]

4. April is the cruellest month, breeding
   Lilacs out of the dead land, mixing
   Memory and desire, stirring
   Dull roots with spring rain. [*The Waste Land* (1922), 'The Burial of
   the Dead']

5. We are the hollow men
   We are the stuffed men

   This is the way the world ends
   Not with a bang but a whimper. ['The Hollow Men' (1925)]

6. The Naming of Cats is a difficult matter,
   It isn't just one of your holiday games;
   You may think at first I'm as mad as a hatter
   When I tell you a cat must have THREE DIFFERENT NAMES...
   [*Old Possum's Book of Practical Cats* (1939), 'The Naming of Cats']

7. Human kind
   Cannot bear very much reality...

   At the still point of the turning world. Neither flesh nor fleshless;
   Neither from nor towards; at the still point, there the dance is, [*Four
   Quartets* (1944), 'Burnt Norton']

8. In my beginning is my end...

   In my end is my beginning. [Ib. 'East Coker']

9. Hell is oneself;
   Hell is alone, the other figures in it
   Merely projections. There is nothing to escape from
   And nothing to escape to. One is always alone. [*The Cocktail Party*
   (1950), I.iii]

10. The only way of expressing emotion in the form of art is by finding
    an 'objective correlative'; in other words, a set of objects, a situation, a
    chain of events which shall be the formula of that *particular* emotion;
    such that when the external facts, which must terminate in sensory
    experience, are given, the emotion is immediately evoked. ['Hamlet'
    (1919)]

Elizabeth I (1533–1603)
Queen of England 1558–1603; Daughter of Henry VIII and Anne Boleyn; enforcer of Protestantism; scholar and letter writer

1. I am your anointed Queen. I will never be by violence constrained to do anything. I thank God I am endued with such qualities that if I were turned out of the Realm in my petticoat I were able to live in any place in Christome. [Attr. Speech, 1566]

2. [To Sir Walter Raleigh]
   I have known many persons who turned their gold into smoke, but you are the first to turn smoke into gold. [In F. Chamberlin, *The Sayings of Queen Elizabeth* (1923)]

Elliot, Jean (1727–1805)
Scottish lyricist

1. The Flowers of the Forest are a' wede away. ['The Flowers of the Forest' (1756)]

Elliott, Ebenezer (1781–1849)
English poet and merchant; known as the Corn Law Rhymer

1. What is a communist? One who hath yearnings
   For equal division of unequal earnings. [Epigram, 1850]

Emerson, Ralph Waldo (1803–1882)
American poet, essayist, transcendentalist and teacher

1. There is properly no history; only biography. [*Essays, First Series* (1841), 'History']

2. A foolish consistency is the hobgoblin of little minds, adored by little statesmen and philosophers and divines. With consistency a great soul has simply nothing to do. [Ib. 'Self-Reliance']

3. All mankind love a lover. [Ib. 'Love']

4. The only reward of virtue is virtue; the only way to have a friend is to be one. [Ib. 'Friendship']

5. In skating over thin ice, our safety is in our speed. [Ib. 'Prudence']

6. People wish to be settled; only as far as they are unsettled is there any hope for them. [Ib. 'Circles']

7. Next to the originator of a good sentence is the first quoter of it.
[*Letters and Social Aims* (1875), 'Quotation and Originality']

8. What is a weed? A plant whose virtues have not yet been discovered.
[*Fortune of the Republic* (1878)]

Epicurus (341–270 BC)
Greek philosopher and teacher; founder of Epicureanism

1. It is not so much our friends' help that helps us as the confident
knowledge that they will help us. [Attr.]

Epstein, Julius J. (1909–)
American screenwriter

1. Major Strasser has been shot. Round up the usual suspects.
[*Casablanca*, film, 1942, words spoken by Claude Rains]

Erasmus, Desiderius (c. 1466–1536)
Dutch Renaissance scholar and humanist

1. *Scitum est inter caecos luscum regnare posse.*
It is well known, that among the blind the one-eyed man is king.
[*Adagia* (1500)]

2. *Dulce bellum inexpertis.*
War is sweet to those who do not fight. [Ib.]

Estienne, Henri (1531–1598)
French classical scholar, lexicographer, printer and publisher

1. *Si jeunesse savoit; si vieillesse pouvoit.*
If only youth knew; if only age could. [*Les Prémices* (1594)]

Euclid (fl. c. 300 BC)
Greek mathematician, founder of the mathematical school at Alexandria

1. *Quod erat demonstrandum.*
Which was to be proved. [*Elements* (Latin version)]

Euripides (c. 485–406 BC)
Greek classical dramatist; tragedian and poet

1. Those whom God wishes to destroy, he first makes mad. [Fragment]

Everett, David (1769–1813)
American lawyer and writer

1. Tall oaks from little acorns grow. ['Lines Written for a School Declamation' (at the age of 7)]

Ewer, William Norman (1885–1976)
English journalist

1. How odd
   Of God
   To choose
   The Jews. [In *Week-End Book* (1924), 'How Odd']

Falkland, Lucius Cary, Second Viscount (c. 1610–1643)
English politician and writer

1. When it is not necessary to change, it is necessary not to change. [Speech concerning Episcopacy, 1641]

Farjeon, Herbert (1887–1945)
English actor, dramatic critic, dramatist and theatrical manager

1. I've danced with a man, who's danced with a girl, who's danced with the Prince of Wales. [*The Picnic* (1927)]

Farquhar, George (1678–1707)
Irish comic dramatist of the Restoration period

1. He answered the description the page gave to a T, Sir. [*Love and a Bottle* (1698), IV.iii]

2. My Lady Bountiful. [*The Beaux' Stratagem* (1707), I.i]

Faulkner, William (1897–1962)
American novelist and short-story writer, his work set in the southern states of the US; Nobel prize 1949

1. The writer's only responsibility is to his art ... If a writer has to rob his mother, he will not hesitate; the 'Ode on a Grecian Urn' is worth any number of old ladies. [*Paris Review*, 1956]

Fawkes, Guy (1570–1606)
English Roman Catholic conspirator, executed for his part in the
Gunpower Plot

1. [On being asked by the King whether he regretted his proposed plot
against Parliament and the royal family]
A desperate disease requires a dangerous remedy ... one of my objects
was to blow the Scots back again into Scotland. [*Dictionary of National
Biography*]

Fearon, George (1901–1972)

1. The 'angry young men' of England (who refuse to write grammatically
and syntactically in order to flaunt their proletarian artistry). [*Times
Literary Supplement*, 1957]

Ferdinand I, Emperor of Austria (1793–1875)
King of Hungary (1830–1848) and Emperor of Austria (1830–48);
abdicated

1. I am the emperor, and I want dumplings. [In E. Crankshaw, *The Fall
of the House of Habsburg* (1963)]

Fern, Fanny (Sara Payson Parton) (1811–1872)
American essayist and children's writer

1. The way to a man's heart is through his stomach. [*Willis Parton*]

Ferrier, Kathleen (1912–1953)
Acclaimed English contralto singer

1. [Said shortly before her death]
Now I'll have *eine kleine Pause*. [In Gerald Moore, *Am I Too Loud?*]

Feuerbach, Ludwig (1804–1872)
German materialist philosopher

1. *Der Mensch ist, was er isst.*
Man is what he eats. [In Jacob Moleschott, *Lehre der Nahrungsmittel:
Für das Volk* (1850)]

Fielding, Henry (1707–1754)
English innovative novelist, comic dramatist and political journalist

1. Yes, I had two strings to my bow; both golden ones, agad! and both cracked. [*Love in Several Masques* (1728), V]

2. I am as sober as a judge. [*Don Quixote in England* (1733), III]

3. Public schools are the nurseries of all vice and immorality. [*Joseph Andrews* (1742), III]

Fields, Dorothy (1904–1974)
American songwriter

1. I Can't Give You Anything But Love. [Title of Song, *Delmars Revels,* 1927]

Fields, W. C. (William Claude Dukenfield) (1880–1946)
American comic film actor

1. On the whole, I'd rather be in Philadelphia. [His own epitaph]

FitzGerald, Edward (1809–1883)
English poet, translator and letter writer

1. Awake! for Morning in the Bowl of Night
Has flung the Stone that puts the Stars to Flight:
And Lo! the Hunter of the East has caught
The Sultan's Turret in a Noose of Light. [*The Rubáiyát of Omar Khayyám* (1859), 1, 1st Ed.]

2. Here with a Loaf of Bread beneath the Bough,
A Flask of Wine, a Book of Verse – and Thou
Beside me singing in the Wilderness–
And Wilderness is Paradise enow. [Ib. 11, 1st Ed.]

3. Myself when young did eagerly frequent
Doctor and Saint, and heard great argument
About it and about: but evermore
Came out by the same Door as in I went. [Ib. 27, 1st Ed.]

4. For in and out, above, about, below,
'Tis nothing but a Magic Shadow-show,
Played in a Box whose Candle is the Sun,
Round which we Phantom Figures come and go. [Ib. 46, 1st Ed.]

5. The Moving Finger writes; and, having writ,
Moves on: nor all thy Piety nor Wit
Shall lure it back to cancel half a Line,
Nor all thy Tears wash out a Word of it. [Ib. 51, 1st Ed.]

Fitzgerald, F. Scott (1896–1940)
American novelist, short-story writer and screenwriter

1. In the real dark night of the soul it is always three o'clock in the morning. [*The Crack-Up* (1945)]

2. *Fitzgerald*: The rich are different from us.
Hemingway: Yes, they have more money. [Ib. 'Notebooks, E']

Fitzsimmons, Robert (1862–1917)
English-born New Zealand world champion boxer

1. [Remark before a boxing match, 1900]
The bigger they come, the harder they fall. [Attr.]

Flanders, Michael (1922–1975)
English actor and lyricist
and **Swann,** Donald (1923–1994)

1. Mud, mud, glorious mud,
Nothing quite like it for cooling the blood. ['The Hippopotamus Song', 1953]

Flaubert, Gustave (1821–1880)
French realist novelist

1. *Tout ce qu'on invente est vrai, soi-en sûre. La poésie est une chose aussi précise que la géométrie.*
Everything one invents is true, you can be sure of that. Poetry is as exact a science as geometry. [Letter to Louise Colet, 1853]

2. *L'artiste doit être dans son oeuvre comme Dieu dans la création, invisible et tout-puissant; qu'on le sente partout, mais qu'on ne le voie pas.*
The artist must be in his work as God is in creation, invisible and all-powerful; his presence should be felt everywhere, but he should never be seen. [Letter to Mlle Leroyer de Chantepie, 1857]

Fleming, Marjory (1803–1811)
Scottish child diarist

1. A direful death indeed they had
   That would put any parent mad
   But she was more than usual calm
   She did not give a singel dam. [In A. Esdaile (ed.), *Journals, Letters and Verses* (1934)]

2. The most devilish thing is 8 times 8 and 7 times 7 it is what nature itselfe cant endure. [Ib.]

Fletcher, John (1579–1625)
English dramatist; collaborated with Francis Beaumont and Philip Massinger; cousin of Phineas Fletcher

1. I'll put a spoke among your wheels. [*The Mad Lover* (produced before 1619), III]

2. Let's meet, and either do, or die. [*The Island Princess* (1621), II.ii]

3. I find the medicine worse than the malady. [*The Lover's Progress* (revised by Philip Massinger, produced 1623, published 1647), III.ii]

de Florian, Jean-Pierre Claris (1755–1794)
French novelist and poet

1. *Plaisir d'amour ne dure qu'un moment,*
   Chagrin d'amour dure toute la vie.
   Love's pleasure only lasts a moment; love's sorrow lasts one's whole life long. ['Célestine' (1784)]

Fontaine, Jean de la (1621–1695)
French poet and fabulist

1. *Je plie et ne romps pas.*
   I bend and do not break. [*Fables*, 'Le Chêne et le Roseau']

2. *Mais les ouvrages les plus courts*
   Sont toujours les meilleurs.
   But the shortest works are always the best. [Ib. 'Les lapins']

3. *Celui-ci ne voyait pas plus loin que son nez.*
   This fellow could not see further than his own nose. [Ib. 'Le renard et le bouc']

Ford, Ford Madox (1873–1939)
English novelist, critic and editor

1. This is the saddest story I have ever heard. [*The Good Soldier* (1915), first sentence]

Ford, Henry (1863–1947)
American car manufacturer, pioneer of mass production; pacifist

1. [Popularly remembered as History is bunk]
   History is more or less bunk. It's tradition. We don't want tradition. We want to live in the present and the only history that is worth a tinker's damn is the history we make today. [*Chicago Tribune*, 1916]

2. [On the Model T Ford motor car]
   People can have it any colour – so long as its black. [In Allan Nevins, *Ford* (1957), II, 15]

Ford, Lena (1870–1916)
Songwriter

1. Keep the home fires burning,
   While your hearts are yearning. ['Till the Boys Come Home', song (1914)]

Forgy, Howell (1908–1983)
American naval chaplain

1. [Remark at Pearl Harbour, 1941]
   Praise the Lord and pass the ammunition. [Attr.]

Forster, E. M. (1879–1970)
English novelist, short-story writer, essayist and literary critic

1. Only connect! That was the whole of her sermon. Only connect the prose and the passion, and both will be exalted, and human love will be seen at its highest. [*Howard's End* (1910), 22]

2. I hate the idea of causes, and if I had to choose between betraying my country and betraying my friend, I hope I should have the guts to betray my country. [*Two Cheers for Democracy* (1951), 'What I Believe']

Fowles, John (1926–)
English novelist

1. We all write poems; it is simply that poets are the ones who write in words. [*The French Lieutenant's Woman* (1969), 19]

Fox, Charles James (1749–1806)
English statesman; Whig politician, foreign secretary (1806) and abolitionist

1. [On the Fall of the Bastille]
How much the greatest event it is that ever happened in the world! and how much the best! [Letter, 1789]

Franklin, Benjamin (1706–1790)
American statesman, scientist, political critic and printer

1. Remember that time is money. [*Advice to a Young Tradesman* (1748)]

2. The golden age never was the present age. [*Poor Richard's Almanac*, 1750]

3. A little neglect may breed mischief ... for want of a nail, the shoe was lost; for want of a shoe, the horse was lost; and for want of a horse the rider was lost. [Ib. 1758]

4. Early to bed and early to rise,
Makes a man healthy, wealthy and wise. [Ib. 1758]

5. Creditors have better memories than debtors. [Ib. 1758]

6. But in this world nothing can be said to be certain, except death and taxes. [Letter to Jean Baptiste Le Roy, 1789]

Frazer, Sir James George (1854–1941)
Scottish anthropologist, author of books on primitive religions and magic

1. The awe and dread with which the untutored savage contemplates his mother-in-law are amongst the most familiar facts of anthropology. [*The Golden Bough* (ed. 2, 1900), I]

Frederick the Great (1712–1786)
King of Prussia 1740–86; patron of the arts

1. [Command to hesitant troops]

Ihr verfluchten Kerls, wollt ihr denn ewig leben?
You rogues, do you want to live for ever? [Attr.]

Freud, Sigmund (1856–1939)
Austrian psychiatrist and founder of psychoanalysis

1. Conscience is the internal perception of the rejection of a particular wish operating within us. [*Totem and Taboo*]

2. Religion is an illusion and it derives its strength from the fact that it falls in with our instinctual desires. [*New Introductory Lectures on Psychoanalysis* (1933), 'A Philosophy of Life']

3. The great question ... which I have not been able to answer, despite my thirty years of research into the feminine soul, is 'What does a woman want?' [In Charles Robb, *Psychiatry in American Life*]

Frost, Robert (1874–1963)
American lyric poet, noted for his verse on New England life

1. The woods are lovely, dark and deep,
But I have promises to keep,
And miles to go before I sleep,
And miles to go before I sleep. ['Stopping by Woods on a Snowy Evening' (1923)]

2. He only says, 'Good fences make good neighbours'. ['Mending Wall' (1914)]

3. I never dared be radical when young
For fear it would make me conservative when old. ['Precaution' (1936)]

4. No tears in the writer, no tears in the reader. [*Collected Poems* (1939), Preface]

5. Writing free verse is like playing tennis with the net down. [Address, 1935]

6. Poetry is what is lost in translation. [In Untermeyer, *Robert Frost: a Backward Look* (1964)]

Fuller, Richard Buckminster (1895–1983)
American architect and engineer

1. I am a passenger on the spaceship, Earth. [*Operating Manual for Spaceship Earth* (1969)]

Fyleman, Rose (1877–1957)
English children's poet and dramatist

1. There are fairies at the bottom of our garden! [*Fairies and Chimneys* (1918), 'Fairies']

Gable, Clark (1901–1960)
American leading film actor; Academy Award 1934

1. Frankly, my dear, I don't give a damn. [*Gone With the Wind*, film, 1939; script by Sidney Howard from Margaret Mitchell's novel]

Gaitskell, Hugh (1906–1963)
English socialist; Labour politician (Chancellor of the Exchequer 1950–51) and party leader

1. All terrorists, at the invitation of the Government, end up with drinks at the Dorchester. [Letter to *The Guardian*, 1977]

Galbraith J. K. (1908–)
Canadian-born American Keynesian economist; diplomat and author

1. In the affluent society, no sharp distinction can be made between luxuries and necessaries. [*The Affluent Society* (1958), 21]

Galsworthy, John (1867–1933)
English novelist, noted for the 'Forsyte Saga'; short-story writer and dramatist; Nobel prize 1932

1. [James Forsyte]
Nobody tells me anything. [*The Man of Property* (1906), I, 1]

2. Oh, your precious 'lame ducks'! [Ib. II, 12]

Gandhi, Indira (1917–1984)
Indian stateswoman and Congress Party leader; Prime Minister of India 1966–77, 1980–84; assassinated

1. You cannot shake hands with a clenched fist. [Remark at a press conference, 1971]

Gandhi, Mohandas Karamchand (Mahatma Gandhi) (1869–1948)
Indian political leader, instrumental in achieving independence from Britain; sought reform by non-violent means

1. [When asked what he thought of Western civilization]
I think it would be an excellent idea. [Attr.]

Garbo, Greta (Greta Louisa Gustafsson) (1905–1990)
Swedish-born American film actress of 1930s; Academy Award 1954

1. I want to be alone. [*Grand Hotel*, film, 1932; script by William A. Drake]

Garland, Judy (Frances Gumm) (1922–1969)
American film actress and singer; Academy Award 1939

1. I was born at the age of twelve on a Metro-Goldwyn-Mayer lot. [*The Observer*, 'Sayings of the Week', 1951]

2. If ever I go looking for my heart's desire again, I won't look any further than my own backyard, because if it isn't there, I never really lost it to begin with. [*The Wizard of Oz* (1939), screenplay by Noel Langley, Florence Ryerson and Edgar Allan Woolf]

Gaskell, Elizabeth (1810–1865)
English novelist, short-story writer and biographer of Charlotte Brontë

1. A man ... is *so* in the way in the house! [*Cranford* (1853), 1]

Gay, John (1685–1732)
English poet, dramatist and librettist

1. Do you think your mother and I should have liv'd comfortably so long together, if ever we had been married? [*The Beggar's Opera* (1728), I.viii]

2. Those, who in quarrels interpose,
Must often wipe a bloody nose. [*Fables* (1727), I, 34, 'The Mastiffs']

George II (1683–1760)
King of Great Britain and Ireland, 1727–1760; son of George I

1. [Reply to the Duke of Newcastle who complained that General Wolfe was a madman]
Mad, is he? Then I hope he will *bite* some of my other generals. [In Wilson, *The Life and Letters of James Wolfe* (1909), 17]

George V (1865–1936)
King of Great Britain and Northern Ireland 1910–36; son of Edward VII

1. [To the suggestion that his favourite watering place be dubbed Bognor Regis; not his last words, as often supposed]
   Bugger Bognor! [In K. Rose, *George V*]

George VI (1895–1952)
King of Great Britain and Northern Ireland 1936–52; second son of George V, he succeeded to the throne after the abdication of his brother, Edward VIII

1. We're not a family; we're a firm. [Attr. in Lane, *Our Future King*]

Gerasimov, Gennady (1935–)
Former Soviet Foreign Ministry spokesman and editor of Moscow News

1. We now have the 'Frank Sinatra doctrine'. He had a song, 'I Had It My Way' [*sic*]. So every country decides on its own which road to take [On American television, 25 October 1989, he coined this phrase to explain the Kremlin's attitude to the 1989 revolutions in Eastern Europe]

Gibbon, Edward (1737–1794)
English historian, politician and memoirist

1. History ... is, indeed, little more than the register of the crimes, follies, and misfortunes of mankind. [*Decline and Fall of the Roman Empire* (1776–88), 3]

2. Corruption, the most infallible symptom of constitutional liberty. [Ib. 21]

3. All that is human must retrograde if it does not advance. [Ib. 71]

Gibbon, Lewis Grassic (James Leslie Mitchell) (1901–1935)
Scottish writer

1. Nothing endured at all, nothing but the land ... The land was forever, it moved and changed below you, but was forever. [*Sunset Song* (1932), 3]

Gibbons, Stella (1902–1989)
English novelist, poet and short-story writer

1. I saw something nasty in the woodshed. [*Cold Comfort Farm* (1932), *passim*]

Gilbert, Fred (1850–1903)
British songwriter

1. The man who broke the bank at Monte Carlo. ['The Man who Broke the Bank at Monte Carlo', 1892]

Gilbert, William Schwenck (1836–1911)
English dramatist and humorist; librettist for Arthur Sullivan's operas

1. She may very well pass for forty-three
In the dusk, with a light behind her. [*Trial by Jury* (1875)]

2. And so do his sisters, and his cousins and his aunts!
His sisters and his cousins,
Whom he reckons up by dozens,
And his aunts! [*H.M.S. Pinafore* (1878), I]

3. I am the very model of a modern Major-General. [*The Pirates of Penzance* (1880), I]

4. When constabulary duty's to be done,
A policeman's lot is not a happy one... [Ib. II]

5. Pooh-Bah (Lord High Everything Else) [*The Mikado* (1885), Dramatis Personae]

6. A wandering minstrel I [Ib. I]

7. Three little maids from school are we, [Ib.]

8. Awaiting the sensation of a short, sharp shock,
From a cheap and chippy chopper on a big black block! [Ib.]

9. The flowers that bloom in the spring,
Tra la, [Ib. II]

Ginsberg, Allen (1926–)
American 'Beat' poet

1. I saw the best minds of my generation destroyed by madness, starving hysterical naked. [*Howl* (1956), first line]

Gladstone, William Ewart (1809–1898)
English statesman and reformer; Liberal Prime Minister 1868–1874, 1880–85, 1892–94

1. You cannot fight against the future. Time is on our side. [Speech on the Reform Bill, 1866]

2. All the world over, I will back the masses against the classes. [Speech, Liverpool, 1886]

Gloucester, William, Duke of (1743–1805)
English Field Marshal; brother of George III

1. Another damned, thick, square book. Always scribble, scribble, scribble! Eh! Mr. Gibbon? [In Henry Best, *Personal and Literary Memorials* (1829)]

Godard, Jean-Luc (1930–)
French 'New Wave' film director and writer

1. *La photographie, c'est la vérité. Le cinéma: la vérité vingt-quatre fois par seconde.*
Photography is truth. Cinema is truth twenty-four times a second. [*Le Petit Soldat*, film, 1960]

Goebbels, Joseph (1897–1945)
German Nazi politician, Minister of Propaganda from 1933; committed suicide

1. *. . . mir in Bälde einen Gesamtentwurf über die organisatorischen, sachlichen und materiellen Vorausmassnahmen zur Durchführung der angestrebten Endlösung der Judenfrage vorzulegen.*
. . . to place before me soon a complete proposal for the organisational, practical and material preliminary measures which have to be taken in order to bring about the desired Final Solution to the Jewish question. [Letter to Reinhard Heydrich, 1941]

Goethe, Johann Wolfgang von (1749–1832)
German Romantic poet, novelist, dramatist and scientist; greatly influenced European literature

1. *Ich [nenne] die Baukunst eine erstarrte Musik.*
I [call] architecture a kind of petrified music. [*Gespräche mit Eckermann* 1829]

2. *Das Klassische nenne ich das Gesunde, and das Romantische das Kranke.*
Classicism I call health, and romanticism disease. [Ib.]

Goldsmith, Oliver (c. 1728–1774)
Irish dramatist, poet, novelist and journalist

1. When lovely woman stoops to folly
And finds too late that men betray,
What charm can soothe her melancholy,
What art can wash her guilt away? [*The Vicar of Wakefield* (1766),
Song, 24]

2. Ill fares the land, to hastening ills a prey,
Where wealth accumulates, and men decay; [*The Deserted Village*
(1770)]

3. Truth from his lips prevailed with double sway,
And fools, who came to scoff, remained to pray... [Ib.]

4. And still they gazed, and still the wonder grew,
That one small head could carry all he knew... [Ib.]

5. The true use of speech is not so much to express our wants as to
conceal them. [*The Bee* (1759), 3, 'On the Use of Language']

6. I was ever of opinion, that the honest man who married and brought
up a large family, did more service than he who continued single, and
only talked of population. [*The Vicar of Wakefield* (1766), 1]

Goldwyn, Samuel (1882–1974)
Polish-American film producer

1. Any man who goes to a psychiatrist should have his head examined.
[In Zierold, *Moguls* (1969), 3, 'Samuel Goldwyn Presents']

2. [To Jack L. Warner, when Goldwyn discovered that one of his directors
was moonlighting for Warner Bros.; one of the few genuine
Goldwynisms]
How can we sit together and deal with this industry if you're going
to do things like that to me? If this is the way you do it, gentlemen,
include me out! [Quoted by S. Goldwyn Jnr, *TV Times*, 13 November
1982]

3. I'll give you a definite maybe. [In Colombo, *Wit and Wisdom of the
Moviemakers*]

Grahame, Kenneth (1859–1932)
Scottish essayist and children's writer; Secretary to the Bank of England

1. Believe me, my young friend, there is *nothing* – absolutely nothing – half so much worth doing as simply messing about in boats. [*The Wind in the Willows* (1908), 1]

Granville, Lord (1819–1907)

1. Spheres of action. [Letter to Count Münster, 1885]

Graves, Robert (1895–1985)
English poet, novelist, critic, autobiographer, translator and mythologist; noted for his love poetry

1. Children are dumb to say how hot the day is,
   How hot the scent is of the summer rose. ['The Cool Web' (1927)]

2. Goodbye to All That. [Title of book, 1929]

Gray, Thomas (1716–1771)
Renowned English 'graveyard' poet and scholar

1. Alas, regardless of their doom.
   The little victims play!
   No sense have they of ills to come,
   Nor care beyond to-day...

   No more; where ignorance is bliss,
   'Tis folly to be wise. ['Ode on a Distant Prospect of Eton College' (1742)]

2. The Curfew tolls the knell of parting day,
   The lowing herd wind slowly o'er the lea,
   The plowman homeward plods his weary way,
   And leaves the world to darkness and to me.

   The short and simple annals of the poor.

   The paths of glory lead but to the grave...

   Full many a flower is born to blush unseen,
   And waste its sweetness on the desert air.

   Far from the madding crowd's ignoble strife,

Their sober wishes never learn'd to stray;
Along the cool sequester'd vale of life
They kept the noiseless tenor of their way... ['Elegy Written in a
Country Churchyard' (1751)]

Greeley, Horace (1811–1872)
*American founding editor of the New York Tribune; presidential
candidate and supporter of Fourierism*

1. Go West, young man, and grow up with the country. [*Hints toward
Reform* (1850)]

Greene, Graham (1904–1991)
*English novelist, dramatist, screen and travel writer, his work often
concerned with moral dilemmas*

1. They had been corrupted by money, and he had been corrupted by
sentiment. Sentiment was the more dangerous, because you couldn't
name its price. A man open to bribes was to be relied upon below a
certain figure, but sentiment might uncoil in the heart at a name, a
photograph, even a smell remembered. [*The Heart of the Matter* (1948),
bk I, I, 2]

Greer, Germaine (1939–)
Australian feminist, critic, English scholar and journalist

1. Love, love, love – all the wretched cant of it, masking egotism, lust,
masochism, fantasy under a mythology of sentimental postures, a welter
of self induced miseries and joys, blinding and masking the essential
personalities in the frozen gestures of courtship, in the kissing and the
dating and the desire, the compliments and the quarrels which vivify
its barrenness. [*The Female Eunuch* (1970)]

Grellet, Stephen (1773–1855)
French missionary

1. I expect to pass through this world but once; any good thing therefore
that I can do, or any kindness that I can show to any fellow-creature,
let me do it now; let me not defer or neglect it, for I shall not pass
this way again. [Attr.]

Grey, Edward, Viscount of Fallodon (1862–1933)
English statesman; Liberal Foreign Secretary 1905–16; writer on nature

1. [To a caller at the Foreign Office in August 1914]
   The lamps are going out all over Europe; we shall not see them lit again in our lifetime. [In *Twenty-five Years*, II, 20]

Griffith-Jones, Mervyn (1909–1979)
British lawyer

1. [At the trial of D. H. Lawrence's novel *Lady Chatterley's Lover*]
   Is it a book you would even wish your wife or your servants to read? [*The Times*, 1960]

Grossmith, George (1847–1912)
English singer, comic songwriter and humorous author

1. I left the room with silent dignity, but caught my foot in the mat. [*Diary of a Nobody* (1894), 12]

Gunn, Thom (1929–)
Anglo-American poet, associated with the Movement

1. One is always nearer by not keeping still. ['On The Move' (1957)]

Gurney, Dorothy (1858–1932)
English poet

1. The kiss of the sun for pardon,
   The song of the birds for mirth,
   One is nearer God's Heart in a garden
   Than anywhere else on earth. ['God's Garden' (1913)]

Haggard, Sir Henry Rider (1856–1925)
English writer of Romantic adventure novels and agriculturalist

1. She-who-must-be-obeyed. [*She* (1887), *passim*]

Hahnemann, C. F. S. (1755–1843)
German physician and founder of homeopathy

1. *Similia similibus curantur.*
   Like cures like. [Motto of homeopathic medicine]

Haig, Douglas, First Earl of Bemersyde (1861–1928)
Scottish Commander of British forces in France and Flanders 1915–18

1. Every position must be held to the last man: there must be no retirement. With our backs to the wall, and believing in the justice of our cause, each one of us must fight on to the end. [Order given to British troops on 12 April 1918]

Hamerton, P. G. (1834–1894)
British artist and essayist

1. The art of reading is to skip judiciously. [*The Intellectual Life* (1873), IV, Letter 4]

Hamilton, Gail (Mary A. Dodge) (1838–1896)
American teacher, essayist and journalist

1. The total depravity of inanimate things. [Epigram]

Hammerstein II, Oscar (1895–1960)
American librettist and lyricist

1. Oh, what a beautiful mornin'!
   Oh, what a beautiful day! ['Oh, What a Beautiful Mornin'', song, 1943, from the musical *Oklahoma*]

2. Ol' man river, dat ol' man river,
   He must know sumpin', but don't say nothin',
   He jus' keeps rollin',
   He jus' keeps rollin' along. ['Ol' Man River', song, 1927, from the musical *Show Boat*]

3. The hills are alive with the sound of music [Title song, 1959, from the musical *The Sound of Music*]

Hanrahan, Brian (1949–)
Television news correspondent and reporter

1. [Reporting the British attack on Port Stanley airport, during the Falklands war]
   I'm not allowed to say how many planes joined the raid but I counted them all out and I counted them all back. [Report broadcast by BBC, 1 May 1982]

Haraucourt, Edmond (1856–1941)
French poet

1. *Partir c'est mourir un peu,*
   C'est mourir à ce qu'on aime:
   On laisse un peu de soi-même
   En toute heure et dans tout lieu.
   Leaving is dying a little,
   Dying to one's loves:
   One leaves behind a little of oneself
   At every moment, everywhere. [*Seul* (1891), 'Rondel de l'Adieu']

Harbach, Otto (1873–1963)
American librettist and dramatist

1. Tea for Two, and Two for Tea. [Song title, from the musical *No! No! Nanette*]

Harburg, E. Y. (1896–1981)
American songwriter

1. Somewhere over the rainbow, ['Over the Rainbow', song, 1939, from the musical *The Wizard of Oz*]

Hardy, Oliver (1892–1957)
American comedian, known for his film partnership with Stan Laurel;
Academy Award, 1932

1. [Catch phrase from many of his films (scripts by Stan Laurel) of the 1930s and 1940s]
   Here's another fine mess you've gotten me into. [In Colombo, *Wit and Wisdom of the Moviemakers* (1979), 11]

Hardy, Thomas (1840–1928)
English poet, novelist, short-story writer and dramatist, best known
for his Wessex novels set in rural England

1. My argument is that War makes rattling good history; but Peace is poor reading. [*The Dynasts*, Part I (1903), II.v]

2. Dialect words – those terrible marks of the beast to the truly genteel. [*The Mayor of Casterbridge* (1886), 20]

3. 'Justice' was done, and the President of the Immortals, in Aeschylean

phrase, had ended his sport with Tess. [*Tess of the D'Urbervilles* (1891), VII, 59]

Harlow, Jean (1911–1937)
American leading film actress and platinum blonde

1. Excuse me while I slip into something more comfortable. [*Hell's Angels*, film, 1930; script by Howard Estabrook and Harry Behn]

Harris, Joel Chandler (1848–1908)
American humorist; journalist, short-story writer and novelist

1. Tar-baby ain't sayin' nuthin', en Brer Fox, he lay low [*Uncle Remus* (1881), 'Legends of the Old Plantation', 2, 'The Wonderful Tar-Baby']

2. Bred en bawn in a brier-patch! [Ib. 'Legends of the Old Plantation', 4, 'How Mr Rabbit Was Too Sharp for Mr Fox']

Hart, Lorenz (1895–1943)
American lyricist; wrote musical shows with composer Richard Rodgers

1. Bewitched, Bothered and Bewildered. [Song title, from the musical *Babes in Arms*]

2. That's why the lady is a tramp. [Song title, 1937, from the musical *Babes in Arms*]

Hartley, L. P. (1895–1972)
English novelist, short-story writer and critic

1. The past is a foreign country: they do things differently there. [*The Go-Between* (1953), first sentence]

Harvey, William (1578–1657)
English physician; discovered the circulation of the blood

1. *Ex ovo omnia.*
Everything is from an egg. [*Exercitationes de Generatione Animalium* (1651)]

Haskins, Minnie Louise (1875–1957)
English teacher and writer

1. [Quoted by King George VI in his Christmas broadcast, 1939]

And I said to a man who stood at the gate of the year: 'Give me a light that I may tread safely into the unknown.' And he replied: 'Go out into the darkness and put your hand into the hand of God. That shall be to you better than a light, and safer than a known way.' [*The Desert* (1908), 'God Knows']

Hastings, H. de Cronin (1902–1986)
British editor of architectural journals and writer

1. Worm's eye view. [Caption to photograph in the *Architectural Review*, c. 1932 and *passim*]

Hawthorne, Nathaniel (1804–1864)
Great American allegorical novelist, short-story and children's writer

1. What other dungeon is so dark as one's own heart! What jailer so inexorable as one's self! [*The House of the Seven Gables* (1851), 11]

Hay, Ian (John Hay Beith) (1876–1952)
Scottish novelist and dramatist

1. Funny-peculiar or funny-ha-ha? [*The Housemaster* (1938), III]

Hayes, J. Milton (1884–1940)
British writer

1. There's a one-eyed yellow idol to the north of Khatmandu, ['The Green Eye of the Yellow God' (1911)]

Hazlitt, William (1778–1830)
English essayist, critic and journalist

1. The least pain in our little finger gives us more concern and uneasiness, than the destruction of millions of our fellow-beings. [In the *Edinburgh Review* (1829), 50, 'American Literature – Dr Channing']

2. Man is an intellectual animal, and therefore an everlasting contradiction to himself. His senses centre in himself, his ideas reach to the ends of the universe; so that he is torn in pieces between the two, without a possibility of its ever being otherwise. [*Characteristics* (1823), 158]

3. There is nothing good to be had in the country, or, if there is, they

will not let you have it. [*The Round Table* (1817), 'Observations on Mr Wordsworth's Poem The Excursion']

4. Violent antipathies are always suspicious, and betray a secret affinity. [*Table-Talk* (1822), 'On Vulgarity and Affection']

5. Without the aid of prejudice and custom, I should not be able to find my way across the room. [*Sketches and Essays*, 'On Prejudice']

Healey, Denis (1917–)
English Labour politician; Chancellor of the Exchequer 1974–79

1. [On Geoffrey Howe's attack on his Budget proposals]
Like being savaged by a dead sheep. [Speech, House of Commons, 1978]

Heath, Sir Edward (1916–)
English statesman; Conservative Prime Minister, 1970–74, and author

1. [On the Lonrho affair]
The unpleasant and unacceptable face of capitalism. [Speech, House of Commons, 1973]

Heber, Reginald (1783–1826)
English Bishop of Calcutta, 1822–26; traveller, poet and hymn writer

1. Though every prospect pleases,
And only man is vile. [Hymn, 1821]

Hegel, Georg Wilhelm (1770–1831)
Influential German idealist philosopher, noted for his dialectic

1. *Was die Erfahrung aber und die Geschichte lehren, ist dieses, dass Völker und Regierungen niemals etwas aus der Geschichte gelernt haben.*
What experience and history teach us, however, is this, that peoples and governments have never learned anything from history. [*Vorlesung über die Philosophie der Geschichte* (*Lectures on the Philosophy of History*, 1837), Introduction]

Heine, Heinrich (1797–1856)
German lyric poet; essayist and journalist

1. *Es ist eine alte Geschichte,
Doch bleibt sie immer neu.*

It is an old story, yet it remains forever new. [*Buch der Lieder* (*Book of Songs*), 'Lyrisches Intermezzo' (1822–1823), XXXIX]

2. *Dort, wo man Bücher*
Verbrennt, verbrennt man auch am Ende Menschen.
It is there, where they burn books, that eventually they burn people too. [*Almansor*, 1820–1821]

Heller, Joseph (1923–)
American novelist, noted for his satire

1. There was only one catch and that was Catch-22, which specified that a concern for one's own safety in the face of dangers that were real and immediate was the process of a rational mind. [*Catch-22* (1961), 5]

Helpman, Robert (1909–1986)
Australian ballet dancer and choreographer

1. [Comment on the musical *Oh! Calcutta!*]
The trouble with nude dancing is that not everything stops when the music stops. [Attr.]

Hemans, Felicia Dorothea (1793–1835)
Popular English poet and translator

1. The boy stood on the burning deck
Whence all but he had fled;
The flame that lit the battle's wreck
Shone round him o'er the dead... ['Casabianca' (1829)]

2. The stately Homes of England,
How beautiful they stand!
Amidst their tall ancestral trees,
O'er all the pleasant land!... ['The Homes of England' (1839)]

Heming, John (1556–1630)
English editor of Shakespeare's First Folio; actor and theatrical manager
and Condell, Henry (d. 1627)

1. Well! it is now public, and you will stand for your privileges we know: to read, and censure. Do so, but buy it first. That doth best commend a book, the stationer says. [Preface to the First Folio Shakespeare, 1623]

Hemingway, Ernest (1898–1961)
American novelist, short-story writer and war correspondent; Nobel prize 1954

1. But did thee feel the earth move? [*For Whom the Bell Tolls* (1940), 13]

2. [Definition of 'guts']
   Grace under pressure. [Attr.; phrase first used by Dorothy Parker to describe the Hemingway hero]

Henley, William Ernest (1849–1903)
English poet, dramatist, critic and editor

1. It matters not how strait the gate,
   How charged with punishments the scroll,
   I am the master of my fate:
   I am the captain of my soul. [*Echoes*, 4, 'In Memoriam R.T. Hamilton Bruce' (1875)]

Henri IV of France (1553–1610)
Huguenot leader turned Catholic King of France, from 1589; assassinated

1. *Paris vaut bien une messe.*
   Paris is well worth a mass. [Attr.; also attr. to Sully]

2. [Of James VI and I]
   The wisest fool in Christendom. [Ib.]

Henry II (1133–1189)
First Plantagenet King of England

1. [Of Thomas Becket]
   Will no one rid me of this turbulent priest? [Attr., in Lyttelton, *History of the Life of King Henry* (1769), IV, 3]

Henry, Matthew (1662–1714)
English Nonconformist minister and commentator

1. All this and heaven too. [Attr.]

Henry, O. (William Sydney Porter) (1862–1910)
Prolific American short-story writer

1. It was beautiful and simple as all truly great swindles are. [*The Gentle Grafter* (1908), 'The Octopus Marooned']

Henry, Patrick (1736–1799)
American lawyer, orator and statesman

1. Give me liberty, or give me death! [Speech, 1775]

Henryson, Robert (c. 1425–1505)
Scottish makar; pastoral and allegorical poet, a 'Scottish Chaucerian'

1. The man that will nocht quhen he may
   Sall haif nocht quhen he wald. ['Robene and Makyne' (c. 1560)]

2. Yit efter ioy oftymes cummis cair,
   And troubill efter grit prosperitie. ['The Taill of the Uponlandis Mous and the Burges Mous' (1571)]

3. I lat yow wit, thair is richt few thairout
   Quhome ye may traist to haue trew lufe agane;
   Preif quhen ye will, your labour is in vaine.
   Thairfoir I reid ye tak thame as ye find,
   For thay ar sad as Widdercock in Wind. ['The Testament of Cresseid' (1593)]

Hepburn, Katharine (1907–)
American leading film and stage actress; Academy Awards 1933, 1967, 1968 and 1981

1. I don't care what is written about me as long as it isn't true. [In Cooper and Hartman, *Violets and Vinegar* (1980)]

Heraclitus (c. 540–c. 480 BC)
Greek pre-Socratic philosopher of the Ionian School

1. Everything is on the move, nothing is constant. [In Plato, *Cratylus*]

2. You cannot step twice into the same river. [Ib.]

Herbert, Sir A. P. (1890–1971)
English humorist, novelist, dramatist and politician

1. A highbrow is the kind of person who looks at a sausage and thinks of Picasso. ['The Highbrow']

2. People must not do things for fun. We are not here for fun. There is no reference to fun in any Act of Parliament. [*Uncommon Law* (1935), 'Is it a Free Country?']

Herbert, George (1593–1633)
English Metaphysical poet and priest; brother of Edward Herbert

1. Who aimeth at the sky
   Shoots higher much than he that means a tree... [*The Temple* (1633), 'The Church-Porch']

2. Teach me, my God and King,
   In all things thee to see;
   And what I do in any thing
   To do it as for thee... [Ib. 'The Elixer']

3. He that lives in hope danceth without music. [*Jacula Prudentum; or Outlandish Proverbs, Sentences & c.*, (1640)]

Herrick, Robert (1591–1674)
English lyric poet; royalist and clergyman

1. A sweet disorder in the dresse
   Kindles in cloathes a wantonnesse: [*Hesperides* (1648), 'Delight in Disorder']

2. Gather ye Rose-buds while ye may,
   Old Time is still aflying:
   And this same flower that smiles today,
   Tomorrow will be dying... [Ib. 'To the Virgins, to make much of Time']

3. When as in silks my *Julia* goes,
   Then, then (me thinks) how sweetly flowes
   That liquefaction of her clothes. [Ib. 'Upon Julia's Clothes']

Hewart, Gordon (Viscount Hewart) (1870–1943)
English Liberal politician and Lord Chief Justice of England 1922–40

1. It is not merely of some importance but is of fundamental importance that justice should not only be done, but should manifestly and undoubtedly be seen to be done. [Rex *v.* Sussex Justices, 1923, in *King's Bench Reports* (1924), I]

Hicks, Sir Seymour (1871–1949)
British dramatist, actor-manager, comedian and author

1. You will recognize, my boy, the first sign of old age: it is when you go out into the streets of London and realize for the first time how young the policemen look. [In Pulling, *They Were Singing* (1952), 7]

Hickson, William Edward (1803–1870)
English educationist; author of books on singing

1. 'Tis a lesson you should heed,
   Try, try again.
   If at first you don't succeed,
   Try, try again. ['Try and Try Again']

Hill, Joe (Joel Hägglund) (1879–1914)
Swedish-born American songwriter and workers organizer; convicted of murder and executed

1. You'll get pie in the sky when you die (That's a lie.) ['The Preacher and the Slave', song, 1911]

Hill, Rowland (1744–1833)
English preacher and hymn writer

1. He did not see any reason why the devil should have all the good tunes. [In E.W. Broome, *The Rev. Rowland Hill* (1881), 7]

Hippocrates (c. 460–357 BC)
Greek physician, the 'father of medicine'

1. [Of medicine]
   Life is short, science is lengthy, opportunity is elusive, experience is dangerous, judgement is difficult. [*Aphorisms* (c. 415 BC), 1; the opening phrases are often quoted in Latin in reverse order as *Ars longa, vita brevis*]

2. For extreme illnesses extreme remedies are most fitting. [Ib. 6]

Hitchcock, Alfred (1899–1980)
English film director noted for his mastery of suspense and camera technique

1. What is drama but life with the dull bits cut out? [*The Observer*, 'Sayings of the Week', 1960]

2. I deny that I ever said that actors are cattle. What I said was, 'Actors should be treated like cattle'. [Attr.]

Hitler, Adolf (1889–1945)
Austrian-born German Nazi dictator; leader of the Third Reich from 1934

1. *Die breite Masse eines Volkes... [fällt] einer grossen Lüge leichter zum Opfer fällt als einer kleinen.*
The broad mass of a people ... falls victim to a big lie more easily than to a small one. [*Mein Kampf (My Struggle)*, I (1925), 10]

2. [Said in 1939]
In starting and waging a war it is not right that matters, but victory. [In W.L. Shirer, *The Rise and Fall of the Third Reich* (1960), 16]

Hobbes, Thomas (1588–1679)
Influential English political philosopher; proponent of absolutism and nominalist

1. *True* and *false* are attributes of speech, not of things. And where speech is not, there is neither *truth* nor *falsehood*. [*Leviathan* (1651), I, 4, 'Of Speech']

2. No arts; no letters; no society; and which is worst of all, continual fear, and danger of violent death; and the life of man, solitary, poor, nasty, brutish, and short. [Ib. I, 13, 'Of the natural condition of mankind as concerning their felicity, and misery']

3. [Last words]
I am about to take my last voyage, a great leap in the dark. [In Watkins, *Anecdotes of Men of Learning* (1808)]

Hoffmann, Heinrich (1809–1874)
German author, illustrator and physician

   1. Let me see if Philip can
     Be a little gentleman;
     Let me see, if he is able
     To sit still for once at table... [*Struwwelpeter* (1847), 'Fidgety Philip']

   2. Look at little Johnny there,
     Little Johnny Head-In-Air!... [Ib. 'Johnny Head-in-Air']

Hoffmann, Max (1869–1927)
German general

   1. [Referring to the performance of the British army in World War I]
     Ludendorff: The English soldiers fight like lions.
     Hoffman: True. But don't we know that they are lions led by donkeys.
     [In A. Clark, *The Donkeys* (1962), from Falkenhayn, *Memoirs*]

Hogg, James (1770–1835)
*Scottish poet, ballad writer, novelist and journalist; the Ettrick
Shepherd*

   1. Better lo'ed you'll never be,
     And will you no come back again? [*The Jacobite Relics of Scotland, Second
     Series* (1821), 'Will He No Come Back Again']

   2. There grows a bonny brier bush in our kail-yard. [Ib. 'An Yon Be
     He']

Holmes, Oliver Wendell (1809–1894)
American physician, anatomist, poet, novelist, scientist and essayist

   1. To be seventy years young is sometimes far more cheerful and hopeful
     than to be forty years old. ['On the Seventieth Birthday of Julia Ward
     Howe' (1889)]

Holmes, Rev. John H. (1879–1964)
American Unitarian minister

   1. This universe is not hostile, nor yet is it friendly. It is simply
     indifferent. [*A Sensible Man's View of Religion* (1932), 4]

Home, John (1722–1808)
Scottish dramatist and Church of Scotland minister

1. [On the high duty on French wine, claret being 'the only wine drunk by gentlemen in Scotland']
   Firm and erect the Caledonian stood,
   Old was his mutton, and his claret good;
   Let him drink port, an English statesman cried–
   He drank the poison and his spirit died. [In Mackenzie, *An Account of the Life and Writings of John Home, Esq.* (1822), Appendix]

Homer (fl. c. 8th century BC)
Greek epic poet

1. Rosy-fingered dawn. [*Iliad*, I, opening lines, in Pope's translation and *passim*]

2. Winged words. [Ib.]

3. The wine-dark sea. [Ib.]

4. Like Leaves on Trees the Race of Man is found,
   Now green in Youth, now with'ring on the Ground,
   Another Race the following Spring supplies,
   They fall successive, and successive rise. [Ib. VI, line 146, trans. Pope]

5. The Man, for Wisdom's various arts renown'd,
   Long exercised in woes, Oh Muse! resound.
   Who, when his arms had wrought the destined fall
   Of sacred Troy, and raz'd her heav'n-built wall,
   Wand'ring from clime to clime, observant stray'd
   Their Manners noted, and their States surveyed.
   On stormy seas unnumber'd toils he bore
   Safe with his friends to gain his natal shore. [*Odyssey*, I, line 1, trans. Pope]

Hone, William (1780–1842)
English bookseller, journalist and satirist

1. John Jones may be described as 'one of the *has* beens.' [*Every-Day Book* (1826–1827), II]

Hood, Thomas (1799–1845)
English poet, editor and humorist

1. Ben Battle was a soldier bold,
   And used to war's alarms:
   But a cannon-ball took off his legs,
   So he laid down his arms!... [*Whims and Oddities* (1826), 'Faithless
   Nelly Gray']

2. I remember, I remember,
   The house where I was born,
   The little window where the sun
   Came peeping in at morn; [*The Plea of the Midsummer Fairies and Other
   Poems* (1827), 'I Remember']

Hoover, Herbert Clark (1874–1964)
*American Republican President, 1929–33; engineer, public
administrator and author*

1. The American system of rugged individualism. [Speech, New York,
   1928]

Hope, Laurence (Adela Florence Nicolson) (1865–1904)
English poet

1. Pale hands I loved beside the Shalimar, [*The Garden of Kama* (1901),
   'Kashmiri Song']

Hopkins, Gerard Manley (1844–1889)
*English poet, noted for his experimental sprung rhythm and natural
imagery; classicist and Jesuit priest*

1. Glory be to God for dappled things...

   All things counter, original, spare, strange;
   Whatever is fickle, freckled (who knows how?)
   With swift, slow; sweet, sour; adazzle, dim;
   He fathers-forth whose beauty is past change:
   Praise him. ['Pied Beauty' (1877)]

2. I caught this morning morning's minion, kingdom of daylight's
   dauphin, dapple-dawn-drawn Falcon, in his riding... ['The Windhover'
   (1877)]

3. The poetical language of an age should be the current language heightened. [Letter to Robert Bridges, 1879]

Horace (65–8 BC)
Roman lyric poet and satirist

1. *Parturient montes, nascetur ridiculus mus.*
   Mountains will be in labour, and a ridiculous mouse will be born. [*Ars Poetica*, line 139]

2. *Semper ad eventum festinat et in medias res*
   Non secus ac notas auditorem rapit.
   He always hurries to the main issue and whisks his listener into the middle of things as though it was already known. [Ib. line 148]

3. *Nonumque prematur in annum,*
   Membranis intus positis: delere licebit
   Quod non edideris; nescit vox missa reverti.
   Let it be kept back till the ninth year; the manuscript deposited within: you can destroy what you haven't published; the word once out cannot be recalled. [Ib. line 388]

4. *Ira furor brevis est.*
   Anger is a brief madness. [*Epistles*, I, 2, line 62]

5. *Omnem crede diem tibi diluxisse supremum.*
   Grata superveniet quae non sperabitur hora.
   Believe every day that has dawned is your last. Welcome will come the hour unhoped for. [Ib. I, 4, line 13]

6. *Naturam expelles furca, tamen usque recurret.*
   You may drive out Nature with a pitchfork, but she always comes hurrying back. [Ib. I, 10, line 24]

7. *Dum loquimur, fugerit invida*
   Aetas: carpe diem, quam minimum credula postero.
   While we speak, envious time will have sped away: pluck the fruit of today, putting as little trust as possible in tomorrow. [*Odes*, I, 11, line 7]

8. *Nunc est bibendum, nunc pede libero*
   Pulsanda tellus.
   Now there must be drinking, now must the earth be shaken with unfettered feet in dance. [Ib. I, 37, line 1]

9. *Eheu fugaces, Posthume, Posthume,*
   Labuntur anni.
   Alas, Posthumus, Posthumus, the fleeting years are gliding by. [Ib.
   II, 14, line 1]

10. *Dulce et decorum est pro patria mori.*
    It is sweet and honourable to die for one's country. [Ib. III, 2, line
    13]

11. [Describing how Tigellius would sing 'from the first course to the
    dessert' if the family took him]
    Ab ovo
    Usque ad mala.
    From the egg right through to the apples. [*Satires*, I, 3, line 6]

Horne, Kenneth (1900–1969)
Businessman who became popular through radio comedy

1. Read any good books, lately? [Catch phrase in radio show *Much Binding
   in the Marsh*, 1940s]

Housman, A. E. (1859–1936)
English lyric poet and leading Latin scholar

1. Into my heart an air that kills
   From yon far country blows:
   What are those blue remembered hills,
   What spires, what farms are those?

   That is the land of lost content,
   I see it shining plain,
   The happy highways where I went
   And cannot come again. [*A Shropshire Lad* (1896), 40]

2. Experience has taught me, when I am shaving of a morning, to keep
   watch over my thoughts, because, if a line of poetry strays into my
   memory, my skin bristles so that the razor ceases to act. [The Leslie
   Stephen Lecture, 1933, 'The Name and Nature of Poetry']

Howitt, Mary (1799–1888)
English novelist, translator, children's writer, editor and supporter of
social reform

1. 'Will you walk into my parlour?' said a spider to a fly: ['The Spider
   and the Fly' (1834)]

Hoyle, Edmond (1672–1769)
English writer on card games, chess and backgammon; the Father of Whist

1. When in doubt, win the trick. [*Hoyle's Games* (1756), 'Whist, Twenty-four Short Rules for Learners']

Hubbard, Elbert (1856–1915)
American printer, editor, prose writer and businessman

1. Life is just one damned thing after another. [In *Philistine*, 1909; also attributed to Frank Ward O'Malley (1875–1932), though the saying may pre-date them both]

2. Editor: a person employed by a newspaper whose business it is to separate the wheat from the chaff and to see that the chaff is printed. [*A Thousand and One Epigrams* (1911)]

Hume, David (1711–1776)
Scottish empiricist philosopher, political economist and historian

1. Custom, then, is the great guide of human life. [*Philosophical Essays Concerning Human Understanding* (1748), 5, 'Sceptical Solutions of these Doubts']

2. We soon learn that there is nothing mysterious or supernatural in the case, but that all proceeds from the usual propensity of mankind towards the marvellous, and that, though this inclination may at intervals receive a check from sense and learning, it can never be thoroughly extirpated from human nature. [Ib. 10, 'Of Miracles']

3. Beauty is no quality in things themselves: It exists merely in the mind which contemplates them; and each mind perceives a different beauty. [*Essays, Moral, Political, and Literary*, I (1742), 23, 'Of the Standard of Taste']

4. I am dying as fast as my enemies, if I have any, could wish, and as cheerfully as my best friends could desire. [Last words, 1776]

Hungerford, Margaret Wolfe (c. 1855–1897)
Irish novelist

1. Beauty is altogether in the eye of the beholder. [*Molly Bawn* (1878)]

Hunt, G. W. (1829–1904)
British composer of music hall songs, and painter

1. We don't want to fight, but, by jingo if we do,
   We've got the ships, we've got the men, we've got the money too.
   [Music hall song, 1878]

Hunt, Leigh (1784–1859)
*English essayist, poet, literary editor, journalist and
autobiographer*

1. Abou Ben Adhem (may his tribe increase!)
   Awoke one night from a deep dream of peace,
   And saw, within the moonlight in his room,
   Making it rich, and like a lily in bloom,
   An angel writing in a book of gold:–
   Exceeding peace had made Ben Adhem bold,
   And to the presence in the room he said,
   'What writest thou?' – The vision raised its head,
   And with a look made of all sweet accord,
   Answered, 'The names of those who love the Lord.' ['Abou Ben Adhem'
   (1838)]

2. 'I pray thee then,
   Write me as one that loves his fellow-men.' [Ib.]

Hutcheson, Francis (1694–1746)
Scottish moral philosopher

1. That action is best, which procures the greatest happiness for the
   greatest numbers. [*An Inquiry into the Original of our Ideas of Beauty and
   Virtue* (1725), II, 3]

Huxley, Thomas Henry (1825–1895)
English biologist, Darwinist and agnostic

1. Science is nothing but trained and organized common sense, differing
   from the latter only as a veteran may differ from a raw recruit: and its
   methods differ from those of common sense only as far as the
   guardsman's cut and thrust differ from the manner in which a savage
   wields his club. [*Collected essays*, 'The Method of Zadig']

2. Try to learn something about everything and everything about something. [Memorial stone]

Ibsen, Henrik (1828–1906)
Norwegian founder of modern prose and social drama, and poet

1. One should never put on one's best trousers to go out to battle for freedom and truth. [*An Enemy of the People*, V]

2. People don't do such things! [*Hedda Gabler*, IV]

3. Take the saving lie from the average man and you take his happiness away, too. [*The Wild Duck*, III]

Illich, Ivan (1926–)
Austrian-born American educator, sociologist, writer and priest

1. In a consumer society there are inevitably two kinds of slaves: the prisoners of addiction and the prisoners of envy. [*Tools for Conviviality*]

Inge, William Ralph (Dean Inge) (1860–1954)
English divine, Dean of St Pauls 1911–34; writer and teacher

1. It takes in reality only one to make a quarrel. It is useless for the sheep to pass resolutions in favour of vegetarianism while the wolf remains of a different opinion. [*Outspoken Essays*, 'Patriotism']

Irving, Washington (1783–1859)
American essayist, short-story writer, travel writer and diplomat

1. Whenever a man's friends begin to compliment him about looking young, he may be sure that they think he is growing old. [*Bracebridge Hall*, 'Bachelors']

2. There is a certain relief in change, even though it be from bad to worse; as I have found in travelling in a stage-coach, that it is often a comfort to shift one's position and be bruised in a new place. [*Tales of a Traveller*]

Isherwood, Christopher (1904–1986)
English-born American novelist; collaborated on plays with W. H. Auden and wrote screenplays

1. I am a camera with its shutter open, quite passive, recording, not thinking. [*Goodbye to Berlin*]

Jackson, Laura (Riding) (1901–1991)
American poet

1. There is something to be told about us for the telling of which we all wait. [*The Telling*, (1972)]

Jacobs, Joe (1896–1940)
American boxing manager

1. [Remark made after Max Schmeling, whom he managed, lost his boxing title to Jack Sharkey in 1932]
We was robbed! [Attr.]

James I of Scotland (1394–1437)
King of Scots from 1424 and poet; alienated the nobility and was assassinated

1. The bird, the beast, the fish eke in the sea,
They live in freedom everich in his kind;
And I a man, and lackith liberty ... [*The Kingis Quair*]

James V of Scotland (1512–1542)
King of Scots from 1513; father of Mary, Queen of Scots; King of the Commons

1. [On the rule of the Stuart dynasty in Scotland]
It cam' wi' a lass, and it'll gang wi' a lass. [Remark, 1542]

James VI of Scotland and I of England (1566–1625)
King of Scots from 1567 and of English from 1603; son of Mary, Queen of Scots; father of Charles I, essayist and patron of poetry

1. A custom loathesome to the eye, hateful to the nose, harmful to the brain, dangerous to the lungs, and in the black, stinking fume thereof, nearest resembling the horrible Stygian smoke of the pit that is bottomless. [*A Counterblast to Tobacco* (1604)]

James, Henry (1843–1916)
Great American-born British novelist; short-story writer, critic, dramatist and letter writer

1. We must grant the artist his subject, his idea, his *donnée*: Our criticism is applied only to what he makes of it. [*Partial Portraits* (1888), 'The Art of Fiction']

2. Experience is never limited, and it is never complete; it is an immense sensibility, a kind of huge spider-web of the finest silken threads suspended in the chamber of consciousness, and catching every air-borne particle in its tissue. [Ib.]

3. The time-honoured bread-sauce of the happy ending. [*Theatricals*, 2nd Series]

James, William (1842–1910)
American psychologist and radical empiricist philosopher; brother of Henry and Alice James

1. If merely 'feeling good' could decide, drunkenness would be the supremely valid human experience. [*Varieties of Religious Experience* (1902)]

2. The moral flabbiness born of the exclusive worship of the bitch-goddess *success*. That – with the squalid cash interpretation put on the word success – is our national disease. [Letter to H. G. Wells, 1906]

Jefferson, Thomas (1743–1826)
American statesman; third President, 1801–09, founder of the Democratic Party

1. We hold these truths to be self-evident: that all men are created equal; that they are endowed by their Creator with certain unalienable rights; that among these are life, liberty, and the pursuit of happiness. [Declaration of Independence, 1776]

2. The tree of liberty must be refreshed from time to time with the blood of patriots and tyrants. It is its natural manure. [Letter to W. S. Smith, 1787]

Jennings, Paul (1918–1989)
British humorous writer

1. Of all musicians, flautists are most obviously the ones who know something we don't know. [*The Jenguin Pennings*, 'Flautists Flaunt Afflatus']

Jerome, Saint (c. 342–420)
Christian monk and scholar; translated the Bible into Latin

1. *Noli equi dentes inspicere donati.*
Never look a gift horse in the mouth. [*On the Epistle to the Ephesians*]

Jerome, Jerome K. (1859-1927)
English humorous novelist, dramatist and journalist

1. It is impossible to enjoy idling thoroughly unless one has plenty of work to do. [*Idle Thoughts of an Idle Fellow* (1886)]

2. Love is like the measles; we all have to go through it. [Ib.]

Joad, C. E. M. (1891-1953)
English popularizer of philosophy, scholar and teacher

1. It all depends on what you mean by ... [Response to BBC Brains Trust questions]

St John of the Cross (1542-1591)
Spanish Carmelite monk, poet and mystic

1. *Noche oscura del alma*.
   The dark night of the soul. [Title of poem]

Johnson, Hiram (1866-1945)
American Progressive Republican politician; isolationist in 1930s

1. The first casualty when war comes is truth. [Speech, US Senate, 1917]

Johnson, Lyndon Baines (1908-1973)
American statesman; Democrat President 1963-69, noted for Civil Rights reform

1. [Of J. Edgar Hoover, chief of the FBI]
   I'd much rather have that fellow inside the tent pissing out, than outside pissing in. [Attr.]

Johnson, Philander Chase (1866-1939)
American newspaperman and humorist

1. Cheer up, the worst is yet to come. [*Everybody's Magazine*, 1920]

Johnson, Samuel (1709-1784)
English lexicographer, poet, critic, conversationalist and essayist

1. Men more frequently require to be reminded than informed. [*The Rambler* (1750-1752)]

2. I am not yet so lost in lexicography, as to forget that words are the daughters of the earth, and that things are the sons of heaven. Language

is only the instrument of science, and words are but the signs of ideas: I wish, however, that the instrument might be less apt to decay, and that signs might be permanent, like the things which they denote. [*A Dictionary of the English Language* (1755), Preface]

3. [Of citations of usage in a dictionary]
Every quotation contributes something to the stability or enlargement of the language. [Ib. Preface]

4. *Lexicographer.* A writer of dictionaries, a harmless drudge. [Ib.]

5. *Oats.* A grain, which in England is generally given to horses, but in Scotland supports the people. [Ib.]

6. A hardened and shameless tea-drinker, who has for twenty years diluted his meals with only the infusion of this fascinating plant; whose kettle has scarcely time to cool; who with tea amuses the evening, with tea solaces the midnight, and with tea welcomes the morning. [Review in the *Literary Magazine*, 1757]

7. Pleasure is very seldom found where it is sought; our brightest blazes of gladness are commonly kindled by unexpected sparks. [*The Idler* (1758–1760)]

8. When two Englishmen meet, their first talk is of the weather. [Ib. no. 11]

9. A Scotchman must be a very sturdy moralist who does not love Scotland better than truth. [*A Journey to the Western Islands of Scotland* (1775)]

10. To a poet nothing can be useless. [*Rasselas* (1759), 10]

11. Human life is everywhere a state in which much is to be endured, and little to be enjoyed. [Ib. 11]

12. The only end of writing is to enable the readers better to enjoy life, or better to endure it. [*Works* (1787), X]

13. I am sorry I have not learned to play at cards. It is very useful in life: it generates kindness and consolidates society. [In Boswell, *Journal of a Tour to the Hebrides* (1785), 21 November 1773]

14. I am always sorry when any language is lost, because languages are the pedigree of nations. [Ib. 18 September 1773]

15. The rod produces an effect which terminates in itself. A child is afraid of being whipped, and gets his task, and there's an end on't; whereas, by exciting emulation and comparisons of superiority, you lay the foundation of lasting mischief; you make brothers and sisters hate each other. [In Boswell, *The Life of Samuel Johnson* (1791), I, 1719]

16. [Asked the reason for a mistake in his Dictionary]
Ignorance, madam, sheer ignorance. [Ib. I, 1755]

17. *Boswell*: I do indeed come from Scotland, but I cannot help it...
Johnson: That, Sir, I find, is what a very great many of your countrymen cannot help. [Ib. 1763]

18. Norway, too, has noble wild prospects; and Lapland is remarkable for prodigious noble wild prospects. But, Sir, let me tell you, the noblest prospect which a Scotchman ever sees, is the high road that leads him to England! [Ib. I, 1763]

19. Your levellers wish to level *down* as far as themselves; but they cannot bear levelling *up* to themselves. [Ib. I, 1763]

20. Sir, a woman's preaching is like a dog's walking on his hinder legs. It is not done well; but you are surprised to find it done at all. [Ib. I, 1763]

21. [Kicking a stone in order to disprove Berkeley's theory of the non-existence of matter]
I refute it *thus*. [Ib. I, 1763]

22. It matters not how a man dies, but how he lives. The act of dying is not of importance, it lasts so short a time. [Ib. II, 1769]

23. Read over your compositions, and where ever you meet with a passage which you think is particularly fine, strike it out. [Ib. II, quoting a college tutor, 1773]

24. Patriotism is the last refuge of a scoundrel. [Ib. II, 1775]

25. Knowledge is of two kinds. We know a subject ourselves, or we know where we can find information upon it. [Ib. II, 1775]

26. No man but a blockhead ever wrote, except for money. [Ib. III, 1776]

27. Depend upon it, Sir, when a man knows he is to be hanged in a fortnight, it concentrates his mind wonderfully. [Ib. III, 1777]

28. When a man is tired of London, he is tired of life; for there is in London all that life can afford. [Ib. III, 1777]

29. [Of the Giant's Causeway]
Worth seeing? yes; but not worth going to see. [Ib. III, 1779]

Johnston, Brian (1912–1994)
Broadcaster and commentator on cricket and royal events

1. The bowler's Holding, the batsman's Willey. [Quoted in his obituary, *Sunday Times*]

Johst, Hanns (1890–1978)
German dramatist

1. *Wenn ich Kultur höre ... entsichere ich meinen Browning!*
When I hear the word 'culture' ... I take the safety-catch off my Browning! [*Schlageter* (1933); also attr. Hermann Goering]

Jolson, Al (Asa Yoelson) (1886–1950)
Russian-born American singer; famous for imitations of Negro singers

1. You ain't heard nothin' yet. [*The Jazz Singer*, film, 1927; scriptwriter Alfred A. Cohn]

Jonson, Ben (1572–1637)
English dramatist, poet and author of court masques; noted for comedy of humours

1. I have it here in black and white. [*Every Man in His Humour* (1598), IV.v]

2. Drink to me only with thine eyes,
And I will pledge with mine;
Or leave a kiss upon the cup,
And I'll not look for wine. [*The Forest* (1616), 'To Celia']

3. And though thou hadst small Latin, and less Greek...

He was not of an age, but for all time! ... ['To the Memory of My Beloved, the Author, Mr William Shakespeare' (1623)]

4. She is Venus when she smiles
But she's Juno when she walks,

And Minerva when she talks. [*The Underwood* (1640), 'Celebration of Charis', V]

5. In small proportions we just beauties see;
   And in short measures, life may perfect be. [Ib. 'To the Immortal Memory ... of ... Sir Lucius Carey and Sir H. Morison']

Joyce, James (1882–1941)
Irish novelist, short-story writer and poet; noted for his revolutionary stream of consciousness technique and inventive language

1. Ireland is the old sow that eats her farrow. [*A Portrait of the Artist as a Young Man* (1916), 5]

2. By an epiphany he meant a sudden spiritual manifestation, whether in vulgarity of speech or of gesture or in a memorable phase of the mind itself. He believed that it was for the man of letters to record these epiphanies with extreme care, seeing that they themselves are the most delicate and evanescent of moments. [*Stephen Hero* (1944), 25]

3. And yes I said yes I will Yes. [*Ulysses* (1922), closing words]

4. riverrun, past Eve and Adam's, from swerve of shore to bend of bay, brings us by a commodius vicus of recirculation back to Howth Castle and Environs. [*Finnegans Wake* (1939), first words]

5. All moanday, tearsday, wailsday, thumpsday, frightday, shatterday. [Ib. II]

6. [Replying to Patrick Tuohy's assertion that he wished to capture Joyce's soul in his portrait of him]
   Never mind about my soul, just make sure you get my tie right. [In R. Ellmann, *James Joyce* (1958)]

Jung, Carl Gustav (1875–1961)
Swiss psychiatrist; pupil of Freud and founder of analytic psychology

1. *Soweit wir zu erkennen vermögen, ist es der einzige Sinn der menschlichen Existenz, ein Licht anzuzünden in der Finsternis des blossen Seins.*
   As far as we are able to understand, the only aim of human existence is to kindle a light in the darkness of mere being. [*Erinnerungen, Träume, Gedanken (Memories, Dreams, Thoughts*, 1962), 11, 'On life after death']

Juvenal (c. AD 60–130)
Roman verse satirist and Stoic

1. *Probitas laudatur et alget.*
   Honesty is praised and is left out in the cold. [*Satires*, I]

2. *Sed quis custodiet ipsos*
   Custodes?
   But who will guard the guards themselves? [Ib. VI]

3. *Nobilitas sola est atque unica virtus.*
   The one and only true nobility is virtue. [Ib. VIII]

4. *Duas tantum res anxius optat,*
   Panem et circenses.
   Two things only the people anxiously desire: bread and circuses. [Ib. X]

5. *Orandum est ut sit mens sana in corpore sano.*
   Your prayers should be for a healthy mind in a healthy body. [Ib. X]

Kafka, Franz (1883–1924)
Influential German-speaking novelist and short-story writer; born in Prague

1. *Es ist oft besser, in Ketten, als frei zu sein.*
   It's often better to be in chains than to be free. [*Der Prozess* (*The Trial*, written 1914, published 1925), 8, 'Block the Businessman. Dismissal of the Lawyer']

2. *Im Kampf zwischen dir und der Welt sekundiere der Welt.*
   In the struggle between you and the world, support the world. [*Betrachtungen über Sünde, Leid, Hoffnung und den wahren Weg* (*Reflections on Sin, Sorrow, Hope and the true Way*, first published posthumously by Max Brod in 1953)]

3. In an autobiography one cannot avoid writing 'often' where truth would require that 'once' be written. [Diary 3 January 1912]

Kant, Immanuel (1724–1804)
German idealist philosopher, noted for his idea of the categorical imperative

1. *Endlich gibt es einen Imperativ, der, ohne irgend eine andere durch ein gewisses Verhalten zu erreichende Absicht als Bedingung zum Grunde zu legen, dieses*

Verhalten unmittelbar gebietet. Dieser Imperativ ist kategorisch ... *Dieser Imperativ mag der* der Sittlichkeit *heissen.*

Finally, there is an imperative which immediately dictates a certain mode of behaviour, without having as its condition any other purpose to be achieved by means of that behaviour. This imperative is *categorical* ... This imperative may be called that of *morality*. [*Grundlegung zur Metaphysik der Sitten (Outline of the metaphysics of morals,* 1785), II]

Karr, Alphonse (1808–1890)
French novelist, editor of Figaro and memoirist

1. *Plus ça change, plus c'est la même chose.*
   The more things change the more they remain the same. [*Les Guêpes* (1849)]

Kavanagh, Ted (1892–1958)
New Zealand-born scriptwriter

1. It's that man again. [ITMA (1939–49), BBC Radio]

Kearney, Denis (1847–1907)
American labour leader, born in Ireland

1. Horny-handed sons of toil. [Speech, c. 1878]

Keats, John (1795–1821)
Leading English Romantic poet, noted for his passion for beauty, and letter writer

1. Much have I travell'd in the realms of gold,

   Then felt I like some watcher of the skies
   When a new planet swims into his ken;
   Or like stout Cortez when with eagle eyes
   He star'd at the Pacific – and all his men
   Look'd at each other with a wild surmise—
   Silent, upon a peak in Darien. ['On First Looking into Chapman's Homer' (1816)]

2. A thing of beauty is a joy for ever: ['Endymion' (1818), 1]

3. O what can ail thee, knight-at-arms,
   Alone and palely loitering?

The sedge has wither'd from the lake,
And no birds sing ... ['La Belle Dame Sans Merci' (1819)]

4. 'Beauty is truth, truth beauty,' – that is all
Ye know on earth, and all ye need to know. ['Ode on a Grecian Urn' (1819)]

5. Season of mists and mellow fruitfulness, ['To Autumn' (1819)]

6. *Negative Capability*, that is, when a man is capable of being in uncertainties, mysteries, doubts, without any irritable reaching after fact and reason... [Letter to George and Tom Keats, 21 December 1817]

7. Poetry should surprise by a fine excess and not by Singularity – it should strike the Reader as a wording of his own highest thoughts, and appear almost a Remembrance ... [Letter to John Taylor, 27 February 1818]

Kelvin, William Thomson, 1st Baron (1824–1907)
Irish-born Scottish physicist, noted in the fields of thermodynamics and electricity; inventor of the Kelvin Scale

1. [On realizing that his wife was planning an afternoon excursion]
At what time does the dissipation of energy begin? [In A. Fleming, *Memories of a Scientific Life*]

Kempis, Thomas à (c. 1380–1471)
German mystic, Augustinian monk and writer

1. *O quam cito transit gloria mundi.*
Oh, how quickly the glory in this world passes away. [*De Imitatione Christi* (1892 ed.), I, 3; often quoted as *Sic transit gloria mundi*]

2. *Nam homo proponit, sed Deus disponit.*
For man proposes, but God disposes. [Ib. I, 19]

3. *De duobus malis minus est semper eligendum.*
Of two evils the lesser is always to be chosen. [Ib. III, 12]

Kennedy, John F. (1917–1963)
American Democratic President, 1961–63, noted for his civil rights reform programme; assassinated

1. And so, my fellow Americans: ask not what your country can do for

you – ask what you can do for your country. My fellow citizens of the world: ask not what America will do for you, but what together we can do for the freedom of man. [Inaugural address, 1961]

2. [This speech caused much unintended amusement as *ein Berliner* means a jam doughnut as well as a citizen of Berlin]
As a free man, I take pride in the words *Ich bin ein Berliner*. [Speech, 1963]

Kennedy, Joseph P. (1888'1969)
Irish-American business executive, multi-millionaire and father of President John F. Kennedy

1. When the going gets tough, the tough get going. [In J. H. Cutler, *Honey Fitz* (1962)]

Kerouac, Jack (1922–1969)
American Beat novelist and poet

1. You know, this is really a beat generation. [Phrase borrowed from Herbert Huncke, a drug addict, and recalled in *The Origins of the Beat Generation*]

Kesselring, Joseph (1902–1967)
American dramatist and short-story writer

1. Arsenic and Old Lace. [Title of play, 1941]

Khrushchev, Nikita (1894–1971)
Russian statesman; premier of the Soviet Union 1958–64; noted for his denunciation of Stalin

1. Politicians are the same everywhere. They promise to build a bridge even when there's no river. [Remark to journalists while on a visit to the USA, 1960]

Kilvert, Francis (1840–1879)
English curate and diarist

1. Of all noxious animals, too, the most noxious is a tourist. And of all tourists, the most vulgar, ill-bred, offensive and loathsome is the British tourist. [*Diary*, 1870]

2. It is a fine thing to be out on the hills alone. A man could hardly be a beast or a fool alone on a great mountain. [Ib. 1871]

King, Martin Luther (1929–1968)
American civil rights leader and Baptist minister; advocated non-violence in anti-racist campaigns; Nobel peace prize 1964; assassinated

1. I have a dream that one day this nation will rise up and live out the true meaning of its creed: 'We hold these truths to be self-evident, that all men are created equal'. [Speech, 1963]

Kingsley, Charles (1819–1875)
English historical novelist, poet, lecturer and clergyman

1. More ways of killing a cat than choking her with cream. [*Westward Ho!* (1855), 20]

2. He did not know that a keeper is only a poacher turned outside in, and a poacher a keeper turned inside out. [*The Water Babies* (1863), 1]

Kinnock, Neil (1942–)
Welsh politician and orator; Labour party leader 1983–92

1. Compassion is not a sloppy, sentimental feeling for people who are underprivileged or sick ... it is an absolutely practical belief that, regardless of a person's background, ability or ability to pay, he should be provided with the best that society has to offer. [Maiden speech, House of Commons, 1970]

2. [Of nuclear disarmament]
I would die for my country but I could never let my country die for me. [Speech, 1987]

Kipling, Rudyard (1865–1936)
Indian-born British poet, novelist, short-story and children's writer; Nobel prize 1907

1. Being kissed ... by a man who *didn't* wax his moustache was – like eating an egg without salt. [*The Story of the Gadsbys* (1888), 'Poor Dear Mamma']

2. Steady the Buffs! [Ib.]

3. And he went back through the Wet Wild Woods, waving his wild tail, and walking by his wild lone. But he never told anybody. [*Just So Stories* (1902), 'The Cat That Walked by Himself']

4. And a woman is only a woman, but a good cigar is a Smoke.
[*Departmental Ditties and Other Verses* (1886), 'The Betrothed']

5. Oh, East is East, and West is West, and never the twain shall meet,
['The Ballad of East and West' (1889)]

6. Though I've belted you an' flayed you,
By the livin' Gawd that made you,
You're a better man than I am, Gunga Din! [*Barrack-Room Ballads and Other Verses* (1892), 'Gunga Din']

7. Ye thought? Ye are not paid to think ... ['McAndrew's Hymn' (1893)]

8. For the Colonel's Lady an' Judy O'Grady
Are sisters under their skins! [*The Seven Seas* (1896), 'The Ladies']

9. Take up the White Man's burden—
Send forth the best ye breed—
Go, bind your sons to exile
To serve your captives' need; ['The White Man's Burden' (1899)]

10. I keep six honest serving-men
(They taught me all I knew);
Their names are What and Why and When
And How and Where and Who. [*Just-So Stories* (1902), 'The Elephant's Child']

11. Teach us Delight in simple things,
And Mirth that has no bitter springs. [*Puck of Pook's Hill* (1906), 'The Children's Song']

Klee, Paul (1879–1940)
Swiss painter and engraver; member of Blaue Reiter and teacher at the Bauhaus

1. *Kunst gibt nicht das Sichtbare wieder, sondern macht sichtbar.*
Art does not reproduce what is visible; it makes things visible.
['Schöpferische Konfession' ('Creative Credo', 1920)]

Klinger, Friedrich Maximilian von (1752–1831)
German dramatist

1. [Name adopted by a German literary movement of the late 18th century]
Sturm und Drang.
Storm and stress. [Title of play, 1777]

Knox, John (1505–1572)
Scottish religious reformer, founder of the Presbyterian Church of Scotland (1560) and prose writer

1. The First Blast of the Trumpet Against the Monstrous Regiment of Women [Title of pamphlet, 1558]

Koran

1. There is no doubt in this book. [Chapter 1]

2. Let there be no violence in religion. [Chapter 2]

La Bruyère, Jean de (1645–1696)
French moralist, noted for satirical character studies

1. There are only three events in a man's life; birth, life, and death; he is not conscious of being born, he dies in pain, and he forgets to live. [*Les Caractères*]

2. To endeavour to forget anyone is a certain way of thinking of nothing else. [Ib.]

La Rochefoucauld, François, Duc de (1613–1680)
French moralist and epigrammatist

1. *Dans l'adversité de nos meilleurs amis, nous trouvons toujours quelque chose qui ne nous déplait pas.*
In the misfortune of our best friends, we always find something which is not displeasing to us. [*Réflexions ou Sentences et Maximes Morales*]

2. *On n'est jamais si heureux ni si malheureux qu'on s'imagine.*
One is never so happy or so unhappy as one thinks. [*Maximes*, 49]

3. *On s'ennuie presque toujours avec les gens qui il n'est pas permis de s'ennuyer.*
We are almost always bored by the very people whom we must not find boring. [Ib. 352]

Laing, R. D. (1927–1989)
Scottish pyschiatrist and psychoanalyst, noted for his social theory of mental illness; poet

1. Madness need not be all breakdown. It may also be break-through. It is potential liberation and renewal as well as enslavement and existential death. [*The Politics of Experience*, 16]

Lamb, Lady Caroline (1785–1828)
*English novelist and poet; her marriage to William Lamb Melbourne
was marred by her infatuation with Byron*

1. [Of Byron]
Mad, bad, and dangerous to know. [Journal, 1812]

Lamb, Charles (1775–1834)
English essayist, critic and letter writer

1. Nothing to me is more distasteful than that entire complacency and
satisfaction which beam in the countenance of a new-married couple.
[*Essays of Elia*, 'A Bachelor's Complaint of Married People']

2. In everything that relates to science, I am a whole Encyclopaedia
behind the rest of the world. [Ib. 'The Old and the New
Schoolmaster']

3. The human species, according to the best theory I can form of it, is
composed of two distinct races, *the men who borrow*, and *the men who lend*.
[Ib. 'The Two Races of Men']

4. I mean your *borrowers of books* – those mutilators of collections, spoilers
of the symmetry of shelves, and creators of odd volumes. [Ib. 'The Two
Races of Men']

5. Credulity is the man's weakness, but the child's strength. [Ib. 'Witches
and other Night Fears']

6. [Referring to the nature of a pun]
It is a pistol let off at the ear; not a feather to tickle the intellect. [Ib.
'Popular Fallacies']

7. The greatest pleasure I know, is to do a good action by stealth, and
to have it found out by accident. ['Table Talk by the Late Elia']

8. All, all are gone, the old familiar faces. ['The Old Familiar
Faces']

Lang, Andrew (1844–1912)
*Scottish poet, journalist, mythologist, anthropologist, Greek scholar
and childrens writer*

1. He uses statistics as a drunken man uses lamp-posts – for support
rather than illumination. [*Treasury of Humorous Quotations*]

Lang, Julia S. (1921–)
British broadcaster

1. Are you sitting comfortably? Then I'll begin. [Preamble to children's story in *Listen With Mother*, BBC radio programme, from 1950]

Langbridge, Frederick (1849–1923)
English clergyman, poet and children's writer

1. Two men look out through the same bars:
   One sees the mud, and one the stars. ['A Cluster of Quiet Thoughts']

Langland, William (c. 1330–c. 1400)
English alliterative poet

1. A faire felde ful of folke fonde I there bytwene
   Of all manner of men, the mene and riche,
   Worchyng and wandrying as the world asketh. [*Piers Plowman*, Prologue (B Text)]

2. Grammere, that grounde is of alle. [Ib. Prologue (C Text)]

Lao-tze (c. 604–531 BC)
Chinese philosopher, regarded as founder of Taoism

1. Acting without design, occupying oneself without making a business of it, finding the great in what is small and the many in the few, repaying injury with kindness, effecting difficult things while they are easy, and managing great things in their beginnings: this is the method of Tao. [*Tao Te Ching*]

Larkin, Philip (1922–1985)
English poet, novelist and librarian

1. What will survive of us is love. ['An Arundel Tomb']

2. Nothing, like something, happens anywhere. ['I Remember, I Remember']

3. They fuck you up, your mum and dad.
   They may not mean to, but they do.
   They fill you with the faults they had
   And add some extra, just for you. ['This be the Verse']

4. Get stewed:
Books are a load of crap. ['A Study of Reading Habits']

Lauder, Sir Harry (1870–1950)
Scottish comedian, entertainer and memoirist

1. Just a wee deoch-an-duoris
Before we gang awa'...
If y' can say
It's a braw bricht moonlicht nicht,
Yer a' richt, that's a'. [Song]

2. Roamin' in the gloamin'
By the bonny banks of Clyde. [Song, 1911]

3. Keep right on to the end of the road. [Song, 1924]

Lawrence, D. H. (1885–1930)
English novelist, poet, short-story writer, critic, essayist and traveller

1. You must always be a-waggle with LOVE. [*Bibbles*]

2. Pornography is the attempt to insult sex, to do dirt on it. [*Phoenix* (1936), 'Pornography and Obscenity']

3. Never trust the artist. Trust the tale. The proper function of a critic is to save the tale from the artist who created it. {*Studies in Classic American Literature* (1923), 'The Spirit of Place']

4. How beastly the bourgeois is
especially the male of the species. [*Pansies* (1929), 'How Beastly the Bourgeois Is']

5. A snake came to my water-trough
On a hot, hot day, and I in pyjamas for the heat,
To drink there. [*Birds, Beasts and Flowers* (1923), 'Snake']

Lazarus, Emma (1849–1887)
American poet and translator; champion of Jews

1. Give me your tired, your poor,
Your huddled masses yearning to breathe free. [Verse inscribed on the Statue of Liberty]

Le Corbusier (1887–1965)
Swiss-born French architect and town planner, noted for his functionalist approach

1. *Une maison est une machine-à-habiter.*
   A house is a machine for living in. [*Vers une architecture* (1923)]

Leacock, Stephen Butler (1869–1944)
English-born Canadian humorist, essayist, biographer and economist

1. Lord Ronald said nothing; he flung himself from the room, flung himself upon his horse and rode madly off in all directions. [*Nonsense Novels* (1910), 'Gertrude the Governess']

2. Advertising may be described as the science of arresting the human intelligence long enough to get money from it. [In Prochow, *The Public Speaker's Treasure Chest*]

Lear, Edward (1812–1888)
English nonsense poet, watercolourist, travel writer and ornithologist

1. There was an Old Man with a beard,
   Who said, 'It is just as I feared!–
   Two Owls and a Hen,
   Four Larks and a Wren,
   Have all built their nests in my beard! [*Book of Nonsense* (1846)]

2. 'How pleasant to know Mr. Lear!'
   Who has written such volumes of stuff!
   Some think him ill-tempered and queer,
   But a few think him pleasant enough. [*Nonsense Songs* (1871), Preface]

3. In the middle of the wood,
   Lived the Yonghy-Bonghy-Bó. [Ib. 'The Courtship of the Yonghy-Bonghy-Bó']

4. The wandering dong through the forest goes!
   The Dong! – the Dong!
   The Dong with the Luminous Nose!' [Ib. 'The Dong with the Luminous Nose']

5. Far and few, far and few,
   Are the lands where the Jumblies live;
   Their heads are green, and their hands are blue,
   And they went to sea in a Sieve. [Ib. 'The Jumblies']

6. The Owl and the Pussy-Cat went to sea
   In a beautiful pea-green boat.
   They took some honey, and plenty of money,
   Wrapped up in a five-pound note.
   The Owl looked up to the Stars above
   And sang to a small guitar,
   'Oh lovely Pussy! – O Pussy, my love,
   What a beautiful Pussy you are.' [Ib. 'The Owl and the
   Pussy-Cat']

7. They dined on mince, and slices of quince,
   Which they ate with a runcible spoon;
   And hand in hand, on the edge of the sand,
   They danced by the light of the moon. [Ib. 'The Owl and the
   Pussy-Cat']

Leary, Timothy (1920–)
American psychologist, author and actor

1. Turn on, tune in, and drop out. [*The Politics of Ecstasy*]

Lenin, V. I. (1870–1924)
Russian revolutionary, Marxist theoretician and Bolshevik leader; first Soviet Premier

1. One step forward, two steps back ... It happens in the lives of individuals, and it happens in the history of nations and in the development of parties. [*One Step Forward, Two Steps Back* (1904)]

2. It is true that liberty is precious – so precious that it must be rationed. [In Sidney and Beatrice Webb, *Soviet Communism* (1936)]

Lennon, John (1940–1980)
English pop singer-songwriter and guitarist; member of The Beatles 1962–70

1. It's been a hard day's night. ['A Hard Day's Night' (1964), with Paul McCartney]

2. We're more popular than Jesus Christ now. I don't know which will go first. Rock and roll or Christianity. [*The Beatles Illustrated Lyrics*]

Leonardo da Vinci (1452–1519)
Italian painter, sculptor, architect, engineer, inventor, scientist and musician; outstanding Renaissance figure

1. While I thought that I was learning how to live, I have been learning how to die. [*Notebooks*]

Levant, Oscar (1906–1972)
American pianist; wrote autobiographical works and made film appearances

1. Strip the phony tinsel off Hollywood and you'll find the real tinsel underneath. [In Halliwell, *Filmgoer's Book of Quotes* (1973)]

Leverhulme, Viscount (1851–1925)
English soap manufacturer, philanthropist, Liberal politician and art collector

1. Half the money I spend on advertising is wasted, and the trouble is I don't know which half. [In Ogilvy, *Confessions of an Advertising Man* (1963)]

Lévis, Duc de (1764–1830)
French writer and solider

1. *Noblesse oblige.*
   Nobility has obligations. [*Maximes et réflexions* (1812)]

Ley, Robert (1890–1945)
German Nazi politician; head of labour from 1933

1. *Kraft durch Freude.*
   Strength through joy. [German Labour Front slogan]

Leybourne, George (d.1884)
English songwriter

1. He flies through the air with the greatest of ease,
   This daring young man on the flying trapeze. ['The Man on the Flying Trapeze']

Liberace, Wlaziu Valentino (1920–1987)
American pianist and showman

1. [Remark made after hostile criticism]
   I cried all the way to the bank. [*Autobiography*]

Lincoln, Abraham (1809–1865)
American statesman, lawyer and abolitionist; Republican President 1861–65; assassinated

1. If you don't want to use the army, I should like to borrow it for a while. Yours respectfully, A. Lincoln. [Letter to General George B. McClellan, whose lack of activity during the US Civil War irritated Lincoln]

2. The ballot is stronger than the bullet. [Speech, 1856]

3. ... that this nation, under God, shall have a new birth of freedom; and that government of the people, by the people, and for the people, shall not perish from the earth. [Address at Dedication of National Cemetery at Gettysburg, 1863]

4. You can fool some of the people all of the time, and all of the people some of the time, but you cannot fool all of the people all the time. [Attr. Speech, 1856]

Linklater, Eric (1899–1974)
Scottish novelist, born in Wales; satirist, short-story writer and journalist

1. There won't be any revolution in America ... The people are too clean. They spend all their time changing their shirts and washing themselves. You can't feel fierce and revolutionary in a bathroom. [*Juan in America*, V, 3]

Livy (59 BC– AD 17)
Roman writer, famous for his history of Rome, from its founding to 9 BC

1. *Vae victis.*
   Woe to the vanquished. [*History*, V]

Lloyd George, David (1863–1945)
English-born Welsh Liberal statesman; Chancellor of the Exchequer 1908–15; Prime Minister 1916–22

1. What is our task? To make Britain a fit country for heroes to live in. [Speech, Wolverhampton, 1918]

2. The world is becoming like a lunatic asylum run by lunatics. [*The Observer*, 'Sayings of Our Times', 1933]

Lloyd, Marie (1870–1922)
English music-hall artiste

1. A little of what you fancy does you good. [Music hall song]

Locke, John (1632–1704)
English Liberal philosopher, founder of empiricism

1. It is one thing to show a man that he is in an error, and another to put him in possession of truth. [*Essay concerning Human Understanding*, 4]

2. Wherever Law ends, Tyranny begins. [*Second Treatise of Government*]

Logau, Friedrich von (1605–1655)
German epigrammatist

1. *Gottes Mühlen mahlen langsam, mahlen aber trefflich klein;*
   Ob aus Langmut Er sich säumet, bringt mit Schärf' Er alles ein.
   Though the mills of God grind slowly, yet they grind exceeding small;
   Though with patience He stands waiting, with exactness grinds He all. [*Sinngedichte* (1653), translated Longfellow]

London, Jack (1876–1916)
American adventure novelist, short-story writer, journalist, sailor, socialist and goldminer

1. The Call of the Wild [Title of novel, 1903]

Longfellow, Henry Wadsworth (1807–1882)
American poet, noted for his ballads and narrative poetry; translator and prose writer

1. I shot an arrow into the air,
   It fell to earth, I knew not where. ['The Arrow and the Song']

2. The cares that infest the day
   Shall fold their tents, like the Arabs,
   And as silently steal away. ['The Day is Done']

3. By the shore of Gitche Gumee,
   By the shining Big-Sea-Water,

Stood the wigwam of Nokomis,
Daughter of the Moon, Nokomis. [*The Song of Hiawatha*, 'Hiawatha's Childhood']

4. From the waterfall he named her,
Minnehaha, Laughing Water. [Ib. 'Hiawatha and Mudjekeewis']

5. Ships that pass in the night, and speak each other in passing; [*Tales of a Wayside Inn*, 'The Theologian's Tale. Elizabeth']

6. Under a spreading chestnut-tree
The village smithy stands;
The smith, a mighty man is he,
With large and sinewy hands;
And the muscles on his brawny arms
Are strong as iron bands. ['The Village Blacksmith']

7. There was a little girl
Who had a little curl
Right in the middle of her forehead,
When she was good
She was very, very good,
But when she was bad she was horrid. [In B.R.T. Machetta, *Home Life of Longfellow*, 'There was a Little Girl']

8. It was the schooner Hesperus,
That sailed the wintry sea;
And the skipper had taken his little daughter,
To bear him company. ['The Wreck of the Hesperus']

Loos, Anita (1893–1981)
American humorous novelist and screenwriter

1. Gentlemen Prefer Blondes [Title of book, 1925]

Louis XIV of France (1638–1715)
King of France from 1643 and patron of the arts; the Sun King; established absolute monarchy and waged many wars

1. *L'État c'est moi.*
I am the State. [Attr.]

Louis, Joe (1914–1981)
American boxer; world heavyweight champion 1937–49

1. [Referring to the speed for which his coming opponent, Billy Conn, was renowned]
   He can run, but he can't hide. [Attr.]

Lovelace, Richard (1618–1658)
English Cavalier lyric poet

1. Stone walls do not a prison make
   Nor iron bars a cage; ['To Althea, From Prison']

Lovell, Maria (1803–1877)
English actress and dramatist

1. Two souls with but a single thought,
   Two hearts that beat as one. [*Ingomar the Barbarian*, II]

Lucan (AD 39–65)
Roman epic poet, born in Spain

1. *Etiam periere ruinae.*
   The very ruins have been destroyed. [*Bellum Civile (Civil War)*, IX]

Lucas, George (1945–)
American film director and producer

1. May the Force be with you. [*Star Wars* (1977)]

Lucretius (c. 95–55 BC)
Roman poet and philosopher

1. *Nil posse creari*
   De nilo.
   Nothing can be created from nothing. [*De Rerum Natura*, I]

2. *Augescunt aliae gentes, aliae minuuntur,*
   Inque brevi spatio mutantur saecla animantum
   Et quasi cursores vitai lampada tradunt.
   Some races increase, others are reduced, and in a short while the generations of living creatures are changed and like runners relay the torch of life. [Ib. II]

3. *Nil igitur mors est ad nos neque pertinet hilum,*
   Quandoquidem natura animi mortalis habetur.
   Death therefore is nothing to us nor does it matter a jot, since the
   nature of the soul we have is mortal. [Ib. II]

4. *Vitaque mancipio, nulli datur, omnibus usu.*
   And life is given to none freehold, but it is leasehold for all. [Ib. III]

5. *Ut quod ali cibus est aliis fuat acre venenum.*
   What is food to one is to others bitter poison. [Ib. IV]

Luther, Martin (1483–1546)
German theologian and leader of the Protestant Reformation;
translated the Bible into German

1. Whatever your heart clings to and confides in that is really your God.
   [*Large Catechism*, I]

2. *Hier stehe ich. Ich kann nicht anders. Gott helfe mir. Amen.*
   Here I stand. I can do no other. God help me. Amen. [Speech at the
   Diet of Worms, 1521]

McArthur, Douglas (1880–1964)
American general; Commander of Allied Forces in the Far East and
SW Pacific in World War II

1. [Said on leaving the Philippines, 1942]
   I shall return. [*New York Times*, 1942]

Macaulay, Dame Rose (1889–1958)
English novelist, essayist, journalist and travel writer

1. 'Take my camel, dear,' said my aunt Dot as she climbed down from
   this animal on her return from High Mass. [*The Towers of Trebizond*
   (1956)]

Macaulay, Thomas Babington, Lord (1800–1859)
English historian; Liberal statesman, essayist and poet

1. There is only one cure for the evils which newly acquired freedom
   produces; and that is freedom. [*Literary Essays Contributed to the 'Edinburg
   Review'*, 'Milton' (1825)]

2. Nothing is so useless as a general maxim. [Ib. 'Machiavelli' (1827)]

3. The gallery in which the reporters sit has become a fourth estate of the realm. [*Historical Essays Contributed to the 'Edinburgh Review'*, (1828)]

4. The Puritan hated bear-baiting, not because it gave pain to the bear, but because it gave pleasure to the spectators. [*History of England* (1849), I]

5. Now who will stand on either hand,
   And keep the bridge with me? [*Lays of Ancient Rome* (1842), 'Horatius', 29]

MacCaig, Norman (1910–)
Scottish poet

1. Self under self, a pile of selves I stand
   Threaded on time, and with metaphysic hand
   Lift the farm like a lid and see
   Farm within farm, and in the centre, me. [*Riding Lights* (1955), 'Summer farm']

2. Stop looking like a purse. How could a purse
   squeeze under the rickety door and sit,
   full of satisfaction, in a man's house? [*The Equal Skies* (1980), 'Toad']

McCarthy, Joseph R. (1908–1957)
American Republican politician, known for his investigations of alleged Communists

1. McCarthyism is Americanism with its sleeves rolled. [Speech, 1952]

MacCrae, John (1872–1918)
Canadian physician and poet

1. In Flanders fields the poppies blow
   Between the crosses, row on row,
   That mark our place. ['In Flanders Fields' (1915)]

MacDiarmid, Hugh (1892–1978)
Leading Scottish Renaissance poet; prose writer, Nationalist and Communist

1. Earth, thou bonnie broukit bairn!
   – But greet, an' in your tears ye'll droun
   The haill clanjamfrie! ['The Bonnie Broukit Bairn']

2. It's easier to lo'e Prince Charlie
   Than Scotland — mair's the shame! ['Bonnie Prince Charlie']

3. I'll ha'e nae hauf-way hoose, but aye be whaur
   Extremes meet — it's the only way I ken
   To dodge the curst conceit o' bein' richt
   That damns the vast majority o' men. [*A Drunk Man Looks at the
   Thistle* (1926)]

4. The wee reliefs we ha'e in booze,
   Or wun at times in carnal states,
   May hide frae us but canna cheenge
   The silly horrors o' oor fates. [Ib.]

5. A Scottish poet maun assume
   The burden o' his people's doom,
   And dee to brak' their livin' tomb. [Ib.]

6. God through the wrong end of a telescope. ['Of John Davidson']

7. And I lo'e love
   Wi' a scunner in't. ['Scunner']

8. The rose of all the world is not for me
   I want for my part
   Only the little white rose of Scotland
   That smells sharp and sweet, and breaks the heart. ['The Little White
   Rose']

McGonagall, William (1825–1902)
Scottish doggerel poet; tragedian and actor

1. Beautiful Railway Bridge of the Silv'ry Tay!
   Alas, I am very sorry to say
   That ninety lives have been taken away
   On the last Sabbath day of 1879,
   Which will be remember'd for a very long time. ['The Tay Bridge
   Disaster']

Machiavelli, Niccolo di Bernardo dei (1469–1527)
Florentine statesman, political theorist and historian

1. *Uno principe necessitato sapere bene usare la bestia, debbe di quelle pigliare la
   golpe e il lione; perchè il lione non si defende da'lupi. Bisogna, adunque, essere
   golpe a conoscere e' lacci, e lione a sbigottire e' lupi.*

As a prince must be able to act just like a beast, he should learn from the fox and the lion; because the lion does not defend himself against traps, and the fox does not defend himself against wolves. So one has to be a fox in order to recognize traps, and a lion to frighten off wolves. [*Il Principe*, 18]

Mackenzie, Sir Compton (1883–1972)
Scottish novelist, born in England; journalist, broadcaster, nationalist and autobiographer

1. I don't believe in principles. Principles are only excuses for what we want to think or what we want to do. [*The Adventures of Sylvia Scarlett* (1918)]

Macleod, Fiona (1855–1905)
Scottish neo-Celtic poet, novelist and dramatist

1. My heart is a lonely hunter that hunts on a lonely hill. ['The Lonely Hunter' (1869)]

McLuhan, Marshall (1911–1980)
Canadian communications theorist

1. The new electronic interdependence recreates the world in the image of a global village. [*The Gutenberg Galaxy* (1962)]

2. The medium is the message. [*Understanding Media* (1964), 1]

Macmillan, Harold (1894–1986)
British statesman; Conservative Prime Minister 1957–63

1. Let's be frank about it; most of our people have never had it so good. [Speech, 1957]

2. The most striking of all the impressions I have formed since I left London a month ago is of the strength of this African national consciousness. The wind of change is blowing through this continent. [Speech, 1960]

3. [Referring to privatization of profitable nationalized industries] Selling the family silver. [Speech, House of Lords, 1986]

MacNeice, Louis (1907–1963)
British poet, born in Belfast; radio writer and producer, translator and critic

1. It's no go the merrygoround, it's no go the rickshaw,
   All we want is a limousine and a ticket for the peep show. [*Earth Compels* (1938), 'Bagpipe Music']

2. I am not yet born; O fill me
   With strength against those who would freeze my
   humanity, would dragoon me into a lethal automaton,
   would make me a cog in a machine, a thing with
   one face, a thing, and against all those
   who would dissipate my entirety, would
   blow me like thistledown hither and
   thither or hither and thither
   like water held in the
   hands would spill me.
   let them not make me a stone and let them not spill me
   Otherwise kill me. [*Springboard* (1944), 'Prayer before Birth']

Magidson, Herb (20th century)
American songwriter

1. Music, Maestro, Please. [Song title]

Magna Carta (1215)
Charter granted by King John

1. No free man shall be taken or imprisoned or dispossessed, or outlawed or exiled, or in any way destroyed, nor will we go upon him, nor will we send against him, except by the lawful judgement of his peers or by the law of the land. [Clause 39]

Mahler, Gustav (1860–1911)
Austrian late Romantic composer, known for his symphonies and song cycles

1. [On visiting Niagara]
   Endlich fortissimo!
   At last, *fortissimo*! [In K. Blaukopf, *Gustav Mahler* (1973)]

Mallarmé, Stéphane (1842–1898)
French symbolist poet

1. *Donner un sens plus pur aux mots de la tribu.*
   To give a purer meaning to the language of the tribe. ['Le Tombeau d'Edgar Poe']

Mallory, George Leigh (1886–1924)
English mountaineer and teacher; died attempting to scale Everest

1. [Asked why he wished to climb Mt. Everest]
   Because it is there. [*New York Times*, 1923]

Malory, Sir Thomas (d. 1471)
English writer, celebrated for his Arthurian prose romance translated from the French

1. Whoso pulleth out this sword of this stone and anvil is rightwise King born of all England. [*Le Morte D'Arthur* (1470), I.4]

2. For love that time was not as love is nowadays. [Ib. XX.3]

Malthus, Thomas Robert (1766–1834)
English political economist, noted for his population theory

1. Population, when unchecked, increases in a geometrical ratio. Subsistence only increases in an arithmetical ratio. [*Essay on the Principle of Population* (1798), 1]

2. The perpetual struggle for room and food. [Ib. 3]

Manikan, Ruby (20th century)
Indian church leader

1. If you educate a man you educate a person, but if you educate a woman, you educate a family. [*The Observer*, 'Sayings of the Week', 1947]

Mann, Horace (1796–1859)
American educationist, politician, teacher and writer

1. The object of punishment is, prevention from evil; it never can be made impulsive to good. [*Lectures and Reports on Education* (1845)]

Mansfield, Katherine (1888–1923)
New Zealand-born short-story writer

1. Whenever I prepare for a journey I prepare as though for death. Should I never return, all is in order. That is what life has taught me. [*The Journal of Katherine Mansfield*, 1922]

Mao Tse-Tung (1893–1976)
Chinese Marxist theoretician and statesman; Chairman of the Chinese Communist Party from 1949

1. Imperialism is a paper tiger. [*Quotations from Chairman Mao Tse-Tung*]

2. Political power grows out of the barrel of a gun. [*Selected Works*, II, 'Problems of War and Strategy']

Marie-Antoinette (1755–1793)
Queen of France (1774–93) and wife of Louis XVI; opposed reform and was guillotined in French Revolution

1. *Qu'ils mangent de la brioche.*
Let them eat cake. [Attr. (but much older)]

Marlowe, Christopher (1564–1593)
English poet and dramatist, noted for blank verse plays

1. I count religion but a childish toy,
And hold there is no sin but ignorance. [*The Jew of Malta* (c. 1592), Prologue]

2. *Barnadine*: Thou hast committed—
Barabas: Fornication: but that was in another country;
And besides, the wench is dead. [Ib. IV.i]

3. What doctrine call you this, *Che sera, sera*, What will be, shall be? [*Doctor Faustus* (1604), I.i]

4. Hell hath no limits nor is circumscrib'd
In one self place, where we are is Hell,
And where Hell is, there must we ever be.
And to be short, when all the world dissolves,
And every creature shall be purified,
All places shall be hell that are not heaven. [Ib. II.i]

5. Was this the face that launch'd a thousand ships,
And burnt the topless towers of Ilium? [Ib. V.i]

6. Come live with me, and be my love,
And we will all the pleasures prove, ['The Passionate Shepherd to his Love']

Marquis, Don (1878–1937)
American columnist, satirist and poet

1. but wotthehell archy wotthehell
jamais triste archy jamais triste
that is my motto. [*archy and mehitabel* (1927), 'mehitabel sees paris']

Marryat, Frederick (1792–1848)
English naval officer and novelist, noted for sea stories

1. We always took care of number one. [*Frank Mildmay* (1829), 19]

2. I never knows the children. It's just six of one and half-a-dozen of the other. [*The Pirate*, 4]

Marshall, Arthur (1910–1989)
British journalist

1. It's all part of life's rich pageant. ['The Games Mistress', gramophone record, 1930s]

Marshall, Thomas (1854–1925)
American statesman; Democrat Vice-President 1913–21

1. What this country needs is a good five-cent cigar. [In *New York Tribune*, 1920]

Martial (c. AD 43–c. 104)
Latin epigrammatist and poet, born in Spain

1. *Non amo te, Sabidi, nec possum dicere quare:*
Hoc tantum possum dicere, non amo te.
I don't love you, Sabidius, and I can't tell you why; all I can tell you is this, that I don't love you. [*Epigrammata*, I]

2. *Difficilis facilis, iucundus acerbus es idem:*
Nec tecum possum vivere nec sine te.

Difficult or easy, pleasant or bitter, you are the same you: I cannot live with you – nor without you. [Ib. XII]

3. *Rus in urbe.*
The country in town. [Ib. XII]

Marvell, Andrew (1621–1678)
English Metaphysical lyric poet and prose satirist

1. He nothing common did or mean
Upon that memorable scene:
But with his keener eye
The axe's edge did try. ['An Horatian Ode upon Cromwell's Return from Ireland' (1650)]

2. But at my back I always hear
Time's wingèd chariot hurrying near...
The grave's a fine and private place,
But none I think do there embrace. ['To His Coy Mistress' (1681)]

Marx, Groucho (1895–1977)
American film comedian

1. Either he's dead or my watch has stopped. [*A Day at the Races*, film, 1937; script by Pirosh, Seaton and Oppenheimer]

2. A child of five would understand this. Send somebody to fetch a child of five. [*Duck Soup*]

3. I never forget a face, but I'll make an exception in your case. [*The Guardian*, 1965]

4. I resign. I wouldn't want to belong to any club that would have me as a member. [Attr.]

Marx, Karl (1818–1883)
German political philosopher and economist; founder of Communism

1. Religion ... is the opium of the people. [*A Contribution to the Critique of Hegel's Philosophy of Right* (1843–4)]

2. From each according to his abilities, to each according to his needs. [*Critique of the Gotha Programme* (1875)]

Marx, Karl (1818–1883)
German political philosopher and Communist
and **Engels,** Friedrich (1820–1895)
German socialist and political philosopher

1. A spectre is haunting Europe – the spectre of Communism. [*The Communist Manifesto* (1848)]

2. The history of all hitherto existing society is the history of class struggle. [Ib.]

3. The workers have nothing to lose but their chains in this. They have a world to win. Workers of the world, unite! [Ib.]

Mary, Queen of Scots (1542–1587)
Queen of Scots from 1542–67; daughter of James V; forced to abdicate, imprisoned and executed

1. England is not all the world. [Said at her trial, 1586]

Masefield, John (1878–1966)
English poet, novelist, critic and childrens writer; poet laureate from 1930

1. I must go down to the seas again, to the lonely sea and the sky,
   And all I ask is a tall ship and a star to steer her by, ['Sea Fever' (1902)]

2. Dirty British coaster with a salt-caked smoke stack,
   Butting through the Channel in the mad March days, ['Cargoes' (1903)]

Maugham, William Somerset (1874–1965)
English short-story writer, novelist, dramatist and physician; born in France

1. Life is too short to do anything for oneself that one can pay others to do for one. [*The Summing Up* (1938)]

2. I forget who it was that recommended men for their souls' good to do each day two things they disliked … it is a precept that I have followed scrupulously; for every day I have got up and I have gone to bed. [*The Moon and Sixpence* (1919)]

Mayakovsky, Vladimir (1893–1930)
Russian futurist poet, dramatist and artist; poet of the revolution

1. Art is not a mirror to reflect the world, but a hammer with which to shape it. [*The Guardian*, 1974]

Mearns, Hughes (1875–1965)
American educator and writer

1. As I was going up the stair
   I met a man who wasn't there.
   He wasn't there again to-day.
   I wish, I wish he'd stay away. ['The Psycho-ed' (1910)]

de Medici, Cosimo (1389–1464)
Member of prominent and cultured family of bankers, merchants and rulers of Tuscany and Florence; known as Cosimo the Great

1. We read that we ought to forgive our enemies; but we do not read that we ought to forgive our friends. [In Francis Bacon, *Apophthegms* (1625)]

Melville, Herman (1819–1891)
American novelist, poet and short-story writer, noted for his sea novels

1. Call me Ishmael. [*Moby Dick* (1851), 1, first words]

2. Better sleep with a sober cannibal than a drunken Christian. [Ib. 3]

3. A whale ship was my Yale College and my Harvard. [Ib. 24]

Menander (c. 342–292 BC)
Greek poet and dramatist of New Comedy

1. Whom the gods love dies young. [*Dis Exapaton*]

Mencken, H. L. (1880–1956)
American journalist, ciritc, philologist and satirist

1. Faith may be defined briefly as an illogical belief in the occurrence of the improbable. [*Prejudices* (1922)]

2. Conscience is the inner voice that warns us somebody may be looking. [*A Mencken Chrestomathy* (1949)], [*A Little Book in C Major* (1916)]

3. An idealist is one who, on noticing that a rose smells better than a cabbage, concludes that it will also make better soup. [*Sententiae*]

Mercer, Johnny (1909–1976)
American songwriter and composer; Academy Awards 1946, 1951, 1954

1. That old black magic has me in its spell. ['That Old Black Magic', 1942]

Mercier, Louis-Sébastien (1740–1814)
French playwright and writer on drama

1. *Les extrèmes se touchent.*
Extremes meet. [*Tableau de Paris*, IV, 348, heading]

Meredith, George (1828–1909)
English novelist, poet and critic

1. Kissing don't last: cookery do! [*The Ordeal of Richard Feverel* (1859), 28]

Meredith, Owen (Lord Lytton) (1831–1891)
English statesman; Viceroy of India 1876–1880 and lyric poet

1. Genius does what it must, and Talent does what it can. ['Last Words of a Sensitive Second-Rate Poet']

Merritt, Dixon Lanier (1879–1972)
American editor

1. A wonderful bird is the pelican,
His bill will hold more than his belican.
He can take in his beak
Food enough for a week,
But I'm damned if I see how the helican. [*Nashville Banner*, 1913]

Metternich, Prince Clement (1773–1859)
Austrian statesman; Chancellor of Austria 1821–48

1. When Paris sneezes, Europe catches cold. [Remark, 1830]

Middleton, Thomas (c. 1580–1627)
English dramatist, poet and writer of masques; collaborated with William Rowley, among others

1. By many a happy accident. [*No Wit, No Help, Like a Woman's* (c. 1613), IV.i]

2. Though I be poor, I'm honest. [*The Witch* (1609–16), III.ii]

Mies van der Rohe, Ludwig (1886–1969)
German-born American architect; Bauhaus director 1929–33

1. Less is more. [*New York Herald Tribune*, 1959]

Mikes, George (1912–1987)
Hungarian-born journalist and author

1. Continental people have sex life; the English have hot-water bottles. [*How to be an Alien* (1946)]

Mill, John Stuart (1806–1873)
English utilitarian philosopher; economist, reformer and politician

1. A party of order or stability, and a party of progress or reform, are both necessary elements of a healthy state of political life. [*On Liberty* (1859), 2]

2. I am not aware that any community has a right to force another to be civilized. [Ib. 4]

3. The principle which regulates the existing social relations between the two sexes – the legal subordination of one sex to the other – is wrong in itself, and now one of the chief hindrances to human improvement; and ... it ought to be replaced by a principle of perfect equality, admitting no power or privilege on the one side, nor disability on the other. [*The Subjection of Women* (1869), 1]

Millay, Edna St. Vincent (1892–1950)
American poet and dramatist

1. My candle burns at both ends;
It will not last the night;
But ah, my foes, and oh my friends—
It gives a lovely light! [*A Few Figs from Thistles* (1920), 'First Fig']

Miller, Arthur (1915–)
Leading American dramatist; screenplay writer for his wife, Marilyn Monroe

1. A good newspaper, I suppose, is a nation talking to itself. [*The Observer*, 'Sayings of the Week', 1961]

Miller, William (1810–1872)
Scottish poet; author of nursery rhymes

1. Wee Willie Winkie rins through the town,
   Up stairs and down stairs in his nicht-gown,
   Tirling at the window, crying at the lock,
   Are the weans in their bed, for it's now ten o'clock? ['Willie Winkie' (1841)]

Milligan, Spike (1918–)
Irish radio, stage and screen comedian and writer

1. I'm walking backwards till Christmas. [*The Goon Show*]

2. Money can't buy friends, but you can get a better class of enemy. [*Puckoon* (1963), 6]

Milne, A. A. (1882–1956)
English children's writer; dramatist, novelist, poet and journalist

1. I do like a little bit of butter to my bread! [*When We Were Very Young* (1924), 'The King's Breakfast']

2. Hush! Hush! Whisper who dares!
   Christopher Robin is saying his prayers. [Ib. 'Vespers']

3. Isn't it funny
   How a bear likes honey?
   Buzz! Buzz! Buzz!
   I wonder why he does? [*Winnie-the-Pooh* (1926), 1]

4. I am a Bear of Very Little Brain, and long words Bother me. [Ib. 4]

5. I have decided to catch a Heffalump. [Ib. 5]

6. Time for a little something. [Ib. 6]

Milton, John (1608–1674)
Great English poet; parliamentarian, libertarian and pamphleteer

1. Fame is the spur that the clear spirit doth raise
   (That last infirmity of noble mind)
   To scorn delights, and live laborious days; ['Lycidas' (1638), line 64]

2. At last he rose, and twitch'd his Mantle blue:
   Tomorrow to fresh Woods, and Pastures new. [Ib. line 192]

3. Hence, loathed Melancholy,
   Of Cerberus, and blackest Midnight born,
   In Stygian cave forlorn,
   'Mongst horrid shapes, and shrieks, and sights unholy. ['L'Allegro' (1645), line 1]

4. Sport that wrinkled Care derides,
   And Laughter holding both his sides.
   Come, and trip it as ye go
   On the light fantastic toe,
   And in thy right hand lead with thee
   The mountain nymph, sweet Liberty. [Ib. line 31]

5. Or sweetest Shakespeare, Fancy's child,
   Warble his native wood-notes wild, [Ib. line 127]

6. Peace hath her victories
   No less renowned than war. [*Sonnets*, 'To the Lord General Cromwell' (1652)]

7. They also serve who only stand and wait. [Ib. 'When I consider how my light is spent']

8. Farewell happy fields
   Where joy for ever dwells: Hail horrors, hail
   Infernal world, and thou profoundest Hell
   Receive thy new possessor: one who brings
   A mind not to be changed by place or time.
   The mind is its own place, and in it self
   Can make a Heav'n of Hell, a Hell of Heav'n. [*Paradise Lost* (1667), I, line 249]

9. Better to reign in hell, then serve in heav'n. [Ib. I, line 261]

10. Space may produce new Worlds. [Ib. I, line 650]

11. ... nothing lovelier can be found
In woman, than to study household good,
And good works in her Husband to promote. [Ib. IX, line 232]

12. What thou art is mine;
Our state cannot be sever'd, we are one,
One flesh; to lose thee were to lose myself. [Ib. IX, line 957]

13. Yet I shall temper so
Justice with Mercy. [Ib. X, line 77]

14. If we think to regulate printing thereby to rectify manners, we must regulate all recreations and pastimes, all that is delightful to man ... It will ask more than the work of twenty licensers to examine all the lutes, the violins, and the guitars in every house ... and who shall silence all the airs and madrigals, that whisper softness in chambers? [*Areopagitica* (1644)]

Mitchell, Margaret (1900–1949)
American novelist

1. After all, tomorrow is another day. [*Gone with the Wind* (1936), closing words]

Mizner, Wilson (1876–1933)
American writer, wit and dramatist

1. [Also attributed to Jimmy Durante]
Be nice to people on your way up because you'll meet 'em on your way down. [In Eric Partridge, *A Dictionary of Catch-Phrases*]

2. When you steal from one author, its plagiarism; if you steal from many, its research. [Attr.]

Molière (1622–1673)
French dramatist, creator of French classical comedy; actor and director

1. *On est aisément dupé par ce qu'on aime.*
One is easily deceived by what one loves. [*Tartuffe* (1664), IV]

2. *Il faut manger pour vivre et non pas vivre pour manger.*
One should eat to live, not live to eat. [*L'Avare* (1669), III.i]

Montaigne, Michel de (1533–1592)
French essayist and moralist

1. *Il faut être toujours botté et prêt à partir.*
   One should always have one's boots on and be ready to go. [*Essais* (1580), I.20]

2. *Il faut noter, que les jeux d'enfants ne sont pas jeux: et les faut juger en eux, comme leurs plus sérieuses actions.*
   It should be noted that children at play are not playing about; their games should be seen as their most serious-minded activity. [Ib. I.23]

3. *Quand je me joue à ma chatte, qui sait si elle passe son temps de moi plus que je ne fais d'elle?*
   When I play with my cat, who knows whether she isn't amusing herself with me more than I am with her? [Ib. II.12]

4. *L'homme est bien insensé. Il ne saurait forger un ciron, et forge des Dieux à douzaines.*
   Man is quite insane. He wouldn't know how to create a maggot, and he creates Gods by the dozen. [Ib. II.12]

5. A man who fears suffering is already suffering from what he fears. [Ib. III]

6. Science without conscience is but death of the soul. [In Simcox, *Treasury of Quotations on Christian Themes*]

Montesquieu, Charles, Baron de (1689–1755)
French social and political philosopher and jurist

1. An empire founded by war has to maintain itself by war. [*Considérations sur les causes de la grandeur et de la décadence des romains*, 8]

2. Liberty is the right of doing whatever the laws permit. [*De l'esprit des lois*, XI.3]

3. No kingdom has ever had as many civil wars as the kingdom of Christ. [*Lettres persanes* (1721)]

Moore, Clement C. (1779–1863)
American Hebrew scholar and poet

1. T'was the night before Christmas, when all through the house
   Not a creature was stirring, not even a mouse;
   The stockings were hung by the chimney with care,

In hopes that St Nicholas soon would be there. ['A Visit from St. Nicholas' (1823)]

Moore, Edward (1712–1757)
English dramatist, fabulist and editor

1. This is adding insult to injuries. [*The Foundling*, (1748), V.v]

2. I am rich beyond the dreams of avarice. [*The Gamester* (1753), II.ii]

Moore, George (1852–1933)
Irish realist novelist, dramatist and critic

1. A man travels the world over in search of what he needs and returns home to find it. [*The Brook Kerith* (1916), 11]

Moore, Marianne (1887–1972)
American poet, essayist and editor

1. Not till the poets among us can be
'literalists of
the imagination' – above
insolence and triviality and can present
for inspection, imaginary gardens with real toads in them, shall we have
it. ['Poetry', first version]

Moore, Thomas (1779–1852)
Irish poet, lyricist and biographer

1. The harp that once through Tara's halls
The soul of music shed,
Now hangs as mute on Tara's walls
As if that soul were fled, [*Irish Melodies* (1807), 'The Harp that Once']

2. No, there's nothing half so sweet in life
As love's young dream. [Ib. 'Love's Young Dream']

3. My only books
Were woman's looks,
And folly's all they've taught me. [Ib. 'The Time I've Lost']

More, Sir Thomas (1478–1535)
English statesman and humanist; Lord Chancellor 1529–1532;
executed for refusing to recognize Henry VIII as head of the Church

1. [On reading an unremarkable book recently rendered into verse by a friend of his]
Yea, marry, now it is somewhat, for now it is rhyme; before, it was neither rhyme nor reason. [In Francis Bacon, *Apophthegms New and Old* (1625)]

Morell, Thomas (1703–1784)
English classical scholar, librettist, editor and clergyman

1. See, the conquering hero comes!
Sound the trumpets, beat the drums! [*Joshua* (1748)]

Morgan, Edwin (1920–)
Scottish poet and translator

1. let the storm wash the plates [*The Second Life* (1968), 'Strawberries']

2. ...and washed his hands, and watched his hands, and washed his hands, and watched his hands. [*Sonnets from Scotland* (1984), 'Pilate at Fortingall']

3. The bougainvillea milleniums
may come and go, but then in thistle days
a strengthed seed outlives the hardest blasts. [Ib. 'A Golden Age']

Morris, William (1834–1896)
English poet, designer, craftsman, Pre-Raphaelite, artist and socialist

1. Love is enough: though the world be a-waning,
And the woods have no voice but the voice of complaining. ['Love is Enough']

2. If you want a golden rule that will fit everybody, this is it: Have nothing in your houses that you do not know to be useful, or believe to be beautiful. [*Hopes and Fears for Art* (1882), 'The Beauty of Life']

Morse, Samuel (1791–1872)
American painter, inventor of electric telegraphy and memoirist

1. What God hath wrought. [First message sent on his telegraph, 1844]

Morton, J. B. ('Beachcomber') (1893–1979)
English journalist, humorist and author

1. Dr Strabismus (Whom God Preserve) of Utrecht is carrying out
   research work with a view to crossing salmon with mosquitoes. He says
   it will mean a bite every time for fishermen. [*By the Way* (1931),
   'January Tail-piece']

Mountbatten, Louis, (1st Earl Mountbatten of Burma) (1900–1979)
British naval commander; great-grandson of Queen Victoria

1. In my experience, I have always found that you cannot have an efficient
   ship unless you have a happy ship, and you cannot have a happy ship
   unless you have an efficient ship. That is the way I intend to start this
   commision, and that is the way I intend to go on – with a happy and
   an efficient ship. [Initial address to crew of *HMS Kelly*, 1939, adopted
   verbatim by Noel Coward in the script of the film *In which We Serve*]

Muggeridge, Kitty (1903–1994)
British writer, wife of Malcolm Muggeridge

1. [On David Frost]
   He rose without a trace. [Attr. 1960s]

Muir, Edwin (1887–1959)
Scottish poet, critic, translator, novelist and autobiographer

1. We have seen
   Good men made evil wrangling with the evil,
   Straight minds grown crooked fighting crooked minds.
   Our peace betrayed us; we betrayed our peace.
   Look at it well. This was the good town once. ['The Good Town']

2. Oh these deceits are strong almost as life.
   Last night I dreamt I was in the labyrinth,
   And woke far on. I did not know the place. ['The Labyrinth']

Murdoch, Iris (1919–)
Irish-born British novelist, philosopher and dramatist

1. 'What are you famous *for*?'
   'For nothing. I am just famous.' [*The Flight from the Enchanter*]

Musset, Alfred de (1810–1857)
French Romantic poet, dramatist and novelist

1. *Les grands artistes n'ont pas de patrie.*
   Great artists have no country. [*Lorenzaccio*, I.v]

Nairn, Ian (1930–1983)
English writer on architecture and journalist

1. [Making an ideal of suburbia]
   If what is called development is allowed to multiply at the present rate, then by the end of the century Great Britain will consist of isolated oases of preserved monuments in a desert of wire, concrete roads, cosy plots and bungalows ... Upon this new Britain the REVIEW bestows a name in the hope that it will stick – SUBTOPIA. [*Architectural Review*, 1955]

Nairne, Carolina, Baroness (1766–1845)
Scottish song and ballad writer

1. [Referring to Bonnie Prince Charlie]
   Better lo'ed ye canna be,
   Will ye no come back again? [*Lays from Strathearn* (1846), 'Bonnie Charlie's now awa!']

Napoleon I (1769–1821)
Emperor of the French (1804–15) and much of Europe; brilliant general and reforming administrator

1. *L'Angleterre est une nation de boutiquiers.*
   England is a nation of shopkeepers. [In O'Meara, *Napoleon in Exile* (1822)]

2. *Tout soldat français porte dans sa giberne le bâton de maréchal de France.*
   Every French soldier carries a French marshal's baton in his knapsack. [In E. Blaze, *La Vie Militaire sous l'Empire*, I, v]

3. An army marches on its stomach. [Attr.]

4. Not tonight, Josephine! [Attr.]

Nash, Ogden (1902–1971)
American humorous poet

1. Candy
   Is dandy

But liquor
Is quicker. [*Hard Lines* (1931), 'Reflections on Ice-Breaking']

2. Children aren't happy with nothing to ignore,
And that's what parents were created for. [*Happy Days* (1933), 'The Parent']

Nation, Terry
Original scriptwriter of Dr Who

1. Ex-ter-min-ate! [Robotic watchword of the Daleks, evil creatures housed in a metal casing, first featured in the BBC TV Dr Who adventure, 'The Daleks', December 1963]

Nelson, Horatio (Lord Nelson) (1758–1805)
English admiral, noted for his naval victories in the Napoleonic wars

1. [Nelson's last signal at the Battle of Trafalgar, 1805]
ENGLAND EXPECTS EVERY MAN TO DO HIS DUTY. [In Robert Southey, *The Life of Nelson* (1860 edition), 9]

Newbolt, Sir Henry John (1862–1938)
English poet, man of letters and lawyer

1. There's a breathless hush in the Close to-night—

But the voice of the schoolboy rallies the ranks:
'Play up! play up! and play the game!' [*The Island Race* (1898), 'Vitaï Lampada']

Niebuhr, Reinhold (1892–1971)
American Protestant theologian and writer on political morality

1. God grant me the serenity to accept the things I cannot change, the courage to change the things I can, and the wisdom to distinguish the one from the other. [Prayer adopted by Alcoholics Anonymous, attributed to but not accepted by Niebuhr]

Nietzsche, Friedrich Wilhelm (1844–1900)
German philosopher, critic and poet, noted for his rejection of Christianity and concept of the Superman

1. *Ich lehre euch den Übermenschen. Der Mensch ist etwas, das überwinden werden soll. Was habt ihr getan, ihn zu überwinden?*
Mine is the doctrine of the superman. Man is something to be

overcome. What have you done to overcome him? [*Also Sprach Zarathustra* (*Thus Spake Zarathustra*, 1883–84), I, Prologue, 3]

2. *Gott ist tot: aber so wie die Art der Menschen ist, wird es vielleicht noch jahrtausendelang Höhlen geben, in denen man seinen Schatten zeigt.*
God is dead: but men's natures are such that for thousands of years yet there will perhaps be caves in which his shadow will be seen. [*Die fröhliche Wissenschaft* (*The Gay Science*, 2nd edition, 1887), III, 108]

3. *Glaubt es mir! – das Geheimnis, um die grösste Fruchtbarkeit und den grössten Genuss vom Dasein einzuernten, heisst: gefährlich leben!*
Believe me! – the secret of gathering in the greatest fruitfulness and the greatest enjoyment from existence is *living dangerously*! [Ib. IV, 283]

Nivelle, Général Robert (1856–1924)
French general

1. *Ils ne passeront pas.*
They shall not pass. [Statement at Battle of Verdun, 1916; often attr. to Pétain]

Nixon, Richard (1913–1994)
American politician and lawyer; Republican President 1969–74; resigned after Watergate scandal

1. It is time for the great silent majority of Americans to stand up and be counted. [Speech, 1970]

2. There can be no whitewash at the White House. [*The Observer*, 'Sayings of the Week', 1973]

North, Christopher (John Wilson) (1785–1854)
Scottish poet, novelist, editor, essayist and critic

1. Minds like ours, my dear James, must always be above national prejudices, and in all companies it gives me true pleasure to declare, that, as a people, the English are very little indeed inferior to the Scotch. [*Blackwood's Edinburgh Magazine*, 1826, 'Noctes Ambrosianae', 9]

2. His Majesty's dominions, on which the sun never sets. [Ib. 1829, 'Noctes Ambrosianae', 20]

3. Laws were made to be broken. [Ib. 1830, 'Noctes Ambrosianae', 24]

Oates, Captain Lawrence (1880–1912)
English Antarctic explorer and army captain

1. I am just going outside, and may be some time. [Last words, quoted in Captain Scott's diary]

O'Casey, Sean (1880–1964)
Irish dramatist, author of realist tragi-comedies and autobiographer

1. Th' whole worl's in a terrible state o' chassis! [*Juno and the Paycock* (1924), I]

2. There's no reason to bring religion into it. I think we ought to have as great a regard for religion as we can, so as to keep it out of as many things as possible. [*The Plough and the Stars* (1926), I]

Occam, William of (c. 1280–1349)
English nominalist philosopher and Franciscan friar

1. *Entia non sunt multiplicanda praeter necessitatem.*
   Entities should not be needlessly multiplied. [*Quodlibeta* (c. 1324), V]

O'Connell, Daniel (1775–1847)
Irish politician, 'The Liberator', and nationalist; founder of the Catholic Association 1823

1. [Of Sir Robert Peel's smile; quoting J. P. Curran, Irish politician and lawyer]
   ...like the silver plate on a coffin. [*Hansard*, 1835]

Ogilvy, James, First Earl of Seafield (1663–1730)
Scottish politician and lawyer; Lord Chancellor of Scotland 1702–04, 1705–07

1. [On signing the Act of Union]
   Now there's an end of ane old song. [Remark, 1707]

O'Keefe, Patrick (1872–1934)
American advertising agent

1. Say it with flowers [Advertisement for the Society of American florists, 1917]

Oppenheimer, J. Robert (1904–1967)
American nuclear physicist involved in atomic bomb research

1. [On the consequences of the first atomic test]
   We knew the world would not be the same. [In Giovanitti and Freed,
   The Decision to Drop the Bomb (1965)]

Orczy, Baroness (1865–1947)
*Hungarian-born British historical novelist, short-story writer and
illustrator*

1. We seek him here, we seek him there,
   Those Frenchies seek him everywhere.
   Is he in heaven? – Is he in hell?
   That demmed, elusive Pimpernel? [*The Scarlet Pimpernel* (1905), 12]

Orwell, George (Eric Blair) (1903–1950)
English satirical novelist, essayist and critic, born in India

1. I'm fat, but I'm thin inside. Has it ever struck you that there's a thin
   man inside every fat man, just as they say there's a statue inside every
   block of stone? [*Coming Up For Air* (1939), I, 3]

2. Whatever is funny is subversive, every joke is ultimately a custard pie
   ... A dirty joke is not ... a serious attack upon morality, but it is a
   sort of mental rebellion, a momentary wish that things were otherwise.
   [*Horizon*, 1941, 'The Art of Donald McGill']

3. Four legs good, two legs bad. [*Animal Farm* (1945), 3]

4. All animals are equal, but some animals are more equal than others.
   [Ib. 10]

5. Big Brother is watching you. [*Nineteen Eighty-Four* (1949), I, 1]

6. Only the Thought Police mattered. [Ib. I, 1]

7. Newspeak was the official language of Oceania. [Ib. footnote]

8. *Doublethink* means the power of holding two contradictory beliefs in
   one's mind simultaneously, and accepting both of them. [Ib. II, 9]

9. If you want a picture of the future, imagine a boot stamping on a
   human face -- for ever. [Ib. III, 3]

10. At 50, everyone has the face he deserves. [Closing words, notebook, 1949]

O'Shaughnessy, Arthur (1844–1881)
English poet and herpetologist

1. We are the music makers,
   And we are the dreamers of dreams, . . .
   Yet we are the movers and shakers
   Of the world for ever, it seems. ['Ode' (1874)]

Otis, James (1725–1783)
American lawyer, politician and pamphleteer

1. Taxation without representation is tyranny. [Attr.]

Ovid (43 BC– AD 18)
Roman poet, noted for his love poetry

1. *Spectatum veniunt, veniunt spectentur ut ipsae.*
   The women come to see, they come that they may be seen. [*Art Amatoria*, I, line 99]

2. *Medio tutissimus ibis.*
   The middle way is the safest for you. [*Metamorphoses*, II, line 137]

3. *Video meliora, proboque;*
   Deteriora sequor.
   I see the better way, and approve it, but I follow the worse. [Ib. VII, line 20]

4. *Tempus edax rerum.*
   Time, the devourer of all things [Ib. XV, line 234]

Owen, Wilfred (1893–1918)
English war poet

1. My subject is War, and the pity of War. The Poetry is in the pity. [Quoted in *Poems* (1963), Preface]

2. What passing-bells for these who die as cattle?
   Only the monstrous anger of the guns.
   Only the stuttering rifles' rapid rattle
   Can patter out their hasty orisons . . . ['Anthem for Doomed Youth' (1917)]

Paine, Thomas (1737–1809)
English-born American radical journalist, political theorist, deist and pamphleteer

1. Government, even in its best state, is but a necessary evil; in its worst state, an intolerable one. Government, like dress, is the badge of lost innocence; the palaces of kings are built upon the ruins of the bowers of paradise. [*Common Sense* (1776), 1]

2. My country is the world, and my religion is to do good. [*Rights of Man*, II]

3. The sublime and the ridiculous are often so nearly related, that it is difficult to class them separately. One step above the sublime, makes the ridiculous; and one step above the ridiculous, makes the sublime again. [*The Age of Reason*, II]

Palmerston, Henry John Temple, Viscount (1784–1865)
English statesman; Whig Prime Minister 1855–58, 1859–65

1. [Of the Schleswig-Holstein question]
There are only three men who have ever understood it: one was Prince Albert, who is dead; the second was a German professor, who became mad. I am the third – and I have forgotten all about it. [Attr. in Palmer, *Quotations in History*]

Pankhurst, Dame Christabel (1880–1958)
English suffragette and Women's Social and Political Union (WSPU) organizer; daughter of Emmeline Pankhurst

1. We are here to claim our rights as women, not only to be free, but to fight for freedom. It is our privilege, as well as our pride and our joy, to take some part in this militant movement, which, as we believe, means the regeneration of all humanity. [Speech, 1911]

Pankhurst, Emmeline (1858–1928)
English suffragette, founder of the militant Women's Social and Political Union, 1903

1. The argument of the broken pane of glass is the most valuable argument in modern politics. [*Votes for Women*]

Papprill, Ross F. (1908–1975)

1. There are two kinds of people in the world: those who believe there

are two kinds of people in the world, and those who don't. [Attr.]

Parker, Charlie (1920–1955)
American jazz alto saxophonist and composer; leading exponent of bepop

1. Music is your own experience, your thoughts, your wisdom. If you don't live it, it won't come out of your horn. [In Nat Shapiro and Nat Hentoff, *Hear Me Talkin' to Ya* (1955)]

Parker, Dorothy (1893–1967)
American poet, short-story writer, critic and wit

1. Men seldom make passes
   At girls who wear glasses. [*Not So Deep as a Well*, 'News Item']

2. This is not a novel to be tossed aside lightly. It should be thrown with great force. [In R.E. Drennan, *Wit's End*]

3. [Remark on a performance by Katharine Hepburn]
   She ran the whole gamut of the emotions from A to B. [In G. Carey, *Katharine Hepburn* (1985)]

4. Excuse my dust. [Her own epitaph]

Parkinson, Cyril Northcote (1909–)
English political scientist and historian

1. Work expands so as to fill the time available for its completion. [*Parkinson's Law* (1958)]

Pascal, Blaise (1623–1662)
French philosopher and scientist; mathematician, physicist, theologian and moralist

1. *Je n'ai fait celle-ci plus longue que parce que je n'ai pas eu le loisir de la faire plus courte.*
   I have made this letter longer only because I have not had time to make it shorter. [*Lettres Provinciales* (1657)]

2. *Tout le malheur des hommes vient d'une seule chose, qui est de ne savoir pas demeurer en repos dans une chambre.*
   All the troubles of men are caused by one single thing, which is their inability to stay quietly in a room. [*Pensées*, II.139]

3. *Le coeur a ses raisons que la raison ne connaît point.*
The heart has its reasons which the mind knows nothing of.
[Ib. IV.277]

Pater, Walter (1839–1894)
English critic, essayist and lecturer, associated with the Pre-Raphaelites

1. [Of the Mona Lisa]
She is older than the rocks among which she sits. [*Studies in the History of the Renaissance*, 'Leonardo da Vinci']

2. All art constantly aspires towards the condition of music. [Ib. 'Giorgione']

Payn, James (1830–1898)
Prolific English novelist; editor and poet

1. I had never had a piece of toast
Particularly long and wide,
But fell upon the sanded floor,
And always on the buttered side. [*Chamber's Journal* (1884)]

Péguy, Charles Pierre (1873–1914)
French Catholic socialist, poet, political writer, publisher and nationalist

1. It is impossible to write ancient history because we do not have enough sources, and impossible to write modern history because we have far too many. [*Clio*]

Penn, William (1644–1718)
English Quaker, founder of Pennsylvania; religious and political writer

1. No pain; no palm; no thorns, no throne; no gall, no glory; no cross, no crown. [*No Cross, No Crown* (1669)]

Pepys, Samuel (1633–1703)
English diarist (1660–69), naval administrator and politician

1. And so to bed. [*Diary*, 1660]

2. Music and women I cannot but give way to, whatever my business is. [Ib. 1666]

Peter, Laurence J. (1919–)
Canadian educationist and writer

1. Work is accomplished by those employees who have not yet reached their level of incompetence. [*The Peter Principle*]

Petronius Arbiter (d. AD 66)
Roman prose and verse satirist

1. '*Cave canem.*'
'Beware of the dog.' [*Satyricon*]

Phelps, E. J. (1822–1900)
American lawyer, diplomat and Democrat politician

1. The man who makes no mistakes does not usually make anything. [Speech, 1899]

Philippe, Charles-Louis (1874–1909)
French novelist, noted for his portrayal of poverty

1. One always has the air of someone who is lying when one speaks to a policeman. [*Les Chroniques du canard sauvage*]

Picasso, Pablo (1881–1973)
Spanish painter, sculptor and graphic artist; pioneer of Cubism

1. Painting is a blind man's profession. He paints not what he sees, but what he feels, what he tells himself about what he has seen. [In Jean Cocteau, *Journals*, 'Childhood']

2. [Remark made at an exhibition of children's drawings]
When I was their age, I could draw like Raphael, but it took me a lifetime to learn to draw like them. [In Ronald Penrose, *Picasso: His Life and Work*]

Pindar (518–438 BC)
Greek lyric poet, known for his victory odes

1. Water is best. But gold shines like fire blazing in the night, supreme of lordly wealth. [*Olympian Odes*, I]

2. My soul, do not search for immortal life, but exhaust the boundaries of possibility. [*Pythian Odes*, III]

Pitt, William, Earl of Chatham (1708–1778)
English Whig politician; Prime Minister 1756–61, 1766–68

1. Unlimited power is apt to corrupt the minds of those who possess it. [Speech, House of Commons, 1770]

Pitt, William (1759–1806)
English Tory politician and fiscal reformer; Prime Minister 1783–1801, 1804–1806; son of William Pitt, Earl of Chatham

1. Necessity is the plea for every infringement of human freedom. It is the argument of tyrants; it is the creed of slaves. [Speech, 1783]

Plath, Sylvia (1932–1963)
American poet and novelist; short-story writer, essayist and diarist

1. Every woman adores a Fascist,
   The boot in the face, the brute
   Brute heart of a brute like you. [*Encounter* (1963), 'Daddy']

2. Daddy, daddy, you bastard, I'm through. ['Daddy']

3. Dying
   Is an art, like everything else.
   I do it exceptionally well. ['Lady Lazarus' (1963)]

Plato (c. 429–347 BC)
Great Greek philosopher, noted for his concept of forms; founder of the Academy, pupil of Socrates and teacher of Aristotle

1. That man is wisest who, like Socrates, realizes that his wisdom is worthless. [*Apologia of Socrates*]

2. The good is the beautiful. [*Lysis*]

3. Poets utter great and wise things which they do not themselves understand. [*Republic*, II]

4. The rulers of the State are the only ones who should have the privilege of lying, either at home or abroad; they may be allowed to lie for the good of the State. [Ib. III]

5. Our object in the construction of the state is the greatest happiness of the whole, and not that of any one class. [Ib. IV]

6. They see only their own shadows, or the shadows of one another, which the fire throws on the opposite wall of the cave. [Ib. VII]

Plautus, Titus Maccius (c. 254–184 BC)
Roman comic dramatist and poet

1. *Tetigisti acu.*
You've hit the nail on the head. (*lit.* You have touched it with a needle.) [*Rudens*]

Pliny the Elder (AD 23–79)
Roman scientist, historian and soldier

1. *Ex Africa semper aliquid novi.*
There is always something new out of Africa. [*Historia Naturalis*, VIII (altered)]

2. *In vino veritas.*
Truth is in wine. [Ib. XIV]

3. *Cum grano salis.*
With a grain of salt. [Ib. XXIII]

Plutarch (c. AD 46–120)
Greek biographer and philosopher

1. Alexander wept when he heard from Anaxarchus that there was an infinite number of worlds ... he said: 'Do you not think it lamentable that with such a vast multitude of worlds, we have not yet conquered one?' [*On the Tranquility of the Mind*]

Poe, Edgar Allan (1809–1849)
American poet, author of often macabre short stories, and editor

1. Take thy beak from out my heart, and take thy form from off my door!
Quoth the Raven, 'Nevermore'. ['The Raven' (1845)]

2. All that we see or seem
Is but a dream within a dream. ['A Dream within a Dream' (1849)]

Pomfret, John (1667–1702)
English poet and clergyman

1. We live and learn, but not the wiser grow. [*Reason* (1700)]

Pompadour, Madame de (1721–1764)
French mistress of Louis XV; patron of the arts

1. [Remark after Battle of Rossbach, 1757]
   Après nous le déluge.
   After us the flood. [In Madame du Hausset, *Mémoires* (1824)]

Pope, Alexander (1688–1744)
English satirical poet; translator and editor

1. A *little learning* is a dang'rous thing; [*An Essay on Criticism*, 215]

2. True Wit is Nature to advantage dress'd,
   What oft was thought, but ne'er so well express'd. [Ib. 297]

3. True ease in writing comes from art, not chance,
   As those move easiest who have learn'd to dance.
   'Tis not enough no harshness gives offence,
   The sound must seem an echo to the sense. [Ib. 362]

4. Good-nature and good-sense must ever join;
   To err is human, to forgive, divine. [Ib. 524]

5. For Fools rush in where Angels fear to tread. [Ib. 625]

6. The hungry judges soon the sentence sign,
   And wretches hang that jury-men may dine. [*The Rape of the Lock*, III, 21]

7. True friendship's laws are by this rule express'd,
   Welcome the coming, speed the parting guest. [*Odyssey*, (1725–26), XV]

8. Hope springs eternal in the human breast; [*Essay on Man*, I, 95]

9. Shall then this verse to future age pretend
   Thou wert my guide, philosopher, and friend? [Ib. 389]

10. Not to go back, is somewhat to advance,
    And men must walk at least before they dance. [*Imitations of Horace*, I.1, 'To Lord Bolingbroke', 53]

11. It is with narrow-souled people as with narrow-necked bottles: the less they have in them, the more noise they make in pouring it out. [*Miscellanies* (1727), 'Thoughts on Various Subjects']

Porson, Richard (1759–1808)
English scholar of Greek, noted for his study of Euripides

1. Life is too short to learn German. [In Thomas Love Peacock, *Gryll Grange* (1861, 3]

2. [Giving his opinion of the poems of Robert Southey]
   Your works will be read after Shakespeare and Milton are forgotten – and not till then. [In L. Meissen, *Quotable Anecdotes*]

Porter, Cole (1893–1964)
American composer and lyricist of musical comedies

1. Now, heaven knows, anything goes. [Title song, 1934, from the musical *Anything Goes*]

2. I've Got You Under My Skin. [Song title, 1936, from the musical *Born to Dance*]

3. Who Wants to Be a Millionaire? I don't. [Title song, 1956, from the musical *Who Wants to be a Millionaire?*]

Potter, Beatrix (1866–1943)
English writer and illustrator of children's stories; sheep farmer

1. Once upon a time there were four little Rabbits, and their names were Flopsy, Mopsy, Cottontail, and Peter. [*The Tale of Peter Rabbit*]

2. You may go into the field or down the lane, but don't go into Mr. McGregor's garden: your Father had an accident there; he was put in a pie by Mrs McGregor. [Ib.]

Potter, Stephen (1900–1969)
English humorous writer, radio producer, critic and lecturer

1. Gamesmanship or, The Art of Winning Games without actually Cheating [Title of book, 1947]

2. *How to be one up* – how to make the other man feel that something has gone wrong, however slightly. [*Lifemanship* (1950)]

Pound, Ezra (1885–1972)
American imagist poet, translator and critic; indicted for treason 1945

1. The apparition of these faces in the crowd;
   Petals on a wet, black bough. [*Lustra*, 'In a Station of the Metro']

2. The ant's a centaur in his dragon world.
Pull down thy vanity, it is not man
Made courage, or made order, or made grace. [*Cantos*, 81]

3. Music begins to atrophy when it departs too far from the dance; ...
poetry begins to atrophy when it gets too far from music. [*ABC of Reading* (1934)]

4. Literature is news that STAYS news. [Ib.]

Powell, Enoch (1912–)
English Conservative, later Ulster Unionist, politician and Greek scholar

1. [On race relations in Britain]
As I look ahead I am filled with foreboding. Like the Roman I seem to see 'The River Tiber foaming with much blood.' [Speech, Birmingham, 1968]

Priestley, J. B. (1894–1984)
English novelist, dramatist, critic, essayist and autobiographical writer

1. Comedy, we may say, is society protecting itself – with a smile. [*George Meredith*]

2. [Of politicians]
A number of anxious dwarfs trying to grill a whale. [*Outcries and Asides*]

Protagoras (c. 485–c. 410 BC)
First Greek Sophist

1. Man is the measure of all things. [In Plato, *Theaetetus*]

Proudhon, Pierre-Joseph (1809–1865)
French social reformer and anarchist; politician and writer, imprisoned for his beliefs

1. If I were asked to answer the following question: 'What is slavery?' and I should answer in one word, 'Murder!' my meaning would be understood at once. No further argument would be required to show that the power to take from a man his thought, his will, his personality is a power of life and death, and that to enslave a man is to kill him. Why, then, to this other question: 'What is property?' may I not likewise answer 'Theft'? [*Qu'est-ce que la propriété?* (1840),1]

Proust, Marcel (1871–1922)
Great French novelist; critic and letter writer

1. *Ce goût c'était celui du petit morceau de madeleine que le dimanche matin à
   Combray ... ma tante Léonie m'offrait après l'avoir trempé dans son infusion
   de thé ou de tilleul.*
   The taste was that of the little crumb of madeleine which on Sunday
   mornings at Combray..., my aunt Léonie used to give me, dipping it
   first in her own cup of real or of lime-flower tea. [*A la recherche du
   temps perdu, Du côté de chez Swann*, 1]

2. *Les vrais paradis sont les paradis qu'on a perdus.*
   The true paradises are paradises we have lost. [Ib. *Le temps retrouvé*]

3. *Le bonheur seul est salutaire pour le corps, mais c'est le chagrin qui développe
   les forces de l'esprit.*
   Happiness is beneficial for the body, but it is grief that develops the
   powers of the mind. [Ib.]

Punch
British humorous periodical, founded 1841

1. Advice to persons about to marry – 'Don't!' [1845]

2. You pays your money and you takes your choice. [1846]

3. Never do to-day what you can put off till tomorrow. [1849]

4. What sort of a doctor is he?
   Oh, well, I don't know very much about his ability; but he's got a
   very good bedside manner! [1884]

5. Nearly all our best men are dead! Carlyle, Tennyson, Browning,
   George Eliot! – I'm not feeling very well myself. [1893]

6. Look here, Steward, if this is coffee, I want tea; but if this is tea, then
   I wish for coffee. [1902]

Putnam, Israel (1718–1790)
American Revolutionary general and writer

1. [Said at the Battle of Bunker Hill, 1775]
   Men, you are all marksmen – don't one of you fire until you see the
   whites of their eyes. [In R. Frothingham, *History of the Siege of Boston*
   (1873)]

Puzo, Mario (1920–)
American novelist

1. He's a businessman. I'll make him an offer he can't refuse. [*The Godfather* (1969)]

Pyrrhus (319–272 BC)
King of Epirus from 306 BC and army commander

1. [After a hard-won battle]
Another such victory and we are lost. [In Plutarch, *Life*]

Rabelais, François (c. 1494–c. 1553)
French satirist; humanist, physician and monk

1. [Referring to the fictional Abbey of Thélème]
In their rules there was only one clause. Do what you will. [*Gargantua*, I.57]

2. [Last words]
I owe much; I have nothing; the rest I leave to the poor. [Attr.]

Raleigh, Sir Walter (c. 1552–1618)
English courtier, explorer, military commander, poet, historian and essayist; beheaded after a failed expedition

1. Now what is love? I pray thee, tell.
It is that fountain and that well,
Where pleasure and repentance dwell.
It is perhaps that sauncing bell,
That tolls all in to heaven or hell:
And this is love, as I hear tell. ['A Description of Love']

2. Give me my scallop-shell of quiet,
My staff of faith to walk upon,
My scrip of joy, immortal diet,
My bottle of salvation,
My gown of glory, hope's true gage,
And thus I'll make my pilgrimage. ['The Passionate Man's Pilgrimage']

Ralph, Julian (1853–1903)
American journalist, short-story writer and autobiographer

1. News value. [Lecture to Brander Matthew's English Class, Columbia, 1892]

Ramsay, Allan (1686–1758)
*Scottish poet, satirist, dramatist, song collector and bookseller;
founded first circulating library in Britain*

1. A Scots mist will weet an Englishman to the skin. [*Scots Proverbs*]

Reade, Charles (1814–1884)
English novelist and dramatist; collaborated with Dion Boucicault

1. Make 'em laugh; make 'em cry; make 'em wait. [Attr. programme for
   serial novel]

Reed, Henry (1914–1986)
English poet, radio dramatist and translator

1. As we get older we do not get any younger.
   Seasons return, and today I am fifty-five,
   And this time last year I was fifty-four,
   And this time next year I shall be sixty-two. ['Chard Whitlow', parody
   of T.S. Eliot (1946)]

2. To-day we have naming of parts. Yesterday
   We had daily cleaning. And tomorrow morning,
   We shall have what to do after firing. But to-day,
   To-day we have naming of parts. ['Lessons of the War: 1, Naming of
   Parts' (1946)]

Remarque, Erich Maria (1898–1970)
German-born American novelist

1. *Im Westen nichts Neues.*
   All Quiet on the Western Front. [Title of book, 1929]

Rendall, Montague John (1862–1950)
English teacher and BBC administrator

1. Nation shall speak peace unto nation. [Motto of BBC]

Reuben, David (1933–)
American doctor and writer

1. Everything You've Always Wanted to Know About Sex, But Were
   Afraid to Ask. [Title of book, 1969]

Rexford, Eben (1848–1916)
American poet and writer on gardening

   1. Darling, I am growing old,
      Silver threads among the gold. ['Silver Threads Among the Gold']

Rhodes, Cecil John (1853–1902)
English imperialist, financier and statesman in South Africa; Prime Minister of Cape Colony 1890–96

   1. So little done, so much to do! [Last words, in Lewis Mitchell, *Life of Rhodes* (1910)]

Rice, Grantland (1880–1954)
American sports journalist and poet

   1. For when the One Great Scorer comes
      To write against your name,
      He marks – not that you won or lost–
      But how you played the game. ['Alumnus Football' (1941)]

Rice, Sir Stephen (1637–1715)
Irish lawyer; Chief Baron of the Exchequer in Ireland

   1. I will drive a coach and six horses through the Act of Settlement. [In W. King, *State of the Protestants of Ireland* (1672)]

Richards, Frank (1875–1961)
British writer

   1. The rottenfulness is terrific! [Story in *The Magnet* no. 400]

Richard I (1157–1199)
King of England from 1189 and a leader of the Third Crusade, 1191; son of Henry II and known as Lionheart; poet

   1. *Dieu et mon droit.*
      God and my right. [Attr., 1198]

Richards, I.A. (1893–1979)
English literary critic, linguist, poet and teacher; co-founder of Basic English with C.K. Ogden

   1. [Of poetry]
      It is a perfectly possible means of overcoming chaos. [*Science and Poetry*

Ripley, R.L. (1893–1949)
American cartoonist

1. Believe it or not. [Title of newspaper feature, from 1918]

Roberts, Tommy Rhys, QC (1901–1975)
Welsh lawyer

1. Lloyd George knew my father. [Song, to the tune of 'Onward Christian Soldiers', which was his party piece at legal dinners from the 1940s on]

Robin, Leo (1899–)
American songwriter; Academy Award 1938

1. Diamonds Are A Girl's Best Friend. [Song title, 1949]

Rochefoucauld, François, Duc de la (1613–1680)
French moralist

1. If we had no faults of our own, we would not take so much pleasure in noticing those of others. [*Maximes*, 31]

2. To succeed in the world, we do everything we can to appear successful. [Ib. 50]

3. One gives nothing so freely as advice. [Ib. 110]

4. We only confess our little faults to persuade people that we have no large ones. [Ib. 327]

Rochester, John Wilmot, Earl of (1647–1680)
English lyric poet, satirist, courtier and libertine

1. For all men would be cowards if they durst. ['A Satire Against Mankind' (1679)]

2. Here lies our sovereign lord the King
Whose word no man relies on,
Who never said a foolish thing,
Nor ever did a wise one. [Epitaph written for Charles II (1706); *see* Charles II, 'This is very true...']

Roddenberry, Gene (1921–1991)
American film producer

1. Space – the final frontier. These are the voyages of the starship

Enterprise. Its five year mission: to explore strange new worlds, to seek out new life and civilizations, to boldly go where no man has gone before. [Preamble to U.S. TV series, *Star Trek*, first shown 1966]

Rogers, E. W. (1864–1913)
Songwriter

1. If you want to know the time,
   Ask a P'liceman! ['Ask a P'liceman']

Rogers, Samuel (1763–1855)
English poet, wit and banker

1. When a new book is published, read an old one. [Attr.]

Rogers, Will (1879–1935)
American humorist, comic actor, rancher, writer and wit

1. Communism is like prohibition, it's a good idea but it won't work.
   [*Weekly Articles* (1981), first published 1927]

2. [Message written on a postcard of the Venus de Milo that he sent to
   his young niece]
   See what will happen to you if you don't stop biting your fingernails.
   [Attr.]

Roland, Madame (1754–1793)
French revolutionary; memoirist and letter writer; executed

1. [Remark on mounting the scaffold]
   O liberté! O liberté! que de crimes on commet en ton nom!
   O liberty! O liberty! what crimes are committed in thy name! [In A.
   de Lamartine, *Histoire des Girondins* (1847)]

Roosevelt, Franklin Delano (1882–1945)
*American lawyer and statesman; Democrat President 1933–1945,
noted for his New Deal reforms and wartime leadership*

1. The only thing we have to fear is fear itself. [First Inaugural Address,
   1933]

2. In the future days, which we seek to make secure, we look forward to
   a world founded upon four essential human freedoms.
   The first is freedom of speech and expression – everywhere in the
   world.

The second is freedom of every person to worship God in his own way
– everywhere in the world.
The third is freedom from want...
The fourth is freedom from fear. [Address to Congress, 1941]

Roosevelt, Theodore (1858–1919)
*American statesman, soldier and writer; Republican President
1901–9; Nobel peace prize 1906 for mediating in the Russo-Japanese
war; distant cousin of Franklin Delano Roosevelt*

1. There is a homely adage which runs 'Speak softly and carry a big stick;
   you will go far.' [Minnesota State Fair, 1901], [Speech, Chicago, 1903]

2. The men with the muck-rakes are often indispensable to the well-
   being of society; but only if they know when to stop raking the muck.
   [Speech at the laying of the corner-stone of the Office Building of
   House of Representatives, 1906]

Ross, Alan S.C. (1907–1980)
British linguistics scholar and editor

1. U and Non-U. An Essay in Sociological Linguistics. [Title of essay,
   1954, included in *Noblesse Oblige* (1956)]

Ross, Harold (1892–1951)
Editor of the New Yorker

1. [Customary query on finding a name he did not know in an article]
   Who he? [Quoted in J. Thurber, *The Years With Ross*]

Rossetti, Christina Georgina (1830–1894)
*English Pre-Raphaelite poet, noted for her lyric and religious verse;
sister of Dante Gabriel Rossetti*

1. My heart is like a singing bird
   Whose nest is in a watered shoot;
   My heart is like an apple-tree
   Whose boughs are bent with thickset fruit;
   My heart is like a rainbow shell
   That paddles in a halcyon sea;
   My heart is gladder than all these
   Because my love is come to me. ['A Birthday' (1862)]

2. In the bleak mid-winter
Frosty wind made moan,
Earth stood hard as iron,
Water like a stone;
Snow had fallen, snow on snow,
Snow on snow,
In the bleak mid-winter,
Long ago. ['Mid-Winter' (1875)]

3. Remember me when I am gone away,
Gone far away into the silent land. ['Remember' (1862)]

4. Better by far you should forget and smile
Than you should remember and be sad. [Ib.]

5. Who has seen the wind?
Neither you nor I:
But when the trees bow down their heads,
The wind is passing by. ['Who Has Seen the Wind?']

Rossini, Gioacchino (1792–1868)
Italian composer, noted for his operas

1. Give me a laundry-list and I will set it to music. [Attr.]

Rostand, Jean (1894–1977)
French biologist

1. A married couple are well suited when both partners usually feel the
need for a quarrel at the same time. [*Le Mariage*]

2. Kill a man, and you are a murderer. Kill millions of men, and you
are a conqueror. Kill everyone, and you are a god. [*Pensées d'un biologiste*
(1939)]

Rosten, Leo C. (1908–)
Polish-born American social scientist, writer and humorist

1. [Of W.C. Fields and often attributed to him]
Any man who hates dogs and babies can't be all bad. [Speech at
Masquers' Club dinner, 1939]

Rousseau, Jean-Jacques (1712–1778)
Influential French social and political philosopher, educationist and essayist; born in Switzerland

1. *L'homme est né libre, et partout il est dans les fers.*
   Man is born free, and everywhere is in chains. [*Du Contrat Social* (1762)]

Rowland, Helen (1875–1950)
American writer

1. The follies which a man regrets most in his life are those which he didn't commit when he had the opportunity. [*A Guide to Men* (1922)]

2. Before marriage, a man will lie awake thinking about something you said; after marriage, he'll fall asleep before you finish saying it. [In Cowan, *The Wit of Women*]

Runyon, Damon (1884–1946)
American journalist and short-story writer, known for his Broadway stories

1. More than somewhat. [Phrase used frequently in Runyon's work, and adopted as book title in 1937]

2. A free-loader is a confirmed guest. He is the man who is always willing to come to dinner. [*Short Takes*, 'Free-Loading Ethics']

3. He is without strict doubt a Hoorah Henry, and he is generally figured as nothing but a lob as far as doing anything useful in this world is concerned. [Ib. 'Tight Shoes']

Ruskin, John (1819–1900)
English art critic, social philosopher and reformer; essayist and champion of the Pre-Raphaelites

1. Remember that the most beautiful things in the world are the most useless; peacocks and lilies for instance. [*The Stones of Venice* (1851), I.2]

2. All violent feelings ... produce in us a falseness in all our impressions of external things, which I would generally characterize as the 'Pathetic Fallacy'. [*Modern Painters* (1856), III]

3. Fine art is that in which the hand, the head, and the heart of man go together. [*The Two Paths* (1859), 2]

4. Whereas it has long been known and declared that the poor have no
right to the property of the rich, I wish it also to be known and declared
that the rich have no right to the property of the poor. [*Unto this Last*
(1862), 3]

5. All books are divisible into two classes: the books of the hour, and
the books of all time. [*Sesame and Lilies* (1865), 'Of Kings' Treasuries']

6. Life without industry is guilt, and industry without art is brutality.
[*Lectures on Art* (1870), 3, 'The Relation of Art to Morals']

Russell, Bertrand (1872–1970)
*English philosopher, logician, mathematician, controversialist,
essayist and social reformer; Nobel prize for literature 1950*

1. Every man, wherever he goes, is encompassed by a cloud of comforting
convictions, which move with him like flies on a summer day. [*Sceptical
Essays* (1928), 'Dreams and Facts']

2. One of the symptoms of approaching nervous breakdowns is the belief
that one's work is terribly important. If I were a medical man, I should
prescribe a holiday to any patient who considered his work important.
[*The Autobiography of Bertrand Russell* (1968), II.5]

Ryle, Gilbert (1900–1976)
English metaphysical philosopher

1. The dogma of the Ghost in the Machine. [*The Concept of Mind* (1949), 1]

Sahl, Mort (1926–)
American comedian, born in Canada

1. [Of President Nixon]
Would you buy a second-hand car from this man? [Attr.]

Sainte-Beuve, Charles-Augustin (1804–1869)
Leading French literary critic; essayist and poet

1. *Le silence seul est le souverain mépris.*
Silence is the supreme contempt. ['Mes Poisons']

Saki (Hector Hugh Munro) (1870–1916)
Burmese-born British journalist, novelist and writer of humorous and macabre short stories

1. Never be a pioneer. It's the Early Christian that gets the fattest lion. [*Reginald* (1904), 'Reginald's Choir Treat']

2. The cook was a good cook, as cooks go; and as cooks go she went. [Ib. 'Reginald on Besetting Sins']

3. He's simply got the instinct for being unhappy highly developed. [*Chronicles of Clovis* (1911), 'The Match-Maker']

4. A little inaccuracy sometimes saves tons of explanation. ['The Comments of Maung Ka'] [*The Square Egg* (1924), 'Clovis on the Alleged Romance of Business']

5. In baiting a mouse-trap with cheese, always leave room for the mouse. [Ib. 'The Infernal Parliament']

Sallust (86–34 BC)
Roman historian and statesman

1. *Alieni appetens, sui profusus.*
Greedy for others' possessions, prodigal of his own. [*Catiline*, 5]

2. *Quieta movere magna merces videbatur.*
Just to stir things up seemed a great reward in itself. [Ib. 21]

Sandburg, Carl (1878–1967)
American poet, noted for his free verse; journalist, song collector and biographer of Lincoln

1. Sometime they'll give a war and nobody will come. [*The People, Yes* (1936)]

Santayana, George (1863–1952)
Spanish-born American philosopher, poet, critic and novelist

1. Those who cannot remember the past are condemned to repeat it. [*The Life of Reason* (1905), I.12]

2. Music is essentially useless, as life is: but both have an ideal extension which lends utility to its conditions. [Ib. IV.4]

3. The Bible is literature, not dogma. [*Introduction to the Ethics of Spinoza*]

Sappho (b. c. 612 BC)
Greek lyric poet, known for her love poetry

1. [Of a girl before her marriage]
   Just as the sweet-apple reddens on the high branch, high on the
   highest, and the apple-pickers missed it, or rather did not miss it out,
   but dared not reach it. [In D.L. Page (ed.), *Lyrica Selecta Graeca* (1968)]

Sargent, John Singer (1856–1925)
American painter, born in Florence; noted for his society portraits

1. Every time I paint a portrait I lose a friend. [In N. Bentley and E.
   Esar, *Treasury of Humorous Quotations* (1951)]

Sartre, Jean-Paul (1905–1980)
*French existentialist, philosopher, novelist, dramatist, critic and left-
wing intellectual; declined Nobel prize 1964; companion of Simone de
Beauvoir*

1. Things are entirely what they appear to be and *behind them* ... there
   is nothing. [*La Nausée* (1938)]

2. *Alors, c'est ça l'Enfer. Je n'aurais jamais cru ... Vous vous rappelez: le
   soufre, le bûcher, le gril ... Ah! quelle plaisanterie. Pas besoin de gril, l'Enfer,
   c'est les Autres.*
   So that's what Hell is. I'd never have believed it ... Do you remember,
   brimstone, the stake, the gridiron? ... What a joke! No need of a
   gridiron, Hell is other people. [*Huis Clos (In Camera*, 1944), v]

Sassoon, Vidal (1928–)
Internationally known British hair stylist and businessman

1. The only place where success comes before work is a dictionary.
   [Quoting one of his teachers in a BBC radio broadcast]

Satie, Erik (1866–1925)
French experimental composer

1. [Direction on one of his piano pieces]
   To be played with both hands in the pocket. [In O. Levant, *The
   Unimportance of Being Oscar*]

Schiller, Friedrich von (1759–1805)
Leading writer of German romanticism; dramatist, critic, lyric poet and historian

1. *Freude, schöner Götterfunken,*
   Tochter aus Elysium,
   Wir betreten feuertrunken,
   Himmlische, dein Heiligtum.
   Deine Zauber binden wieder,
   Was die Mode streng geteilt,
   Alle Menschen werden Brüder
   Wo dein sanfter Flügel weilt.
   Joy, beautiful radiance of the gods, daughter of Elysium, we set foot in your heavenly shrine dazzled by your brilliance. Your charms re-unite what common use has harshly divided: all men become brothers under your tender wing. ['An die Freude' (1785); set to music by Beethoven in the last movement of his Ninth Symphony]

Schopenhauer, Arthur (1788–1860)
German pessimist philosopher

1. Every parting gives a foretaste of death; every coming together again a foretaste of the resurrection. [*Gedanken über vielerlei Gegenstände*]

2. To expect a man to retain everything that he has ever read is like expecting him to carry about in his body everything that he has ever eaten. [*Parerga and Paralipomena* (1851)]

Schultz, Charles (1922–)
American cartoonist

1. I love mankind – it's people I can't stand. [*Go Fly a Kite, Charlie Brown*]

Schumacher, E.F. (1911–1977)
German-born British economist, essayist and lecturer; noted for work in developing countries

1. Small is Beautiful [Title of book, 1973]

Scott, Alexander (c. 1525–c. 1584)
Scottish lyric poet and musician

1. Love is ane fervent fire,

Kindled without desire,
Short pleasure, long displeasure;
Repentance is the hire;
And pure treasure without measure.
Love is ane fervent fire. ['Lo, What it is to Love' (c. 1568)]

Scott, Alexander (1920–1989)
Scottish writer and poet

1. I tellt ye
   I tellt ye. [*Scotched*, Scotch Education]

Scott, Robert Falcon (1868–1912)
English naval officer, Antarctic explorer and writer

1. For God's sake look after our people. [*Journal*, 25 Mar. 1912]

Scott, Sir Walter (1771–1832)
Scottish Romantic novelist, poet, short-story writer, historian, folklorist, dramatist, editor, critic and translator

1. Breathes there the man, with soul so dead,
   Who never to himself hath said,
   This is my own, my native land! [*The Lay of the Last Minstrel* (1805), VI]

2. O Caledonia! stern and wild,
   Meet nurse for a poetic child!
   Land of brown heath and shaggy wood,
   Land of the mountain and the flood,
   Land of my sires! what mortal hand
   Can e'er untie the filial band
   That knits me to thy rugged strand! [Ib. VI]

3. And come he slow, or come he fast,
   It is but Death who comes at last. [*Marmion* (1808), II]

4. O what a tangled web we weave,
   When first we practise to deceive. [Ib. VI]

5. Hail to the Chief who in triumph advances. [*The Lady of the Lake* (1810), II]

6. But answer came there none. [*The Bridal of Triermain* (1813), Canto 3]

7. There's a gude time coming. [*Rob Roy* (1817), 32]

8. The hour is come, but not the man. [*The Heart of Midlothian* (1818), 4]

9. It's ill taking the breeks aff a wild Highlandman. [*The Fortunes of Nigel* (1822), 5]

Segal, Erich (1937–)
American scholar, lecturer, novelist, screenwriter and essayist

1. Love means never having to say you're sorry. [*Love Story*]

Selden, John (1584–1654)
English historian, antiquary, jurist, orientalist and politician; imprisoned for his opposition to King James

1. Ignorance of the law excuses no man; not that all men know the law, but because 'tis an excuse every man will plead, and no man can tell how to confute him. [*Table Talk* (1689), 'Law']

2. Take a straw and throw it up into the air, you shall see by that which way the wind is. [Ib. 'Libels']

Selfridge, H. Gordon (1858–1947)
American-born British businessman, founder of London's first large department store

1. The customer is always right. [Slogan in A.H. Williams, *No Name on the Door; A Memoir of Gordon Selfridge* (1956)]

2. There are … shopping days to Christmas. [Ib.]

Sellar, Walter Carruthers (1898–1951)
and Yeatman, Robert Julian (1897–1968)
British humorous writers

1. 1066, And All That. [Title of book, 1930]

2. The Roman Conquest was, however, a *Good Thing*, since the Britons were only natives at the time. [*1066, And All That* (1930), 1]

Seneca (c. 4 BC– AD 65)
Roman Stoic philosopher, tragic poet and dramatist; essayist, rhetorician, statesman and tutor of Nero

1. *Homines dum docent discunt.*
   Even while they teach, men learn. [*Epistulae Morales*, 7]

2. *Eripere vitam nemo non homini potest,*
   At nemo mortem; mille ad hanc aditus patent.
   Anyone can stop a man's life, but no one his death; a thousand doors open on to it. [*Phoenissae*]

Service, Robert W. (1874–1958)
British-born Canadian poet, novelist, journalist and autobiographical writer

1. Back of the bar, in a solo game, sat Dangerous Dan McGrew,
   And watching his luck was his light-o'-love, the lady that's known as Lou. ['The Shooting of Dan McGrew' (1907)]

2. Ah! the clock is always slow;
   It is later than you think. ['It is Later than You Think' (1921)]

Shakespeare, William (1564–1616)
Greatest English dramatist and poet; author of comedies, tragedies, historical plays and sonnets; actor

All's Well That Ends Well
1. Our remedies oft in ourselves do lie,
   Which we ascribe to heaven. [I.i]

Antony and Cleopatra
1. My salad days,
   When I was green in judgment, cold in blood, [I.v]

2. Age cannot wither her, nor custom stale
   Her infinite variety. [II.ii]

As You Like It
1. Sweet are the uses of adversity;
   Which, like the toad, ugly and venomous,
   Wears yet a precious jewel in his head;
   And this our life, exempt from public haunt,
   Finds tongues in trees, books in the running brooks,

Sermons in stones, and good in everything. [II.i]

2. All the world's a stage,
And all the men and women merely players;
They have their exits and their entrances;
And one man in his time plays many parts,
His acts being seven ages. [II.vii]

3. Blow, blow, thou winter wind,
Thou art not so unkind
As man's ingratitude; [II.vii]

4. It was a lover and his lass,
With a hey, and a ho, and a hey nonino, [V.iii]

Coriolanus

1. Let me have war, say I; it exceeds peace as far as day does night; it's
spritely, waking, audible, and full of vent. Peace is a very apoplexy,
lethargy; mull'd, deaf, sleepy, insensible; a getter of more bastard
children than war's a destroyer of men. [IV.v]

Cymbeline

1. Fear no more the heat o' th' sun
Nor the furious winter's rages;
Thou thy worldly task hast done,
Home art gone, and ta'en thy wages.
Golden lads and girls all must,
As chimney-sweepers, come to dust. [IV.ii]

Hamlet

1. A little more than kin, and less than kind. [I.ii]

2. O, that this too too solid flesh would melt,
Thaw, and resolve itself into a dew!
Or that the Everlasting had not fix'd
His canon 'gainst self-slaughter! O God! God!
How weary, stale, flat, and unprofitable,
Seem to me all the uses of this world!...
...Frailty, thy name is woman! [I.ii]

3. 'A was a man, take him for all in all,
I shall not look upon his like again. [I.ii]

4. Neither a borrower nor a lender be;
For loan oft loses both itself and friend,
And borrowing dulls the edge of husbandry.
This above all – to thine own self be true,
And it must follow, as the night the day,
Thou canst not then be false to any man. [I.iii]

5. But to my mind, though I am native here
And to the manner born, it is a custom
More honour'd in the breach than the observance. [I.iv]

6. Something is rotten in the state of Denmark. [I.iv]

7. There are more things in heaven and earth, Horatio,
Than are dreamt of in your philosophy. [I.v]

8. The time is out of joint. [I.v]

9. Brevity is the soul of wit. [II.ii]

10. Though this be madness, yet there is method in't. [II.ii]

11. There is nothing either good or bad, but thinking makes it so. [II.ii]

12. What a piece of work is a man! [II.ii]

13. The play's the thing [II.ii]

14. To be, or not to be – that is the question;
Whether 'tis nobler in the mind to suffer
The slings and arrows of outrageous fortune,
Or to take arms against a sea of troubles,
And by opposing end them? [III.i]

15. Get thee to a nunnery. [III.i]

16. O, what a noble mind is here o'erthrown! [III.i]

17. ... it out-herods Herod. [III.ii]

18. The lady doth protest too much, methinks. [III.ii]

19. How now! a rat? Dead, for a ducat, dead! [III.iv]

20. I must be cruel, only to be kind. [III.iv]

21. For 'tis the sport to have the engineer
Hoist with his own petar; [III.iv]

22. A man may fish with the worm that hath eat of a king, and eat of the fish that hath fed of that worm. [IV.iii]

23. Lord, we know what we are, but know not what we may be. [IV.v]

24. Good night, ladies; good night, sweet ladies, good night, good night. [IV.v]

25. There's rosemary, that's for remembrance; pray you, love, remember. And there is pansies, that's for thoughts. [IV.v]

26. Alas, poor Yorick! I knew him, Horatio: a fellow of infinite jest, of most excellent fancy [V.i]

27. There's a divinity that shapes our ends, Rough-hew them how we will. [V.ii]

28. The rest is silence. [V.ii]

29. Now cracks a noble heart. Good night, sweet prince, And flights of angels sing thee to thy rest! [V.ii]

Henry IV, Part 1
1. Out of this nettle, danger, we pluck this flower, safety. [II.iii]

2. O, while you live, tell truth, and shame the devil! [III.i]

3. The better part of valour is discretion [V.iv]

Henry V
1. ... for his nose was as sharp as a pen, and 'a babbl'd of green fields. [II.iii]

2. Once more unto the breach, dear friends, once more;
   Or close the wall up with our English dead.
   In peace there's nothing so becomes a man
   As modest stillness and humility;
   But when the blast of war blows in our ears,
   Then imitate the action of the tiger:
   Stiffen the sinews, summon up the blood,
   Disguise fair nature with hard-favour'd rage;
   Then lend the eye a terrible aspect. [III.i]

3. I see you stand like greyhounds in the slips,
   Straining upon the start. The game's afoot:
   Follow your spirit; and upon this charge
   Cry 'God for Harry, England, and Saint George!' [III.i]

4. We few, we happy few, we band of brothers;
   For he to-day that sheds his blood with me
   Shall be my brother; be he ne'er so vile,
   This day shall gentle his condition;
   And gentlemen in England now a-bed
   Shall think themselves accurs'd they were not here,
   And hold their manhoods cheap whiles any speaks
   That fought with us upon Saint Crispin's day. [IV.iii]

Henry VI, Part 1

1. Away with him, away with him! He speaks Latin. [IV.vii]

Julius Caesar

1. Beware the ides of March. [I.ii]

2. Why, man, he doth bestride the narrow world
   Like a Colossus, and we petty men
   Walk under his huge legs, and peep about
   To find ourselves dishonourable graves.
   Men at some time are masters of their fates:
   The fault, dear Brutus, is not in our stars,
   But in ourselves, that we are underlings. [I.ii]

3. Let me have men about me that are fat;
   Sleek-headed men, and such as sleep o' nights.
   Yon Cassius has a lean and hungry look;
   He thinks too much. Such men are dangerous. [I.ii]

4. ...but for mine own part, it was Greek to me. [I.ii]

5. Cowards die many times before their deaths:
   The valiant never taste of death but once.
   Of all the wonders that I yet have heard,
   It seems to me most strange that men should fear,
   Seeing that death, a necessary end,
   Will come when it will come. [II.ii]

6. O, pardon me, thou bleeding piece of earth,
   That I am meek and gentle with these butchers!
   Thou art the ruins of the noblest man
   That ever lived in the tide of times. [III.i]

7. Not that I lov'd Caesar less, but that I lov'd Rome more. [III.ii]

8. Friends, Romans, countrymen, lend me your ears;
I come to bury Caesar, not to praise him.
The evil that men do lives after them;
The good is oft interred with their bones; [III.ii]

9. This was the most unkindest cut of all;
O, what a fall was there, my countrymen! [III.ii]

10. This was the noblest Roman of them all.
His life was gentle; and the elements
So mix'd in him that Nature might stand up
And say to all the world 'This was a man!' [V.v]

King Lear

1. Nothing will come of nothing. Speak again. [I.i]

2. Have more than thou showest,
Speak less than thou knowest,
Lend less than thou owest. [I.iv]

3. I am a man
More sinn'd against then sinning. [III.ii]

4. As flies to wanton boys are we to th' gods—
They kill us for their sport. [IV.i]

Macbeth

1. *First Witch*: When shall we three meet again?
In thunder, lightning, or in rain?
Second Witch: When the hurlyburly's done,
When the battle's lost and won.
All: Fair is foul, and foul is fair:
Hover through the fog and filthy air. [I.i]

2. Present fears
Are less than horrible imaginings. [I.iii]

3. *Malcolm*: Nothing in his life
Became him like the leaving it: he died
As one that had been studied in his death
To throw away the dearest thing he ow'd
As 'twere a careless trifle.

Duncan: There's no art
To find the mind's construction in the face. [I.iv]

4. Yet do I fear thy nature;
It is too full o' th' milk of human kindness
To catch the nearest way. Thou wouldst be great;
Art not without ambition, but without
The illness should attend it. [I.v]

5. False face must hide what the false heart doth know. [I.vii]

6. Methought I heard a voice cry 'Sleep no more;
Macbeth does murder sleep' – the innocent sleep,
Sleep that knits up the ravell'd sleave of care,
The death of each day's life, sore labour's bath,
Balm of hurt minds, great nature's second course,
Chief nourisher in life's feast. [II.ii]

7. Will all great Neptune's ocean wash this blood
Clean from my hand? No; this my hand will rather
The multitudinous seas incarnadine,
Making the green one red. [II.ii]

8. A little water clears us of this deed.
How easy is it then! [II.ii]

9. *Porter*: Drink, sir, is a great provoker of three things.
Macduff: What three things does drink especially provoke?
Porter: Marry, sir, nose-painting, sleep, and urine. Lechery, sir, it
provokes, and unprovokes: it provokes the desire, but it takes away the
performance. [II.iii]

10. Double, double toil and trouble;
Fire burn, and cauldron bubble. [IV.i]

11. By the pricking of my thumbs,
Something wicked this way comes. [IV.i]

12. Be bloody, bold, and resolute; laugh to scorn
The pow'r of man, for none of woman born
Shall harm Macbeth. [IV.i]

13. *Macduff*: Stands Scotland where it did?
Ross: Alas, poor country,
Almost afraid to know itself! It cannot

Be call'd our mother, but our grave. [IV.iii]

14. Out, damned spot! out, I say!
Yet who would have thought the old man to have had so much blood
in him? [V.i]

15. Here's the smell of the blood still. All the perfumes of Arabia will
not sweeten this little hand. Oh, oh, oh! [V.i]

16. She should have died hereafter;
There would have been a time for such a word.
To-morrow, and to-morrow, and to-morrow,
Creeps in this petty pace from day to day
To the last syllable of recorded time,
And all our yesterdays have lighted fools
The way to dusty death. Out, out, brief candle!
Life's but a walking shadow, a poor player,
That struts and frets his hour upon the stage,
And then is heard no more; it is a tale
Told by an idiot, full of sound and fury,
Signifying nothing. [V.v]

17. Lay on, Macduff;
And damn'd be him that first cries 'Hold,
enough!' [V.vii]

Measure for Measure
1. They say best men are moulded out of faults;
And, for the most, become much more the better
For being a little bad; so may my husband. [V.i]

2. What's mine is yours, and what is yours is mine. [V.i]

The Merchant of Venice
1. God made him, and therefore let him pass for a man. [I.ii]

2. The devil can cite Scripture for his purpose. [I.iii]

3. It is a wise father that knows his own child. [II.ii]

4. All that glisters is not gold,
Often have you heard that told. [II.vii]

5. Hath not a Jew eyes? Hath not a Jew hands, organs, dimensions,
senses, affections, passions, fed with the same food, hurt with the same

weapons, subject to the same diseases, healed by the same means, warmed and cooled by the same winter and summer, as a Christian is? If you prick us, do we not bleed? If you tickle us, do we not laugh? If you poison us, do we not die? And if you wrong us, shall we not revenge? If we are like you in the rest, we will resemble you in that. [III.i]

6. The pound of flesh which I demand of him
   Is dearly bought, 'tis mine, and I will have it. [IV.i]

7. The quality of mercy is not strain'd;
   It droppeth as the gentle rain from heaven
   Upon the place beneath. It is twice blest:
   It blesseth him that gives and him that takes. [IV.i]

A Midsummer Night's Dream

1. The course of true love never did run smooth. [I.i]

2. Ill met by moonlight, proud Titania. [II.i]

3. Lord, what fools these mortals be! [III.ii]

4. The lunatic, the lover, and the poet,
   Are of imagination all compact. [V.i]

Much Ado About Nothing

1. Sigh no more, ladies, sigh no more,
   Men were deceivers ever, [II.iii]

Othello

1. But I will wear my heart upon my sleeve
   For daws to peck at: I am not what I am. [I.i]

2. Virtue? A fig! 'Tis in ourselves that we are thus or thus. Our bodies are our gardens to the which our wills are gardeners. [I.iii]

3. Good name in man and woman, dear my lord,
   Is the immediate jewel of their souls:
   Who steals my purse steals trash; 'tis something, nothing;
   'Twas mine, 'tis his, and has been slave to thousands;
   But he that filches from me my good name
   Robs me of that which not enriches him
   And makes me poor indeed. [III.iii]

Richard II

1. This royal throne of kings, this scept'red isle,
   This earth of majesty, this seat of Mars,
   This other Eden, demi-paradise,
   This fortress built by Nature for herself
   Against infection and the hand of war,
   This happy breed of men, this little world,
   This precious stone set in the silver sea,
   Which serves it in the office of a wall,
   Or as a moat defensive to a house,
   Against the envy of less happier lands;
   This blessed plot, this earth, this realm, this England, [II.i]

Richard III

1. Now is the winter of our discontent
   Made glorious summer by this sun of York. [I.i]

2. And thus I clothe my naked villainy
   With odd old ends stol'n forth of holy writ,
   And seem a saint when most I play the devil. [I.iii]

3. A horse! a horse! my kingdom for a horse! [V.iv]

Romeo and Juliet

1. From forth the fatal loins of these two foes
   A pair of star-cross'd lovers take their life. [Prologue]

2. But, soft! What light through yonder window breaks?
   It is the east, and Juliet is the sun. [II.ii]

3. O Romeo, Romeo! wherefore art thou Romeo?
   Deny thy father and refuse thy name;
   Or, if thou wilt not, be but sworn my love,
   And I'll no longer be a Capulet. [II.ii]

4. What's in a name? That which we call a rose
   By any other name would smell as sweet. [II.ii]

The Tempest

1. Full fathom five thy father lies;
   Of his bones are coral made;
   Those are pearls that were his eyes;
   Nothing of him that doth fade

But doth suffer a sea-change
Into something rich and strange.
Sea-nymphs hourly ring his knell:
Ding-dong.
Hark! now I hear them – Ding-dong, bell. [I.ii]

2. Misery acquaints a man with strange bedfellows. [II.ii]

3. Be not afeard. The isle is full of noises,
Sounds, and sweet airs, that give delight, and hurt not.
Sometimes a thousand twangling instruments
Will hum about mine ears; and sometime voices,
That, if I then had wak'd after long sleep,
Will make me sleep again; and then, in dreaming,
The clouds methought would open and show riches
Ready to drop upon me, that, when I wak'd,
I cried to dream again. [III.ii]

Twelfth Night

1. If music be the food of love, play on,
Give me excess of it, that, surfeiting,
The appetite may sicken and so die. [I.i]

2. O mistress mine, where are you roaming?
O, stay and hear; your true love's coming,
That can sing both high and low.
Trip no further, pretty sweeting;
Journeys end in lovers meeting,
Every wise man's son doth know... [II.iii]

3. Come away, come away, death;
And in sad cypress let me be laid; [II.iv]

4. She never told her love,
But let concealment, like a worm i' th' bud,
Feed on her damask cheek. She pin'd in thought;
And with a green and yellow melancholy
She sat like Patience on a monument,
Smiling at grief. Was not this love indeed?
We men may say more, swear more, but indeed
Our shows are more than will; for still we prove
Much in our vows, but little in our love. [II.iv]

5. Be not afraid of greatness. Some are born great, some achieve greatness, and some have greatness thrust upon 'em. [II.v]

The Two Gentlemen of Verona
1. Who is Sylvia? What is she, [IV.ii]

The Winter's Tale
1. Exit, pursued by a bear. [III.iii, stage direction]

2. I would there were no age between ten and three and twenty, or that youth would sleep out the rest; for there is nothing in the between but getting wenches with child, wronging the ancientry, stealing, fighting. [III.iii]

3. My father nam'd me Autolycus; who, being, as I am, litter'd under Mercury, was likewise a snapper-up of unconsidered trifles. [IV.iii]

Sonnets
1. Shall I compare thee to a summer's day?
Thou art more lovely and more temperate.
Rough winds do shake the darling buds of May,
And summer's lease hath all too short a date: [18]

2. Let me not to the marriage of true minds
Admit impediments. Love is not love
Which alters when it alteration finds,
Or bends with the remover to remove. [116]

3. Th' expense of spirit in a waste of shame
Is lust in action; and till action, lust
Is perjur'd, murd'rous, bloody, full of blame,
Savage, extreme, rude, cruel, not to trust;
Enjoyed no sooner but despised straight;
Past reason hunted; and, no sooner had,
Past reason hated, as a swallowed bait,
On purpose laid to make the taker mad—
Mad in pursuit, and in possession so;
Had, having, and in quest to have, extreme;
A bliss in proof, and prov'd, a very woe;
Before, a joy propos'd; behind, a dream.
All this the world well knows; yet none knows well
To shun the heaven that leads men to this hell. [129]

1. [Contained in his will]
Item, I give unto my wife my second best bed. [Attr.]

Shankly, Bill (1914–1981)
Scottish footballer and manager

1. Some people think football is a matter of life and death. I don't like that attitude. I can assure them it is much more serious than that. [Remark on BBC T.V., 1981]

Shaw, George Bernard (1856–1950)
Irish novelist, dramatist, essayist, critic, pamphleteer, socialist and letter writer; Nobel prize 1925

1. The Gospel of Getting On. [*Mrs. Warren's Profession* (1893), IV]

2. The worst sin towards our fellow creatures is not to hate them, but to be indifferent to them: that's the essence of inhumanity. [*The Devil's Disciple* (1901), II]

3. A lifetime of happiness! No man alive could bear it: it would be hell on earth. [*Man and Superman* (1903), I]

4. The true artist will let his wife starve, his children go barefoot, his mother drudge for his living at seventy, sooner than work at anything but his art. [Ib. I]

5. Very nice sort of place, Oxford, I should think, for people who like that sort of place. [Ib. II]

6. Hell is full of musical amateurs: music is the brandy of the damned. [Ib. III]

7. There are two tragedies in life. One is not to get your heart's desire. The other is to get it. [Ib. IV]

8. The golden rule is that there are no golden rules. [Ib. 'Maxims for Revolutionists: The Golden Rule']

9. He who can, does. He who cannot teaches. [Ib. 'Maxims for Revolutionists: Education']

10. If you strike a child, take care that you strike it in anger, even at the risk of maiming it for life. A blow in cold blood neither can nor should be forgiven. [Ib. 'Maxims for Revolutionists: How to Beat Children']

11. The universal regard for money is the one hopeful fact in our civilization, the one sound spot in our social conscience. Money is the most important thing in the world. It represents health, strength, honour, generosity, and beauty as conspicuously as the want of it represents illness, weakness, disgrace, meanness, and ugliness. [*Major Barbara* (1907), Preface]

12. Nobody can say a word against Greek: it stamps a man at once as an educated gentleman. [Ib. I]

13. I am a sort of collector of religions: and the curious thing is that I find I can believe in them all. [Ib. II]

14. *Pickering*: Have you no morals, man?
    Doolittle: Can't afford them, Governor. [*Pygmalion* (1916), II]

15. I'm one of the undeserving poor: that's what I am. Think of what that means to a man. It means that he's up agen middle class morality all the time ... What is middle class morality? Just an excuse for never giving me anything. [Ib. II]

16. [Reflecting upon youth]
    Far too good to waste on children. [In L. Copeland, *10,000 Jokes, Toasts, and Stories*]

Shelley, Percy Bysshe (1792–1822)
English Romantic poet and dramatist, known for his lyrics; essayist and letter writer; husband of Mary Wollstonecraft Shelley

1. I love all waste
   And solitary places; where we taste
   The pleasures of believing what we see
   Is boundless, as we wish our souls to be... ['Julian and Maddalo' (1818)]

2. I met Murder on the way—
   He had a mask like Castlereagh... ['The Mask of Anarchy' (1819)]

3. O, Wind,
   If Winter comes, can Spring be far behind? ['Ode to the West Wind' (1819)]

4. I met a traveller from an antique land
   Who said: Two vast and trunkless legs of stone

Stand in the desert ... Near them, on the sand,
Half sunk, a shattered visage lies, whose frown,
And wrinkled lip, and sneer of cold command,
Tell that its sculptor well those passions read
Which yet survive, stamped on these lifeless things...

'My name is Ozymandias, king of kings:
Look on my works, ye Mighty, and despair!'
Nothing beside remains. Round the decay
Of that colossal wreck, boundless and bare
The lone and level sands stretch far away. ['Ozymandias' (1817)]

5. Hail to thee, blithe Spirit!
Bird thou never wert,
That from Heaven, or near it,
Pourest thy full heart
In profuse strains of unpremeditated art... ['To a Skylark'
(1820)]

6. To suffer woes which Hope thinks infinite;
To forgive wrongs darker than death or night;
To defy Power, which seems omnipotent;
To love, and bear; to hope till Hope creates
From its own wreck the thing it contemplates;
Neither to change, nor falter, nor repent;
This, like thy glory, Titan, is to be
Good, great and joyous, beautiful and free;
This is alone Life, Joy, Empire and Victory. [*Prometheus Unbound*
(1820), IV, line 570]

7. He has outsoared the shadow of our night;
Envy and calumny and hate and pain,
And that unrest which men miscall delight,
Can touch him not and torture not again;
From the contagion of the world's slow stain
He is secure, and now can never mourn
A heart grown cold, a head grown gray in vain. [*Adonais* (1821), 40]

8. Poets are the unacknowledged legislators of the world. [*A Defence of Poetry* (1821)]

9. Poetry is the record of the happiest and best moments of the happiest and best minds. [Ib.]

Sheridan, Philip Henry (1831–1888)
American Union general in the Civil War

1. The only good Indian is a dead Indian. [Attr.]

Sheridan, Richard Brinsley (1751–1816)
Irish comic dramatist and theatre manager; politician and orator

1. Illiterate him, I say, quite from your memory. [*The Rivals* (1775), I.ii]

2. He is the very pine-apple of politeness! [Ib. III.iii]

3. *Mrs. Candour*: I'll swear her colour is natural: I have seen it come and go.
   Lady Teazle: I dare swear you have ma'am; it goes off at night, and comes again in the morning. [*The School for Scandal* (1777), II.ii]

Sieyès, Abbé Emmanuel Joseph (1748–1836)
French statesman, political theorist, pamphleteer and priest

1. [Reply when asked what he did during the French Revolution]
   J'ai vécu.
   I survived. [In F.A.M. Mignet, *Notice historique sur la vie et les travaux de M. le Comte de Sieyès* (1836)]

Simonides (c. 556–468 BC)
Greek lyric poet and epigrammatist, known for his elegies and choral odes

1. Go, tell the Spartans, thou who passest by,
   That here, obedient to their laws, we lie. [In Herodotus, *Histories*]

Sims, George R. (1847–1922)
English journalist, dramatist and novelist

1. It is Christmas Day in the Workhouse. ['In the Workhouse – Christmas Day' (1879)]

Singer, Isaac Bashevis (1904–)
American Yiddish novelist and short-story writer, born in Poland; Nobel prize 1978

1. We have to believe in free will. We've got no choice. [*The Times*, 1982]

Sitting Bull (c. 1834–1890)
Sioux chief, known for his defeat of General Custer in 1876

1. The white man knows how to make everything, but he does not know how to distribute it. [Attr.]

Sitwell, Sir Osbert (1892–1969)
English poet, novelist, short-story and autobiographical writer; brother of Edith Sitwell

1. *Educ*: during the holidays from Eton. [*Who's Who* (1929)]

Smart, Christopher (1722–1771)
English poet and translator, noted for his religious lyrics

1. For I will consider my Cat Jeoffry.
   For he is the servant of the Living God, duly and daily serving Him. [*Jubilate Agno* (c. 1758–63), 19]

Smith, Adam (1723–1790)
Scottish economist, moral philosopher and essayist; founder of modern political economy

1. No society can surely be flourishing and happy, of which the far greate part of the members are poor and miserable. [*Wealth of Nations* (1776) I.8]

2. People of the same trade seldom meet together, even for merriment and diversion, but the conversation ends in a conspiracy against the public, or in some contrivance to raise prices. [Ib. I.10]

3. There is no art which one government sooner learns of another than that of draining money from the pockets of the people. [Ib. V.2]

Smith, Logan Pearsall (1865–1946)
American-born British epigrammatist, essayist, critic and short-story writer

1. A best-seller is the gilded tomb of a mediocre talent. [*Afterthoughts* (1931), 5, 'Art and Letters']

2. People say that life is the thing, but I prefer reading. [Ib. 'Myself'], [*All Trivia* (1933)]

3. Thank heavens, the sun has gone in, and I don't have to go out and enjoy it. [Ib.]

Smith, Stevie (1902–1971)
English novelist, poet and illustrator of her verse

1. I was much further out than you thought
And not waving but drowning. ['Not Waving But Drowning' (1957)]

Smith, Sydney (1771–1845)
English clergyman and wit

1. The motto I proposed for the [*Edinburgh*] *Review* was: *Tenui musam meditamur avena* – 'We cultivate literature upon a little oatmeal.' [*Works* (1859), I, Preface]

2. I have no relish for the country; it is a kind of healthy grave. [*Letters*, To Miss G. Harcourt, 1838]

3. It requires a surgical operation to get a joke well into a Scotch understanding. Their only idea of wit ... is laughing immoderately at stated intervals. [In Lady Holland, *Memoir* (1855), I.2]

4. No furniture so charming as books. [Ib. I.9]

5. I never read a book before reviewing it; it prejudices a man so. [In H. Pearson, *The Smith of Smiths* (1943), 3]

6. My idea of heaven is, eating *pâté de foie gras* to the sound of trumpets. [Ib. 10]

Smollett, Tobias (1721–1771)
Scottish author of picaresque novels; editor, satirist, translator, historian, traveller and physician

1. Some folks are wise, and some are otherwise. [*The Adventures of Roderick Random* (1748), 6]

Snow, C. P. (1905–1980)
English novelist, critic, physicist, biographer and public administrator

1. The official world, the corridors of power, the dilemmas of conscience and egotism – she disliked them all. [*Homecomings* (1956), 22]

Socrates (469–399 BC)
Athenian philosopher, noted for his method of instruction, recorded by Plato; condemned to death for impiety

1. Death is one of two things. Either it is annihilation, and the dead

have no consciousness of anything; or, as we are told, it is really a change: a migration of the soul from this place to another. [In Plato, *Apology*, 41]

Solon (c. 638–c. 559 BC)
Athenian statesman, noted for his legal, political and economic reforms, and poet

1. Call no man happy until he is dead, but only lucky. [In Herodotus, *Histories*]

Sontag, Susan (1933–)
American critic, essayist, novelist and short-story writer

1. Interpretation is the revenge of the intellect upon art. [*Against Interpretation*]

Sophocles (495–406 BC)
Classical Greek dramatist and poet, known for his seven surviving tragedies

1. Not to be born is best. The second best is to have seen the light and then to go back quickly whence we came. [*Oedipus at Colonus*]

Spark, Muriel (1918–)
Scottish novelist, poet, dramatist, short-story and autobiographical writer

1. Give me a girl at an impressionable age, and she is mine for life. [*The Prime of Miss Jean Brodie* (1961), 1]

2. If only you small girls would listen to me, I would make of you the crème de la crème. [Ib.]

Spencer, Herbert (1820–1903)
English evolutionary philosopher and journalist

1. It was remarked to me ... that to play billiards well was a sign of an ill-spent youth. [In Duncan, *Life and Letters of Spencer*]

Spender, Stephen (1909–)
English poet and critic, associated with 1930s left-wing writers; editor, translator, diarist and autobiographer

1. I think continually of those who were truly great—

The names of those who in their lives fought for life,
Who wore at their hearts the fire's centre. ['I think continually of those' (1933)]

Spenser, Edmund (c. 1522–1599)
English poet, noted for his versification, imagery and allegorical poems; the 'poet's poet'

1. And he that strives to touch the stars,
   Oft stumbles at a straw. [*The Shepherd's Calendar* (1579), 'July']

2. The gentle mind by gentle deeds is known.
   For a man by nothing is so well bewray'd,
   As by his manners. [*The Faerie Queen* (1596), VI]

3. Sweet Thames, run softly, till I end my Song. [*Prothalamion* (1596)]

Spinoza, Baruch (1632–1677)
Dutch moral and metaphysical philosopher, and theologian

1. Nature abhors a vacuum. [*Ethics* (1677)]

2. Man is a social animal. [Ib.]

Spooner, William (1844–1930)
English clergyman and university warden

1. Let us drink to the queer old Dean. [Attr.]

2. I remember your name perfectly, but I just can't think of your face. [Attr.]

Squire, J. C. (1884–1958)
English poet and critic; essayist, journalist, editor and short-story writer

1. But I'm not so think as you drunk I am. [In M. Baring and others, *One Hundred and One Ballades* (1931), 'Ballade of Soporific Absorption']

Stalin, Joseph (1879–1953)
Soviet totalitarian dictator, born in Georgia; General Secretary of the Soviet Communist Party 1922–53

1. The state is an instrument in the hands of the ruling class for suppressing the resistance of its class enemies. [In M.R. Werner (ed.), *Stalin's Kampf*]

Stanley, Sir Henry Morton (1841–1904)
Welsh journalist, explorer of Africa, travel writer and politician

1. Dr. Livingstone, I presume? [*How I found Livingstone* (1872), 11]

Steele, Sir Richard (1672–1729)
Irish-born English essayist, comic dramatist, pamphleteer and politician

1. A little in drink, but at all times yr faithful husband. [Letter to his wife, 1708]

2. There are so few who can grow old with a good grace. [*Spectator*, 263, 1712]

3. Reading is to the mind what exercise is to the body. [*The Tatler*, 54, 1710]

Steffens, Lincoln (1866–1936)
American political analyst, journalist and memoirist

1. [Remark after visiting Russia in 1919]
I have seen the future, and it works. [*Letters* (1938), I]

Stein, Gertrude (1874–1946)
American novelist, dramatist, poet, critic and autobiographical writer, noted for her experimental style

1. Rose is a rose is a rose is a rose. [*Sacred Emily* (1913)]

Sterne, Laurence (1713–1768)
Irish-born English novelist, humorist and clergyman, noted for his development of the novel form

1. I wish either my father or my mother, or indeed both of them, as they were in duty both equally bound to it, had minded what they were about when they begot me. [*Tristram Shandy* (1759–67), I.1]

2. Digressions, incontestably, are the sunshine; – they are the life, the soul of reading; – take them out of this book for instance, – you might as well take the book along with them. [Ib. I.22]

3. That's another story, replied my father. [Ib. II.17]

4. A man should know something of his own country, too, before he goes abroad. [Ib. VII.2]

5. They order, said I, this matter better in France. [*Sentimental Journey* (1768), first sentence]

Stevens, Wallace (1879–1955)
American poet

1. The only emperor is the emperor of ice-cream. ['The Emperor of Ice-Cream' (1923)]

2. They said, 'You have a blue guitar,
You do not play things as they are.'
The man replied, 'Things as they are
Are changed upon a blue guitar.' ['The Man with the Blue Guitar' (1937)]

Stevenson, Adlai (1900–1965)
American statesman

1. There is no evil in the atom; only in men's souls. [Speech, Hartford, Connecticut, 1952]

Stevenson, Robert Louis (1850–1894)
Scottish writer

1. For my part, I travel not to go anywhere, but to go. I travel for travel's sake. The great affair is to move. [*Travels with a Donkey* (1879), 'Cheylard and Luc']

2. To travel hopefully is a better thing than to arrive, and the true success is to labour. [*Virginibus Puerisque* (1881), 6]

3. Fifteen men on the dead man's chest
Yo-ho-ho, and a bottle of rum!
Drink and the devil had done for the rest—
Yo-ho-ho, and a bottle of rum. [*Treasure Island* (1883), 1]

4. 'I've a grand memory for forgetting, David.' [*Kidnapped* (1886), 18]

5. I have a little shadow that goes in and out with me,
And what can be the use of him is more than I can see. [*A Child's Garden of Verses* (1885), 'My Shadow']

6. Under the wide and starry sky
Dig the grave and let me lie
Glad did I live and gladly die,

And I laid me down with a will.
This be the verse you grave for me:
'Here he lies where he longed to be;
Home is the sailor, home from sea,
And the hunter home from the hill.' [*Underwoods* (1887), 'Requiem']

7. Give to me the life I love,
Let the lave go by me,
Give the jolly heaven above
And the byway nigh me.
Bed in the bush with stars to see,
Bread I dip in the river—
There's the life for a man like me,
There's the life for ever. [*Songs of Travel* (1896), 'The Vagabond']

Stout, Rex Todhunter (1886–1975)
American detective-story writer

1. There are two kinds of statistics, the kind you look up and the kind you make up. [*Death of a Doxy*, 9]

Stowe, Harriet Beecher (1812–1896)
American novelist

1. 'Do you know who made you?' 'Nobody, as I knows on,' said the child, with a short laugh ... 'I'spect I grow'd.' [Topsy] [*Uncle Tom's Cabin* (1852), 20]

Stravinsky, Igor (1882–1971)
Russian-born American composer

1. A good composer does not imitate; he steals. [In Peter Yates, *Twentieth Century Music*]

Suetonius (fl. AD 75–150)
Roman biographer and historian

1. *Festina lente.*
Hasten slowly. [*Lives of the Caesars*, 'Divus Augustus']

2. *Ave, Imperator, morituri te salutant.*
Hail, Emperor, those about to die salute thee. [*Life of Claudius*]

Sullivan, Sir Arthur (1842–1900)
English composer

1. [Accused of plagiarism]
   We all have the same eight notes to work with. [Attr.]

Swift, Jonathan (1667–1745)
Anglo-Irish satirist and churchman

1. When a true genius appears in the world, you may know him by this sign, that the dunces are all in confederacy against him. [*Thoughts on Various Subjects* (1711)]

2. Every man desires to live long; but no man would be old. [Ib.]

3. We are so fond of one another, because our ailments are the same. [*Journal to Stella*, 1711]

4. He showed me his bill of fare to tempt me to dine with him; poh, said I, I value not your bill of fare, give me your bill of company. [Ib.]

5. I have been assured by a very knowing American of my acquaintance in London, that a young healthy child, well nursed, is, at a year old, a most delicious, nourishing, and wholesome food, whether stewed, roasted, baked, or boiled; and I make no doubt that it will equally serve in a fricassee, or a ragout. [*A Modest Proposal for Preventing the Children of Ireland from being a Burden to their Parents or Country* (1729)]

6. So, naturalists observe, a flea
   Hath smaller fleas that on him prey;
   And these have smaller fleas to bite 'em,
   And so proceed *ad infinitum*.
   Thus every poet, in his kind,
   Is bit by him that comes behind. ['On Poetry' (1733)]

Szasz, Thomas (1920–)
Hungarian-born American psychiatrist

1. If you talk to God, you are praying; if God talks to you, you have schizophrenia. If the dead talk to you, you are a spiritualist; if God talks to you, you are a schizophrenic. [*The Second Sin* (1973)]

Tacitus (c. AD 55–c. 120)
Roman historian, noted for his prose style

1. *Ubi solitudinem faciunt pacem appellant.*
   They create desolation, and call it peace. [*Agricola*, 30]

2. *Proprium humani ingenii est odisse quem laeseris.*
   It is part of human nature to hate the man you have hurt. [Ib. 42]

Talleyrand, Charles-Maurice de (1754–1838)
French statesman; Foreign Minister 1797–1807; memoirist and former prelate

1. [Of America]
   I found there a country with thirty-two religions and only one sauce. [In Pedrazzini, *Autant en apportent les mots*]

2. War is much too serious to be left to the generals. [Attr.]

Taylor, Ann (1782–1866)
English poet and children's writer

1. Twinkle, twinkle, little star,
   How I wonder what you are!
   Up above the world so high,
   Like a diamond in the sky. [*Rhymes for the Nursery* (1806), 'The Star']

Taylor, Bert Leston (1866–1921)
American journalist and columnist

1. A bore is a man who, when you ask him how he is, tells you. [*The So-Called Human Race* (1922)]

Taylor, Bishop Jeremy (1613–1667)
English divine, noted for his devotional writings

1. Every school boy knows it. [*On the Real Presence* (1654)]

Temple, William (1881–1944)
English prelate, social reformer, supporter of ecumenicalism, teacher and writer; son of Frederick Temple

1. Christianity is the most materialistic of all great religions. [*Readings in St John's Gospel* (1939)]

2. [Remark to parents when headmaster of Repton School]
Personally, I have always looked on cricket as organized loafing. [Attr.]

Tennyson, Alfred, Lord (1809–1892)
English poet, noted for his lyric genius; poet laureate from 1850

1. The mirror crack'd from side to side;
'The curse is come upon me,' cried
The Lady of Shalott. ['The Lady of Shalott' (1832, revised 1842), line 109]

2. In the Spring a young man's fancy lightly turns to thoughts of love.
['Locksley Hall' (1842), line 19]

3. Forward, forward let us range,
Let the great world spin for ever down the ringing grooves of change.
[Ib. line 181]

4. ...that which we are, we are;
One equal temper of heroic hearts,
Made weak by time and fate, but strong in will
To strive, to seek, to find, and not to yield. ['Ulysses' (1842), line 44]

5. Now sleeps the crimson petal, now the white;
Nor waves the cypress in the palace walk;
Nor winks the gold fin in the prophyry font:
The fire-fly wakens: waken thou with me. [*The Princess* (1847), VII, Song, added 1850]

6. I hold it true, whate'er befall;
I feel it, when I sorrow most,
'Tis better to have loved and lost
Than never to have loved at all. [*In Memoriam A. H. H.* (1850), 27]

7. Who trusted God was love indeed
And love Creation's final law—
Tho' Nature, red in tooth and claw
With ravine, shrieked against his creed. [Ib. 56]

8. Ring out, wild bells, to the wild sky,
The flying cloud, the frosty light:
The year is dying in the night;
Ring out, wild bells, and let him die.

Ring out the old, ring in the new,

Ring, happy bells, across the snow:
The year is going, let him go;
Ring out the false, ring in the true. [Ib. 106]

9. Half a league, half a league,
Half a league onward,
All in the valley of Death
Rode the six hundred...

'Forward the Light Brigade!'
Was there a man dismay'd?
Not tho' the soldiers knew
Some one had blunder'd:
Their's not to make reply,
Their's not to reason why,
Their's but to do and die:
Into the valley of Death
Rode the six hundred.

Cannon to right of them
Cannon to left of them,
Cannon in front of them
Volley'd and thunder'd;
Stormed at with shot and shell,
Boldly they rode and well,
Into the jaws of Death
Into the mouth of Hell
Rode the six hundred. ['The Charge of the Light Brigade' (1854)]

10. Come into the garden, Maud, [*Maud* (1855), I.22]

11. The days darken round me, and the years,
Among new men, strange faces, other minds.

And slowly answer'd Arthur from the barge:
'The old order changeth, yielding place to new,
And God fulfils himself in many ways,
Lest one good custom should corrupt the world.' [*The Idylls of the King*,
'The Passing of Arthur' (1869), line 405]

Terence (c.190–159 BC)
Carthaginian-born Roman comic dramatist

1. *Nullumst iam dictum quod non dictum sit prius.*

Nothing has yet been said that's not been said before. [*Eunuchus*, Prologue]

2. *Homo sum; humani nil a me alienum puto.*
I am a man, I count nothing human indifferent to me. [*Heauton Timoroumenos*]

3. *Quot homines tot sententiae.*
So many men, so many opinions. [*Phormio*]

4. *Fortis fortuna adiuvat.*
Fortune helps the brave. [Ib.]

Tertullian (c. AD 160–c. 225)
Carthaginian theologian and Latin Church Father; originated much ecclesiastical terminology

1. *De calcaria in carbonarium.*
Out of the frying pan into the fire. [*De Carne Christi*]

2. *Certum est quia impossibile est.*
It is certain because it is impossible. [Ib.]

Tessimond, A.S.J. (1902–1962)
Poet

1. Cats, no less liquid than their shadows,
Offer no angles to the wind.
They slip, diminished, neat, through loopholes
Less than themselves. [*Cats* (1934)]

Thackeray, William Makepeace (1811–1863)
Indian-born English novelist, journalist and lecturer

1. If a man's character is to be abused, say what you will, there's nobody like a relation to do the business. [*Vanity Fair* (1847–8), 19]

2. Them's my sentiments! [Ib. 21]

3. I think I could be a good woman if I had five thousand a year. [Ib. 36]

4. 'No business before breakfast, Glum!' says the King. 'Breakfast first, business next.' [*The Rose and the Ring* (1855), 11]

Thatcher, Margaret (1925–)
English stateswoman; Conservative Prime Minister 1979–90

1. U-turn if you want to. The lady's not for turning. [Speech, Conservative Conference, 1980]

2. Victorian values ... were the values when our country became great. [Television interview, 1982]

3. There is no such thing as society. There are individual men and women and there are families. [*Woman's Own*, 31 October 1989]

Thomas, Brandon (1856–1914)
English comedy actor and dramatist

1. I'm Charley's aunt from Brazil – where the nuts come from. [*Charley's Aunt* (1892), I]

Thomas, Dylan (1914–1953)
Welsh poet, short-story writer, essayist, radio dramatist and journalist

1. The force that through the green fuse drives the flower
   Drives my green age; that blasts the roots of trees
   Is my destroyer. ['The force that through the green fuse drives the flower' (1934)]

2. Oh as I was young and easy in the mercy of his means,
   Time held me green and dying
   Though I sang in my chains like the sea. ['Fern Hill' (1946)]

3. Do not go gentle into that good night,
   Old age should burn and rave at close of day;
   Rage, rage against the dying of the light. ['Do not go gentle into that good night' (1952)]

Thompson, Francis (1859–1907)
English poet, essayist and critic, noted for his religious imagery

1. I fled Him, down the nights and down the days;
   I fled Him, down the arches of the years;
   I fled Him, down the labyrinthine ways
   Of my own mind; and in the mist of tears
   I hid from Him, and under running laughter. ['The Hound of Heaven' (1913), I]

Thompson, Hunter S. (1939–)
American 'new' journalist and writer

1. Fear and Loathing in Las Vegas [Title of two articles in *Rolling Stone*, 1971]

Thompson, William Hepworth (1810–1886)
English scholar of Greek, university lecturer and priest

1. [Of Sir Richard Jebb, Professor of Greek at Cambridge]
   What time he can spare from the adornment of his person he devotes to the neglect of his duties. [In M.R. Bobbit, *With Dearest Love to All* (1960)]

Thomson, James (1700–1748)
Scottish poet and dramatist, noted for his nature poetry

1. 'Rule, Britannia, rule the waves;
   Britons never will be slaves.' [*Alfred: A Masque* (1740), II]

Thomson, James (1834–1882)
Scottish poet, essayist and journalist

1. The City is of Night, but not of Sleep;
   There sweet sleep is not for the weary brain;
   The pitiless hours like years and ages creep,
   A night seems termless hell. [*The City of Dreadful Night* (1870–3), I]

Thomson, Roy, Lord (1894–1977)
Canadian-born British newspaper proprietor; founder of radio and television stations

1. [Of commercial television]
   It's just like having a licence to print your own money. [In R. Braddon, *Roy Thomson* (1965)]

Thoreau, Henry David (1817–1862)
American essayist, social critic, writer on natural history and follower of Emerson

1. The mass of men lead lives of quiet desperation. [*Walden* (1854), 'Economy']

2. I once had a sparrow alight upon my shoulder for a moment while I was hoeing in a village garden, and I felt that I was more distinguished

by that circumstance than I should have been by any epaulet I could have worn. [Ib. 'Winter Animals']

3. Things do not change; we change. [Ib. Conclusion]

4. Some circumstantial evidence is very strong, as when you find a trout in the milk. [Journal, 1850]

5. [On being urged to make his peace with God]
I did not know that we had ever quarrelled. [Attr.]

Thurber, James (1894–1961)
American humorist, essayist, short-story writer, illustrator and dramatist

1. No man ... who has wrestled with a self-adjusting card table can ever quite be the same man he once was. [*Let Your Mind Alone*, 'Sex ex Machina']

2. Early to rise and early to bed makes a male healthy and wealthy and dead. [*New Yorker*, 1939, 'The Shrike and the Chipmunks']

3. All right, have it your way – you heard a seal bark. [Caption to cartoon 'The Seal in the Bedroom', in *New Yorker*, 1932]

4. It's a naïve domestic Burgundy, without any breeding, but I think you'll be amused by its presumption. [Cartoon caption in *New Yorker*, 1937]

5. Well, if I called the wrong number, why did you answer the phone? [Ib.]

Tillich, Paul (1886–1965)
German-born American philosopher and Protestant theologian

1. Neurosis is the way of avoiding non-being by avoiding being. [*The Courage to Be* (1952)]

Tolstoy, Leo (1828–1910)
Great Russian novelist; essayist, short-story writer, philosopher and moralist

1. All happy families resemble one another, but each unhappy family is unhappy in its own way. [*Anna Karenina* (1875–7), I.1; trans. A. and L. Maude]

Toscanini, Arturo (1867–1957)
Great Italian conductor

1. [Criticizing the playing of an Austrian orchestra during rehearsal]
Can't you read? The score demands *con amore*, and what are you doing?
You are playing it like married men! [Attr.]

Trace, Christopher (1933–)
Ex-army officer turned actor, the first presenter of Blue Peter *with
Leila Williams*

1. Here's one I made earlier. [*Blue Peter*]

Traherne, Thomas (c. 1637–1674)
English metaphysical religious poet and prose writer; clergyman

1. You will never enjoy the world aright, till the sea itself floweth in
your veins, till you are clothed with the heavens, and crowned with the
stars: and perceive yourself to be the sole heir of the whole world, and
more than so, because men are in it who are every one sole heirs as well
as you. Till you can sing and rejoice and delight in God, as misers
do in gold, and kings in sceptres, you can never enjoy the world.
[*Centuries of Meditations*, I.29]

Truman, Harry S. (1884–1972)
*American statesman; Democrat President 1945–53; sanctioned the
dropping of the atom bomb on Japan, a post-war loan to Britain and
US involvement in Korea; memoirist*

1. If you can't stand the heat, get out of the kitchen. [*Mr. Citizen* (1960),
15]

2. A statesman is a politician who's been dead ten or fifteen years. [*New
York World Telegram and Sun*, 1958]

3. The buck stops here. [Sign on his desk]

Tucker, Sophie (1884–1966)
Russian-born American vaudeville singer

1. I've been poor and I've been rich. Rich is better. [In Cowan, *The Wit
of Women*]

Tusser, Thomas (c. 1524–1580)
English agricultural writer, poet and musician

1. The stone that is rolling can gather no moss;
   For master and servant oft changing is loss. [*Five Hundred Points of Good Husbandry*]

2. At Christmas play and make good cheer,
   For Christmas comes but once a year. [Ib.]

Twain, Mark (Samuel Langhorne Clemens) (1835–1910)
American humorist and novelist; journalist, lecturer and autobiographer

1. Persons attempting to find a motive in this narrative will be prosecuted; persons attempting to find a moral in it will be banished; persons attempting to find a plot in it will be shot. [*The Adventures of Huckleberry Finn* (1884), Introduction]

2. Hain't we got all the fools in town on our side? and ain't that a big enough majority in any town? [Ib. 26]

3. Cauliflower is nothing but cabbage with a college education. [*Pudd'nhead Wilson's Calendar*]

4. When angry count four; when very angry swear. [Ib.]

5. Some of his words were not Sunday-school words. [*A Tramp Abroad*, 20]

6. I have been told that Wagner's music is better than it sounds. [*Autobiography*]

7. [Definition of a classic]
   Something that everybody wants to have read and nobody wants to read. ['The Disappearance of Literature']

8. The report of my death was an exaggeration. [Cable, 1897]

Valéry, Paul (1871–1945)
French poet; critic, mathematician and philosopher

1. God made everything out of nothing. But the nothingness shows through. [*Mauvaises Pensées et autres*]

2. A poem is never finished, only abandoned. [In Auden, *A Certain World*]

Vanbrugh, Sir John (1664–1726)
English comic dramatist and baroque architect

1. *Belinda*: Ay, but you know we must return good for evil.
   Lady Brute: That may be a mistake in the translation. [*The Provoked Wife* (1697), I.i]

Vaughan, Henry (1622–1695)
Welsh metaphysical poet and physician

1. I saw Eternity the other night,
   Like a great ring of pure and endless light,
   All calm, as it was bright;
   And round beneath it, Time in hours, days, years,
   Driv'n by the spheres
   Like a vast shadow mov'd; in which the world
   And all her train were hurl'd. [*Silex Scintillans* (1650–5), 'The World']

Vespasian (AD 9–79)
Roman emperor from 69, and soldier; consolidated Roman rule in Britain and Germany

1. *Pecunia non olet.*
   Money has no smell. [In Suetonius, *Lives of the Caesars*, 'Vespasian']

Victoria, Queen (1819–1901)
Queen of Great Britain and Ireland from 1837 and Empress of India from 1876; diarist and writer

1. [Of Gladstone]
   He speaks to me as if I was a public meeting. [In G.W.E. Russell, *Collections and Recollections* (1898), 14]

2. We are not amused. [Attr. in Caroline Holland, *Notebooks of a Spinster Lady* (1919), 21]

Virgil (70–19 BC)
Great Roman epic and pastoral poet, also noted for his verse on husbandry

1. *Arma virumque canto,*
   I sing of arms and the man [*Aeneid*, I, line 1]

2. *Infandum, regina, iubes renovare dolorem.*
   You bid me renew, O queen, an unspeakable grief. [Ib. II, line 3]

3. *Equo ne credite, Teucri.*
   Quidquid id est, timeo Danaos et dona ferentis.
   Do not trust the horse, Trojans. Whatever it is, I fear the Greeks even
   when they bring gifts. [Ib. II, line 48]

4. *Varium et mutabile semper*
   Femina.
   Woman is always fickle and changeable. [Ib. IV, line 569]

5. *Hos successus alit: possunt, quia posse videntur.*
   These success encourages: they can because they think they can. [Ib.
   V, line 231]

6. *Bella, horrida bella,*
   Et Thybrim multo spumantem sanguine cerno.
   I see wars, horrible wars, and the Tiber foaming with much blood.
   [Ib. VI, line 86]

7. *Facilis descensus Averni:*
   Noctes atque dies patet atri ianua Ditis;
   Sed revocare gradum superasque evadere ad auras,
   Hoc opus, hic labor est.
   The way to Hell is easy: night and day the gates of black Dis stand
   open; but to retrace the step and reach the breezes above, this is the
   task, and in it the labour. [Ib. VI, line 126]

8. *Omnia vincit Amor: et nos cedamus Amori.*
   Love conquers all: and we succumb to love. [*Eclogues*, X, line 69]

9. *Labor omnia vincit.*
   Work conquers all. [*Georgics*, I]

10. *Sed fugit interea, fugit inreparabile tempus.*
    Time meanwhile flies, flies never to return. [Ib. III, line 284]

Voltaire (François-Marie Arouet) (1694–1778)
*French philosopher, dramatist, poet, historian, novelist, critic and
letter writer; outstanding figure of the Enlightenment*

1. *Tout est pour le mieux dans le meilleur des mondes possibles.*
   All is for the best in the best of all possible worlds. [*Candide* (1759),
   1 (and elsewhere)]

2. *Dans ce pays-ci il est bon de tuer de temps en temps un amiral pour encourager
   les autres.*

In this country [England] it is considered good to kill an admiral from time to time, to encourage the others. [Ib. 23]

3. *Cela est bien dit, répondit Candide, mais il faut cultiver notre jardin.*
   'That is well said,' replied Candide, 'but we must cultivate our garden.'
   (We must attend to our own affairs.) [Ib. 30]

4. *Si Dieu n'existait pas, il faudrait l'inventer.*
   If God did not exist, it would be necessary to invent him. [*Epîtres*, 96]

5. I disapprove of what you say, but I will defend to the death your right to say it. [Attr.]

Voznesensky, Andrei (1933–   )
Russian avant-garde poet

1. The art of creation
   is older than the art of killing. ['Poem with a Footnote']

Wallace, William Ross (c. 1819–1881)
American lawyer and poet

1. The hand that rocks the cradle
   Is the hand that rules the world. [*John o' London's Treasure Trove*]

Walpole, Sir Robert (1676–1745)
English Whig statesman, known as first British Prime Minister, 1721–42; father of Horace Walpole

1. The balance of power. [Speech, House of Commons, 1741]

Ward, Artemus (Charles Farrar Browne) (1834–1867)
American humorist; journalist, editor and lecturer

1. I now bid you a welcome adoo. [*Artemus Ward His Book*]

2. The ground flew up and hit me in the hed. [Ib.]

3. Why is this thus? What is the reason of this thusness? [*Artemus Ward's Lecture* (1869), 'Heber C. Kimball's Harem']

4. Why care for grammar as long as we are good? ['Pyrotechny']

Warhol, Andy (1931–1987)
American 'pop' artist; painter, graphic designer and filmmaker

1. In the future everyone will be famous for fifteen minutes. [In *Andy Warhol* (1968)]

Washington, George (1732–1799)
American general and statesman; first US President 1789–97

1. [On being accused of chopping down a cherry tree]
   Father, I cannot tell a lie; I did it with my little hatchet. [Attr., probably apocryphal]

Watts, Isaac (1674–1748)
English hymn writer, poet and minister

1. 'Tis the voice of the sluggard; I heard him complain,
   'You have wak'd me too soon, I must slumber again'.
   As the door on its hinges, so he on his bed,
   Turns his sides and his shoulders and his heavy head. [*Moral Songs*, 'The Sluggard'], [*Divine Songs for Children* (1715), 'The Sluggard']

Waugh, Evelyn (1903–1966)
English novelist, journalist, travel writer and diarist; noted for his satire

1. Nonconformity and lust stalking hand in hand through the country, wasting and ravaging. [*Decline and Fall* (1928)]

2. Feather-footed through the plashy fen passes the questing vole. [*Scoop* (1938), I.1]

Webster, John (c. 1580–1625)
English dramatist, noted for his tragedies

1. We are merely the stars' tennis-balls, struck and bandied,
   Which way please them. [*The Duchess of Malfi* (1623), V.iv]

Wedgwood, Josiah (1730–1795)
English potter, known for his neo-classical design; manufacturer and pamphleteer

1. Am I not a man and a brother? [Motto adopted by Anti-Slavery Society]

Welles, Orson (1915–1985)
*American actor, director and producer; Academy Awards 1941
(script) and 1970*

1. In Italy for thirty years under the Borgias they had warfare, terror,
   murder, bloodshed – they produced Michelangelo, Leonardo da Vinci
   and the Renaissance. In Switzerland they had brotherly love, five
   hundred years of democracy and peace, and what did they produce...?
   The cuckoo clock. [*The Third Man*, 1949]

2. I started at the top and worked my way down. [In Leslie Halliwell,
   The Filmgoer's Book of Quotes]

Wellington, Arthur Wellesley, Duke of (1769–1852)
*Irish-born British field-marshal and statesman; Tory Prime Minister
1828–30; famous for his victory over Napoleon at Waterloo, 1815*

1. [Of his troops]
   The mere scum of the earth. [In Philip Henry Stanhope, *Notes of
   Conversations with the Duke of Wellington* (1888)]

2. The battle of Waterloo was won on the playing fields of Eton. [Attr.]

3. [Reply to a threat of blackmail]
   Publish and be damned. [Attr.]

Wells, H. G. (1866–1946)
*English novelist, known for his scientific romances and
autobiographical writing; short-story, historical and political writer*

1. The war that will end war. [Title of book, 1914]

2. The Shape of Things to Come [Title of book, 1933]

Wesley, John (1703–1791)
*English theologian and preacher; found of Methodist Church, 1739;
diarist; brother of Charles Wesley*

1. Let it be observed, that slovenliness is no part of religion; that neither
   this, nor any text of Scripture, condemns neatness of apparel. Certainly
   this is a duty, not a sin. 'Cleanliness is, indeed, next to godliness.'
   [*Sermons on Several Occasions* (1788), Sermon No. 93, 'On Dress']

West, Mae (1892–1980)
American leading vaudeville and film actress, and scriptwriter

1. Come up and see me sometime. [*She Done Him Wrong*, 1933; attr. version]

2. Beulah, peel me a grape. [*I'm No Angel*, 1933]

3. Is that a gun in your pocket or are you just pleased to see me? [*My Little Chickadee*], [In Joseph Weintraub, *Peel Me a Grape* (1975)]

Whistler, James McNeill (1834–1903)
American painter and etcher, noted for his portraits and nocturnes, and pamphleteer

1. [Replying to the question 'For two days' labour, you ask two hundred guineas?']
No, I ask it for the knowledge of a lifetime. [In D.C. Seitz, *Whistler Stories* (1913)]

2. *Oscar Wilde*: I wish I had said that.
Whistler: You will, Oscar, you will. [In Ingleby, *Oscar Wilde*], [In R. Ellman, *Oscar Wilde* (1987)]

Whitman, Walt (1819–1892)
American poet, journalist and essayist, noted for his free verse

1. I celebrate myself, and sing myself,
And what I assume you shall assume. ['Song of Myself' (1855), 1]

2. Do I contradict myself?
Very well then I contradict myself,
(I am large, I contain multitudes). [Ib. 51]

3. Out of the cradle endlessly rocking,
Out of the mocking-bird's throat, the musical shuttle...
A reminiscence sing. ['Out of the Cradle Endlessly Rocking' (1860)]

Whittington, Robert (fl. 1520)
English grammarian and translator from Latin

1. [Of Sir Thomas More]
As time requireth, a man of marvellous mirth and pastimes, and sometimes of as sad gravity, as who say: a man for all seasons. [*Vulgaria* (1521), II]

Wilcox, Ella Wheeler (1850–1919)
American poet and novelist; prolific author of romantic verse

1. Laugh and the world laughs with you;
   Weep, and you weep alone; ['Solitude']

Wilde, Oscar (1854–1900)
Irish poet, comic dramatist, novelist, critic, wit and author of fairy tales

1. Art never expresses anything but itself. ['The Decay of Lying' (1889)]

2. There is no such thing as a moral or an immoral book. Books are well written or badly written. [*The Picture of Dorian Gray* (1891), Preface]

3. There is only one thing in the world worse than being talked about, and that is not being talked about. [Ib.]

4. A cigarette is the perfect type of a perfect pleasure. It is exquisite, and it leaves one unsatisfied. What more can one want? [Ib. 6]

5. We are all in the gutter, but some of us are looking at the stars. [*Lady Windermere's Fan* (1892), III]

6. *Cecil Graham*: What is a cynic?
   Lord Darlington: A man who knows the price of everything and the value of nothing. [Ib. II]

7. Children begin by loving their parents. After a time they judge them. Rarely, if ever, do they forgive them. [*A Woman of No Importance* (1893), I]

8. To lose one parent, Mr. Worthing, may be regarded as a misfortune; to lose both looks like carelessness. [*The Importance of Being Earnest* (1895), I]

9. I never travel without my diary. One should always have something sensational to read in the train. [Ib. II]

10. Yet each man kills the thing he loves,
    By each let this be heard,
    Some do it with a bitter look,
    Some with a flattering word,
    The coward does it with a kiss,
    The brave man with a sword! [*The Ballad of Reading Gaol* (1898), I]

11. [At the New York Customs]
I have nothing to declare except my genius. [In F. Harris, *Oscar Wilde* (1918)]

12. Work is the curse of the drinking classes. [In Pearson, *Life of Wilde*]

William of Wykeham (1324–1404)
English Bishop of Winchester from 1367, Chancellor of England, 1368–71, and founder of New College, Oxford (1380)

1. Manners maketh man. [Motto of Winchester College and New College, Oxford]

Williams, Tennessee (1911–1983)
American dramatist, noted for his dialogue, characterization and Deep South settings; novelist and short-story writer

1. I have always depended on the kindness of strangers. [*A Streetcar Named Desire* (1947), II]

Williams, William Carlos (1883–1963)
American objectivist poet, short-story writer, novelist, essayist, letter writer and paediatrician

1. so much depends
upon
a red wheel
barrow
glazed with rain
water
beside the white
chickens. ['The Red Wheelbarrow' (1923)]

2. . . . no ideas but in things. [*Paterson* (1946), I, 1]

Wilson, Harold (1916–)
English statesman; Labour Prime Minister 1964–70, 1974–76, and party leader, 1963–76

1. The little gnomes of Zurich. [Speech, 1956]

2. It does not mean, of course, that the pound here in Britain, in your pocket or purse or in your bank, has been devalued. [T.V. broadcast, 1967]

3. A week is a long time in politics. [Remark, 1965]

Wilson, Woodrow (1856–1924)
American statesman; Democrat President 1913–21; helped found the League of Nations, and awarded Nobel peace prize, 1919

1. The world must be made safe for democracy. [Address, 1917]

Wittgenstein, Ludwig (1889–1951)
Austrian-born British philosopher of linguistics; influential on logical positivism

1. *Wovon man nicht sprechen kann, darüber muss man schweigen.*
   Whereof one cannot speak, thereon one must remain silent. [*Tractatus Logico-Philosophicus* (1922)]

2. *Die Welt ist alles, was der Fall ist.*
   The world is everything that is the case. [Ib.]

Wodehouse, P.G. (1881–1975)
English humorist; novelist, short-story writer and librettist, noted for his literary skill; American citizen from 1955

1. I spent the afternoon musing on Life. If you come to think of it, what a queer thing Life is! So unlike anything else, don't you know, if you see what I mean. [*My Man Jeeves* (1919), 'Rallying Round Old George']

2. Jeeves coughed one soft, low, gentle cough like a sheep with a blade of grass stuck in its throat. [*The Inimitable Jeeves* (1923)]

3. It is never difficult to distinguish between a Scotsman with a grievance and a ray of sunshine. [*Blandings Castle and Elsewhere* (1935), 'The Custody of the Pumpkin']

4. He spoke with a certain what-is-it in his voice, and I could see that, if not actually disgruntled, he was far from being gruntled. [*The Code of the Woosters* (1938), 1]

5. The callous way in which Nature refuses to chip in and do its bit when the human heart is in the soup. [*The Mating Season* (1949)]

Wolfe, Charles (1791–1823)
Irish poet and clergyman

1. Not a drum was heard, not a funeral note,
   As his corse to the rampart we hurried. ['The Burial of Sir John Moore at Corunna' (1817)]

Wolfe, James (1727–1759)
English major-general, noted for the capture of Quebec, during which he was fatally wounded

1. The General ... repeated nearly the whole of Gray's Elegy ... adding, as he concluded, that he would prefer being the author of that poem to the glory of beating the French tomorrow. [In Robinson, *Biographical Account*], [In J. Playfair, *Biographical Account of J. Robinson* (1815)]

Wolfe, Tom (1931–)
American novelist, 'new' journalist and illustrator

1. Radical chic. [Title of essay]

Wollstonecraft, Mary (1759–1797)
English feminist, novelist, essayist, letter writer and teacher; wife of William Godwin and mother of Mary Shelley

1. [Of women]
I do not wish them to have power over men; but over themselves. [*A Vindication of the Rights of Women* (1792), 4]

Wood, Mrs Henry (1814–1887)
English novelist, short-story writer and editor

1. Dead! and ... never called me mother. [*East Lynne* (stage adaptation, 1874)]

Woolf, Virginia (1882–1941)
English novelist and critic; short-story and letter writer, and diarist; known for her stream of consciousness technique

1. A Room of One's Own [Title of book, 1929]

2. I have lost friends, some by death ... others through sheer inability to cross the street. [*The Waves* (1931)]

3. Are not the best critics private people, and is not the only criticism worth having spoken criticism? [*Three Guineas* (1938)]

Wordsworth, Dorothy (1771–1855)
English diarist, letter and travel writer; sister of William Wordsworth

1. When we were in the woods beyond Gowbarrow park we saw a few daffodils close to the waterside ... But as we went along there were

more and yet more and at last under the boughs of the trees, we saw
that there was a long belt of them along the shore, about the breadth
of a country turnpike road. I never saw daffodils so beautiful they
grew among the mossy stones about and about them, some rested their
heads upon these stones as on pillow for weariness and the rest tossed
and reeled and danced and seemed as if they verily laughed with the
wind that blew upon them over the lake. [*Journals*, 'Grasmere Journal',
1802]

Wordsworth, William (1770–1850)
*English Romantic poet, greatly inspired by the Lake District; poet
laureate from 1843*

1. On that best portion of a good man's life;
   His little, nameless, unremembered acts
   Of kindness and of love. ['Lines composed a few miles above Tintern
   Abbey' (1798)]

2. All the mighty world
   Of eye, and ear, – both what they half create,
   And what perceive. [Ib.]

3. She dwelt among the untrodden ways
   Beside the springs of Dove,
   A maid whom there were none to praise
   And very few to love:

   She lived unknown, and few could know
   When Lucy ceased to be;
   But she is in her grave, and, oh,
   The difference to me! ['She dwelt among the untrodden ways' (1800)]

4. The Child is father of the Man; ['My heart leaps up when I behold'
   (1807)]

5. Shades of the prison-house begin to close
   Upon the growing boy,
   But he beholds the light, and whence it flows,
   He sees it in his joy; ['Ode: Intimations of Immortality' (1807), 4]

6. Earth has not anything to show more fair; ['Sonnet composed upon
   Westminster Bridge' (1807)]

7. The world is too much with us; late and soon,

Getting and spending, we lay waste our powers:
Little we see in Nature that is ours;
We have given our hearts away, a sordid boon! ['The world is too
much with us' (1807)]

8. I wandered lonely as a cloud
That floats on high o'er vales and hills,
When all at once I saw a crowd,
A host, of golden daffodils;
Beside the lake, beneath the trees,
Fluttering and dancing in the breeze. ['I Wandered Lonely as a Cloud'
(1815 ed.)]

9. Bliss was it in that dawn to be alive,
But to be young was very heaven. [*The Prelude* (1850), XI]

10. I have said that poetry is the spontaneous overflow of powerful feelings:
it takes its origin from emotion recollected in tranquillity: the emotion
is contemplated till, by a species of reaction, the tranquillity gradually
disappears, and an emotion, kindred to that which was before the subject
of contemplation, is gradually produced, and does itself actually exist
in the mind. [*Lyrical Ballads* (1802), Preface]

Wren, Sir Christopher (1632–1723)
*English architect, mathematician and astronomer; known for his many
buildings, including St Paul's, replacing those destroyed in the Great
Fire of London*

1. *Si monumentum requiris, circumspice.*
If you would see his monument look around. [Inscription, St. Paul's
Cathedral, London]

Wright, Frank Lloyd (1869–1959)
*Influential American architect and writer; known for his organic
architecture*

1. The physician can bury his mistakes, but the architect can only advise
his client to plant vines. [*New York Times Magazine*, 4 October 1953]

Wyatt, Sir Thomas (c. 1503–1542)
English poet, courtier and diplomat

1. They flee from me, that sometime did me seek
With naked foot, stalking in my chamber.

I have seen them gentle, tame, and meek,
That now are wild, and do not remember
That sometime they put themselves in danger
To take bread at my hand. ['They flee from me' (1557)]

Wycherley, William (c. 1640–1716)
English Restoration dramatist and poet

1. With faint praises one another damn. [*The Plain Dealer* (1677),
   Prologue]

Wyntoun, Andrew (c. 1350–c. 1420)
Scottish poet-historian and prior

1. Quhen Alysandyr oure King wes dede
   That Scotland led in luve and lé,
   Away wes sons of Ale and Brede,
   Of wyne and wax, of gamyn and glé,
   Oure gold wes changyd into lede.
   Chryst, born into Virgynyté,
   Succour Scotland, and remede
   That stad in perplexyté. [*Oryginale Cronykille of Scotland*]

Xenophon (c. 430–354 BC)
Greek general, historian and prose writer; disciple of Socrates

1. [The joyful cry of his soldiers after their long march (1000 miles) back
   to the Aegean from the centre of Persia]
   The sea! The sea! [*Anabasis* IV, 7]

Yeames, W. F. (1835–1918)
Russian-born British historical and subject painter

1. And when did you last see your father? [Title of painting, 1878]

Yeats, W. B. (1865–1939)
*Irish lyric poet and dramatist; editor, essayist, letter writer,
autobiographer, a founder of the Irish National Theatre Company and
senator; Nobel prize 1923*

1. I will arise and go now, and go to Innisfree,
   And a small cabin build there, of clay and wattles made:
   Nine bean-rows will I have there, a hive for the honey-bee,

And live alone in the bee-loud glade. [In the *National Observer*, 1890, 'The Lake Isle of Innisfree']

2. Tread softly because you tread on my dreams. [*The Wind Among the Reeds* (1899), 'He wishes for the Cloths of Heaven']

3. And pluck till time and times are done
The silver apples of the moon,
The golden apples of the sun. [In *The Sketch*, 1897, 'The Song of Wandering Aengus']

4. Nor law, nor duty bade me fight,
Nor public men, nor cheering crowds,
A lonely impulse of delight
Drove to this tumult in the clouds;
I balanced all, brought all to mind,
The years to come seemed waste of breath,
A waste of breath the years behind
In balance with this life, this death. [*The Wild Swans at Coole* (1919), 'An Irish Airman Foresees his Death']

5. I have met them at close of day
Coming with vivid faces
From counter or desk among grey
Eighteenth-century houses.
I have passed with a nod of the head
Or polite meaningless words,
Or have lingered awhile and said
Polite meaningless words,
And thought before I had done
Of a mocking tale or a gibe
To please a companion
Around the fire at the club,
Being certain that they and I
But lived where motley is worn:
All changed, changed utterly:
A terrible beauty is born... [*Easter, 1916* (1916), title poem]

6. Turning and turning in the widening gyre
The falcon cannot hear the falconer;
Things fall apart; the centre cannot hold;
Mere anarchy is loosed upon the world,
The blood-dimmed tide is loosed, and everywhere

The ceremony of innocence is drowned;
The best lack all conviction, while the worst
Are full of passionate intensity. [In *The Dial*, 1920, 'The Second
Coming']

7. And what rough beast, its hour come round at last,
Slouches towards Bethlehem to be born? [Ib.]

8. We make out of the quarrel with others, rhetoric; but of the quarrel
with ourselves, poetry. [*Per Amica Silentia Lunae* (1917), 'Anima
Hominis', V]

Young, Edward (1683–1765)
*English graveyard poet, tragic dramatist and satirist; clergyman and
royal chaplain*

1. Procrastination is the Thief of Time...

All men think all men Mortal, but themselves. [*Night-Thoughts on
Life, Death and Immortality* (1742–5), 'Night 1']

Zola, Emile (1840–1902)
*Leading French naturalist novelist, short-story writer and critic;
champion of Dreyfus*

1. *J'accuse.*
I accuse. [Title of open letter to the President of the Republic, 1898,
accusing those in power of making Dreyfus a scapegoat in order to
protect the real traitor]

INDEX

Alpha: I am A. and Omega . . . . BIBLE: REVELATION 1
always: A. suspect everybody . . . . DICKENS 7
am: I a. yet what I am . . . . CLARE 1
A. in Market Harborough . . . . CHESTERTON 7
America: my A.! my new-found-land . . . . DONNE 3
Americanism: McCarthyism is A. . . . . MCCARTHY 1
amor: *Omnia vincit A.* . . . . VIRGIL 8
amused: We are not a. . . . . VICTORIA 2
ammunition: Lord and pass the a. . . . . FORGY 1
angels: flights of a. sing . . . . SHAKESPEARE: HAMLET 29
where A. fear to tread . . . . POPE 5
anger: A. is a brief madness . . . . HORACE 4
angry: a. young men . . . . FEARON 1
animals: A. . . . agreeable friends . . . . ELIOT, G. 1
another: a. fine mess, ... HARDY, O. 1
a. Helen fired a. Troy . . . . DRYDEN 2
answer: a. there came none . . . . SCOTT, W. 6
ant: a.'s a centaur . . . . POUND 2
anyone: A. can stop a man's lie . . . . SENECA 2
anything: heaven knows, a. goes . . . . PORTER 1
I Can't . . . A. But Love . . . . FIELDS, G. 1
In case a. turned up . . . . DICKENS 12
Nobody tells me a. . . . . GALSWORTHY 1
angels: 'twixt air and A.' purity . . . . DONNE 1
angry: When very a. swear . . . . TWAIN 4
animals: All a. are equal, but some . . . . ORWELL 4
aphorisms: great writers of a. . . . . CANETTI 1
April: A. is the cruellest month . . . . ELIOT, T.S. 4
Aprill: Whan that A. with his shoures soote . . . . CHAUCER 1
Arabia: All the perfumes of A. . . . SHAKESPEARE: MACBETH 15
architecture: a. . . . petrified music . . . . GOETHE 1
argument: a. of the broken pane . . . . PANKHURST, E. 1
arise: I will a. and go now . . . . YEATS 1
armies: where ignorant a. clash by night . . . . ARNOLD 1
arms: of a. and the man . . . . VIRGIL 1
arrow: I shot an a. into the air . . . . LONGFELLOW 1
ars: *A. longa, vita brevis* . . . . HIPPOCRATES 1
arsenic: A. and Old Lace . . . . KESSELRING 1
art: a. . . . aspires . . . music . . . . PATER 2
A. is not a mirror . . . . MAYAKOVSKY 1
A. . . . makes things visible . . . . KLEE 1
Fine a . . . .hand, the head and . . . . RUSKIN 3
artful: The a. Dodger . . . . DICKENS 4

artist: a. . . . his wife starve . . . . SHAW 4
  a. must be in his work . . . . FLAUBERT 2
  grant the a. his subject . . . . JAMES , H. 1
artists: Great a. have no country . . . . MUSSET 1
ask: A., and it shall be given . . . . BIBLE: MATTHEW 14
Assyrian: A. came down like . . . . BYRON 2
atom: no evil in the a. . . . . STEVENSON, A. 1
author: a. . . . his own books . . . . DISRAELI 5
avarice: beyond the dreams of a. . . . . MOORE, E. 2
ave: *ave atque vale* . . . . CATULLUS 6
axe: a.'s edge did try . . . . MARVELL 1
babes: Out of the mouth of b. . . . . BIBLE: PSALMS 1
Babylon: B. in all its desolation . . . . DAVIES, S. 1
  by the rivers of B. . . . . BIBLE: PSALMS 6
bachelors: reasons for b. to go out . . . . ELIOT, G. 3
backs: With our b. to the wall . . . . HAIG 1
backyard: won't look further . . . b. . . . . GARLAND 2
ballot: b. stronger than the bullet . . . . LINCOLN 2
bang: Not with a b. but . . . . ELIOT, T.S. 5
bank: cried all the way . . . b. . . . . LIBERACE 1
  man who broke the b. . . . . GILBERT 1
Barkis: B. is willin' . . . . DICKENS 11
bathroom: can't feel fierce . . . in a b. . . . . LINKLATER 1
be: To b. or not to be . . . . SHAKESPEARE: HAMLET 14
  What will b., shall be . . . . MARLOWE 3
bear: B. of Very Little Brain . . . . MILNE 4
  Exit, pursued by a b. . . . . SHAKESPEARE: WINTER'S 1
  gave pain to the b. . . . . MACAULAY 4
  funny/How a b. like honey . . . . MILNE 3
beard: built their nests in my b. . . . . LEAR 1
beast: what rough b. . . . . YEATS 7
beastie: cowrin, tim'rous b. . . . . BURNS 3
beat: b. the iron while it is hot . . . . DRYDEN 1
  really a b. generation . . . . KEROUAC 1
beauty: B. in distress is much . . . . BURKE 1
  B. . . . . eye of the beholder . . . . HUNGERFORD 1
  B. is no quality in things . . . . HUME 3
  B. is truth, truth b. . . . . KEATS 4
  terrible, 4. is born . . . . YEATS 5
  thing of b. is a joy . . . . KEATS 2
beautiful: Oh what a b. mornin' . . . . HAMMERSTEIN 1
  Everything has its b. . . . . CONFUCIUS 2
  most, 2. things . . . most useless . . . . RUSKIN 1

She walks in b. like the . . . . BYRON 3
What a b. Pussy you are . . . . LEAR 6
when a woman isn't b., people say . . . . . CHEKHOV 2
bed: And so to b. . . . . PEPYS 1
my second best b. . . . . SHAKESPEARE: WILL 1
bedfellows: Misery . . . strange b. . . SHAKESPEARE: TEMPEST 2
bedside: b. manner . . . . PUNCH 4
begin: B. at the beginning . . . . CARROLL 11
because: B. it is there . . . . MALLORY 1
beginning: In my b. is my end . . . . ELIOT, T.S. 8
In the b. . . . . BIBLE: GENESIS 1
In the b. was the Word . . . . BIBLE: JOHN 1
believe: B. it or not . . . . RIPLEY 1
bell: I shall b. the cat . . . . DOUGLAS, EARL 1
for whom the b. tolls . . . . DONNE 6
Who will b. the cat? . . . . DESCHAMPS 1
bend: I b. and do not break . . . . FONTAINE 1
Berliner: *Ich bin ein B.* . . . . KENNEDY, J.F. 2
best: b. of all possible worlds . . . . VOLTAIRE 1
It was the b. of times . . . . DICKENS 20
best-seller: b. . . . gilded tomb . . . . SMITH, L. 1
betray: guts to b. my country . . . . FORSTER 2
better: b./For being a little bad . . . SHAKESPEARE: MEASURE 1
b. man than I am, Gunga Din . . . . KIPLING 6
I see the b. way . . . . OVID 3
You are no b. than . . . . BEAUMONT 1
beware: B. of the dog . . . . PETRONIUS 1
B. the ides of March . . . . . SHAKESPEARE: JULIUS CAESAR 1
bewitched: B., Bothered and Bewildered . . . . HART 1
big: b. lie more easily than . . . . HITLER 1
bigger: The b. they come . . . . FITZSIMMONS 1
biography: art of B./is different . . . . BENTLEY, E. 1
no history, only b. . . . . EMERSON 1
birds: And no b. sing . . . . KEATS 3
bisier: seemed b. than he was . . . . CHAUCER 4
bite: *b.* some . . . generals . . . . GEORGE II 1
black: here in b. and white . . . . JONSON 1
so long as it's b., ... FORD, H. 2
That old b. magic has me . . . . MERCER 1
bless: God b. us every one! . . . . DICKENS 9
bleak: In the b. mid-winter . . . . ROSSETTI, C. 1
blessed: B. are the poor in . . . . BIBLE: MATTHEW 3
more b. to give than . . . . BIBLE: ACTS 3

brass: become as sounding b. . . . . BIBLE: I CORINTHIANS 2
Brazil: B. – where the nuts come from . . . . THOMAS, B. 1
brave: None but the b. . . . . DRYDEN 4
braw: b. bricht moonlicht nicht . . . . LAUDER 1
breach: Once more into the b. . . . . . SHAKESPEARE: HENRY V 2
bread: b. and circuses . . . . JUVENAL 4
  Cast thy b. upon the waters . . . . BIBLE: ECCLESIASTES 3
  Man doth not live by b. only . . . . BIBLE: DEUTERONOMY 1
bread-sauce: b. of the happy ending . . . . JAMES, H. 3
brevity: B. is the soul of wit . . . . . . SHAKESPEARE: HAMLET 9
bridge: And keep the b. with me? . . . . MACAULAY 5
brier-patch: Bred and bawn in a b. . . . . HARRIS 2
brigade: Forward the Light B. . . . . TENNYSON 9
brillig: 'Twas b, and the slithy toves . . . . CARROLL 12
bristles: my skin b. . . . . HOUSMAN 2
Britannia: B., rule the waves; . . . . THOMSON, J. 1
British: Dirty B. coaster with . . . . MASEFIELD 2
Britons: B. were only natives . . . . SELLAR & YEATMAN 2
brother: Am I not a man and a b. . . . . WEDGWOOD 1
  Big B. is watching you . . . . ORWELL 5
bruised: be b. in a new place . . . . IRVING 2
Brute: Et tu B.? . . . . CAESAR 4
Brutus: You too, Brutus? . . . . CAESAR 4
buck: b. stops here . . . . TRUMAN 3
bugger: B. Bognor! . . . . GEORGE V 1
burn: B. books . . . b. people too . . . . HEINE 2
burning: boy stood on the b. deck . . . . HEMANS 1
  Keep the home fires b. . . . . FORD, L. 1
business: B. as usual . . . . CHURCHILL 2
  b. of America is b. COOLIDGE 1
  No b. before breakfast . . . . THACKERAY 4
butter: little bit of b. to my bread . . . . MILNE 1
buttered: always on the b. side . . . . PAYN 1
butterfly: float like a b., sting . . . . ALI 1
Byron: b. is dead . . . . CARLYLE, J. 1
cabbage: c. . . . college education . . . . TWAIN 3
cabbages: Of c. and kings . . . . CARROLL 13
Cain: Lord set a mark upon C. . . . . BIBLE: GENESIS 6
cake: Let them eat c. . . . . MARIE-ANTOINETTE 1
Caledonia: O, C.! stern and wild . . . . SCOTT, W. 2
camel: c. . . . eye of a needle . . . . BIBLE: MARK 4
  take my c., dear . . . . MACAULAY, R. 1
camera: I am a c. ISHERWOOD 1

Train up a c. . . . . BIBLE: PROVERBS 4
unto us a c. is born . . . . BIBLE: ISAIAH 4
childhood: Old age is a second c. . . . . ARISTOPHANES 2
children: C. are dumb to say . . . . GRAVES 1
c. at play are not playing . . . . MONTAIGNE 2
C. . . . rarely forgive them . . . . WILDE 7
Far too good to waste on c. . . . . SHAW 16
Suffer the little c. . . . . BIBLE: MARK 3
Christ: civil wars as the kingdom of C. . . . . MONTESQUIEU 3
Christendom: wisest fool in C. . . . . HENRI IV 2
Christianity: C. . . . most materialistic . . . . TEMPLE 1
Christmas: C. comes but once a year . . . . TUSSER 2
C. Day in the Workhouse . . . . SIMS 1
I'm dreaming of a white C. . . . . BERLIN 1
I'm walking backwards till C. . . . . MILLIGAN 1
. . . shopping days to C. . . . . SELFRIDGE 2
Twas the night before C. . . . . MOORE, C. 1
church: Stands the C. clock . . . . BROOKE 1
cigar: a good, five-cent c. . . . . MARSHALL, T. 1
cigarette: c. is the perfect type . . . . WILDE 4
cinema: C. is truth 24 times . . . . GODARD 1
citizen: a c. of the world . . . . DIOGENES 1
city: C. is of Night but not . . . . THOMSON, J. 1
no mean c. . . . . BIBLE: ACTS 4
clanjamfrie: droun/the haill c. . . . . MACDIARMID 2
classicism: C. I call health . . . . GOETHE 2
cleanliness: C. is next to godliness . . . . WESLEY 1
clenched: shake hands with a c. fist . . . . GANDHI, I. 1
Cloudcuckooland: What do you think of C.? . . . ARISTOPHANES 1
club: c. . . . me as a member . . . . MARX, G. 4
coach: drive a c. . . . through the Act . . . . RICE, S. 1
coeur: *Le c. a ses raisons* . . . . PASCAL 3
coffee: if this is c., I want tea . . . . PUNCH 6
coffin: silver plate on a c. . . . . O'CONNELL 1
Cogito: *C. ergo sum* . . . . DESCARTES 1
cold war: in the midst of a c.w. . . . . BARUCH 1
colonnade: whispering sound of the cool c. . . . . . COWPER 3
colour: any c. – so long as it's black, ... FORD, H. 2
colours: All c. will agree in the dark . . . . BACON 8
coat of many c. . . . . BIBLE: GENESIS 9
come: C. up and see me sometime . . . . WEST 1
comedy: C. . . . society protecting . . . . PRIESTLEY 1
comfortable: slip into something more c. . . . . HARLOW 1

comfortably: Are you sitting c.? . . . . LANG, J. 1
common sense: C. is the best distributed . . . . DESCARTES 2
  Science . . . organized c. . . . . HUXLEY 1
communism: C. . . . good idea but it . . . . ROGERS, W. 1
  C. with a human face . . . . DUBCEK 1
  spectre of C. . . . . MARX & ENGELS 1
communist: What is a c.? . . . . ELLIOTT, E. 1
community: any c. has a right . . . . MILL 2
company: give me your bill of c. . . . . SWIFT 4
compare: Shall I c. thee . . . . SHAKESPEARE: SONNETS 1
comparisons: She, and c. are odious . . . . DONNE 2
compassion: C. is not a sloppy . . . . KINNOCK 1
complain: To c. of the age . . . . BURKE 2
conceited: pity for c. people . . . . ELIOT, G. 2
concentrates: c. his mind wonderfully . . . . JOHNSON, S. 27
connect: Only c.! . . . . FORSTER 1
conquered: I came, I saw, I c. . . . . CAESAR 2
conquering: See, the c. hero . . . . MORELL 1
conscience: C. . . . internal perception . . . . FREUD 1
  C. is the inner voice . . . . MENCKEN 2
  Science without c. is . . . . MONTAIGNE 6
consumer: In a c. society . . . . ILLICH 1
contradict: Do I c. myself? . . . . WHITMAN 2
convictions: cloud of comforting c. . . . . RUSSELL 1
cooks: as c. go she went . . . . SAKI 2
correlative: objective c. . . . . ELIOT, T.S. 10
corridors: c. of power . . . . SNOW 1
corruption: C. . . . infallible symptom . . . . GIBBON, E. 2
counted: I c. them all out and . . . . HANRAHAN 1
country: ask not what your c. . . . . KENNEDY, J.F. 1
  c. in town . . . . MARTIAL 3
  c. . . . kind of healthy grave . . . . SMITH SY. 2
  c. . . . with only one sauce . . . . TALLEYRAND 1
  fit c. for heroes to live in . . . . LLOYD GEORGE 1
  know . . . his own c. . . . abroad . . . . STERNE 4
  our c., right or wrong . . . . DECATUR 1
  die for one's c. . . . . HORACE 10
  my c. is the world . . . . PAINE 2
  never let my c. die for me . . . . KINNOCK 2
  nothing good . . . in the c. . . . . HAZLITT 3
  unmapped c. within us, ... ELIOT, G. 6
course: c. of true love never . . . . SHAKESPEARE: MIDSUMMER 1
cow: till the c. comes home . . . . BEAUMONT 3

coward: c. does it with a kiss . . . . WILDE 10
cowards: All men would be c. . . . . ROCHESTER 1
  C. die many times . . . . . . SHAKESPEARE: JULIUS CAESAR 5
cradle: Out of the c. endlessly . . . . WHITMAN 3
creari: *Nil posse c./De nilo* . . . . LUCRETIUS 1
creditors: c. have better memories . . . . FRANKLIN 5
credulity: C. is the man's weakness . . . . LAMB, C. 5
crème: c. de la c. . . . . SPARK 2
cricket: c. as organized loafing . . . . TEMPLE 2
crimes: c., follies and misfortunes . . . . GIBBON, E. 1
critics: best c. private people . . . . WOOLF 3
cruel: c. . . . to be kind . . . . SHAKESPEARE: HAMLET 20
cuckoo: did they produce? the c. clock . . . . WELLES 1
Cui: *C. bono?* . . . . CICERO 5
cultiver: *faut c. notre jardin* . . . . VOLTAIRE 3
culture: c. being pursuit . . . perfection . . . . ARNOLD 2
  c. . . . safety-catch off my Browning . . . . JOHST 1
cup: my c. runneth over . . . . BIBLE: PSALMS 2
cups: the c. that cheer . . . . COWPER 1
curfew: C. tolls the knell of . . . . GRAY 2
curious: the c. incident of the dog . . . . DOYLE 4
curiouser: C. and C.! cried Alice . . . . CARROLL 2
currency: debasing the moral c. . . . . ELIOT, G. 7
custom: C. . . . great guide . . . . HUME 1
  C./More honour'd in the breach . . SHAKESPEARE: HAMLET 5
customer: c. is always right . . . . SELFRIDGE 1
cymbal: brass, or a tinkling c. . . . . . . BIBLE: I CORINTHIANS 2
daddy: D., daddy, you bastard . . . . PLATH 2
daffodils: host of golden d. . . . . WORDSWORTH, W. 8
  we saw a few d. . . . . WORDSWORTH, D. 1
damned: just one d. thing after . . . . HUBBARD 1
dance: can't act, can't sing, can d. . . . . ANON. 1
  men must walk . . . before they d. . . . . POPE 10
danced: d. by the light of the moon . . . . LEAR 7
  girl, who's d. with the Prince . . . . FARJEON 1
dancing: d. in the streets of Raith tonight . . . . ANON. 3
  trouble with nude dancing is . . . . HELPMAN 1
danger: Out of this nettle, d. . . . . SHAKESPEARE: HENRY IV 1
dangerous: D. Dan McGrew . . . . SERVICE 1
dangerously: *living d.* . . . . NIETZSCHE 3
dappled: Glory . . . for d. things . . . . HOPKINS 1
dark: d. night of the soul . . . . FITZGERALD, F.S. 1
  d. night of the soul . . . . JOHN OF THE CROSS 1

great leap in the d. . . . . HOBBES 3
darksome: along the d. road . . . . CATULLUS 1
darling: d. buds of May . . . . SHAKESPEARE: SONNETS 1
daughter: your d. on the stage . . . . COWARD 3
dawn: Rosy-fingered d. . . . . HOMER 1
days: d. are as grass . . . . BIBLE: PSALMS 4
d. darken round me . . . . TENNYSON 11
d. of our years . . . . BIBLE: PSALMS 3
dead: Let the d. bury . . . . BIBLE: MATTHEW 16
death: any man's d. diminishes . . . . DONNE 6
balance with this life, this d. . . . . YEATS 4
come away d. . . . . SHAKESPEARE: TWELFTH 3
d. and taxes . . . . FRANKLIN 6
d., the destroyer of worlds . . . . BHAGAVADGITA 1
d., where is thy sting . . . . BIBLE: I CORINTHIANS 4
I prepare as though for d. . . . . MANSFIELD 1
Into the valley of D. rode . . . . TENNYSON 9
It is but D. who comes at last . . . . SCOTT, W. 3
parting . . . foretaste of d. . . . . SCHOPENHAUER 1
valley of the shadow of d. . . . . BIBLE: PSALMS 2
deceived: d. by what one loves . . . . MOLIERE 1
deeds: Our d. still travel with us . . . . ELIOT, G. 5
defend: d. your right to say it . . . . VOLTAIRE 5
Delenda: *D. est Carthago* . . . . CATO 1
delight: Energy is Eternal D. . . . . BLAKE 2
Teach us D. in simple things . . . . KIPLING 11
déluge: *Après nous le d.* . . . . POMPADOUR 1
democracy: d. . . . government by discussion . . . . ATTLEE 1
safe for d. . . . . WILSON, W. 1
depends: It all d. on what you mean . . . . JOAD 1
so much d./ upon . . . . WILLIAMS, W.C. 1
depravity: total d. of inanimate . . . . HAMILTON 1
desperate: d. disease requires a . . . . FAWKES 1
desperation: lives of quiet d. . . . . THOREAU 1
despond: name of the slough was D. . . . . BUNYAN 1
destroy: whom God wished to d. . . . . EURIPIDES 1
devil: and shame the d.! . . . . SHAKESPEARE: HENRY IV 2
d. . . . all the good tunes . . . . HILL, R. 1
d. can cite Scripture . . . . . . SHAKESPEARE: MERCHANT 2
devilish: most d. thing is 8 . . . . FLEMING 2
diamonds: D. are Girl's Best Friend . . . . ROBIN 1
diapason: d. closing full in Man . . . . DRYDEN 12
die: d. is cast . . . . CAESAR 3

either do, or d. . . . . FLETCHER 2
for these who d. as cattle . . . . OWEN 2
It's not that I'm afraid to d. . . . . ALLEN 1
those about to d. salute thee . . . . SUETONIUS 2
dies: matters not how a man d. . . . . JOHNSON, S. 22
Dieu: *D. et mon droit* . . . . RICHARD I 1
digressions: D. are the sunshine . . . . STERNE 2
directions: rode madly off in all d. . . . . LEACOCK 1
discovery: d. of a new dish . . . . . . BRILLAT-SAVARIN 1
disguise: naked is the best d. . . . . CONGREVE 2
disorder: sweet d. in the dresse . . . . HERRICK 1
distance: d. lends enchantment . . . . CAMPBELL, T. 1
distrust: against despots . . . D. . . . . DEMOSTHENES 1
divinity: d. that shapes our ends . . . SHAKESPEARE: HAMLET 27
doctrine: the 'Frank Sinatra d.' . . . . GERASIMOV 1
dodger: The artful D. DICKENS 4
Dong: D. with the Luminous Nose . . . . LEAR 4
door: I stand at the d. . . . . BIBLE: REVELATION 2
double: D., d. toil and trouble . . . SHAKESPEARE: MACBETH 10
doublethink: *D.* . . . . ORWELL 8
doubt: no d. in this book . . . . KORAN 1
drama: d. . . . . dull bits cut out . . . . HITCHCOCK 1
drawers: d. of water . . . . BIBLE: JOSHUA 1
drawling: D., Stretching and Fainting . . . . CARROLL 8
dream: d. within a dream . . . . POE 2
I have a d. . . . . KING 1
dressed: all d. up and no place . . . . BURT 1
drink: a little in d., but . . . . STEELE 1
D. no longer water . . . . BIBLE: TIMOTHY 2
D. to me only with thine eyes . . . . JONSON 2
Nor any drop to d. . . . . COLERIDGE 2
drinking: D. . . . . soldier's pleasure . . . . DRYDEN 5
Now there must be d. . . . . HORACE 8
Work is the curse of the d. classes . . . . WILDE 12
drunk: I'm not so think as you d. . . . . SQUIRE 1
Man . . . must get d. BYRON 8
drunkard: The rolling English d. . . . . CHESTERTON 6
drunkeness: d. . . . supremely valid human . . . . . . JAMES, W. 1
ducat: Dead, for a d. . . . . SHAKESPEARE: HAMLET 19
duchess: my last D. . . . . BROWNING, R. 2
dulce: *D. bellum inexpertis* . . . . ERASMUS 2
D. et decorum est . . . . HORACE 10
dull: d. prospect of a distant good . . . . DRYDEN 10

dumplings: emperor, and I want d. . . . . FERDINAND I 1
dunces: d. are all in confederacy . . . . SWIFT 1
Dunfermline: The king sits in D. town . . . . BALLADS 2
dungeon: d. . . . one's own heart . . . . HAWTHORNE 1
dwarfs: d. trying to grill a whale . . . . PRIESTLEY 2
dying: d. as fast as my enemies . . . . HUME 4
   D. is an art . . . . PLATH 3
   unconscionable time d. . . . . CHARLES II 2
earlier: Here's one I made e. . . . . TRACE 1
early: E. to bed and e. to rise . . . . FRANKLIN 4
   E. to rise and e. to bed . . . dead . . . . THURBER 2
earnest: not die in sport but in e. . . . . BION 1
earth: E. has not anything to show . . . WORDSWORTH, W. 6
   E., thou bonnie broukit bairn . . . . MACDIARMID 1
   feel the e. move . . . . HEMINGWAY 1
   salt of the e. . . . . BIBLE: MATTHEW 4
   shall inherit the e. . . . . BIBLE: MATTHEW 3
east: Oh, E. is East and . . . . KIPLING 5
eat: e. to live, not live . . . . MOLIERE 2
Educ: E.: during the holidays . . . . SITWELL 1
egg: From the e. . . . to the apples . . . . HORACE 11
egotist: E.: a person of low taste . . . . BIERCE 1
eightfold: E. Path . . . Right view . . . . BUDDHA 1
either: E. he's dead or my watch . . . . MARX, G. 1
elementary: 'E.' said he . . . . DOYLE 3
Emperor: But the E. has nothing on at all! . . . . . . ANDERSEN 2
   Only e. . . . e. of ice-cream . . . . STEVENS 1
encourager: *pour e. les autres* . . . . VOLTAIRE 2
encyclopaedia: a whole E. behind . . . . LAMB, C. 2
end: e. of ane old song . . . . OGILVY 1
endeavour: To e. to forget anyone . . . . LA BRUYERE 2
endlich: *E. fortissimo!* . . . . MAHLER 1
Endlösung: *E. der Judenfrage* . . . . GOEBBELS 1
enemy: better class of e. . . . . MILLIGAN 2
energy: dissipation of e. begin . . . . KELVIN 1
   E. is Eternal Delight . . . . BLAKE 2
enfant: I am the *e. terrible* . . . . BUTLER 1
England: E. EXPECTS EVERY MAN . . . . NELSON 1
   E. is not all the world . . . . MARY, QUEEN OF SCOTS 1
   E. . . . little . . . inferior to the Scotch . . . . NORTH 1
   E. . . . nation of shopkeepers . . . . NAPOLEON I 1
   Oh, to be in E. . . . . BROWNING, R. 3
   road that leads him to E. . . . . JOHNSON, S. 18

fight: I have fought a good f. . . . . BIBLE: II TIMOTHY 1
we shall f. on the beaches . . . . CHURCHILL 4
figures: we Phantom F. come and go . . . . . . FITZGERALD, E. 4
final: F. Solution . . . . GOEBBELS 1
finality: F. . . . language of politics . . . . DISRAELI 3
finest: This was their f. hour . . . . CHURCHILL 5
finger: Moving F. writes: and, ... FITZGERALD, E. 5
pain in our little f. gives . . . . HAZLITT 1
fishers: F. of men . . . . BIBLE: MATTHEW 2
five: fetch a child of f. . . . . MARX, G. 2
flag: keep the red f. flying here . . . . CONNELL 1
flattery: Imitation . . . form of f. . . . . COLTON 2
flautists: Of all musicians, f. . . . . JENNINGS 1
fleas: flea/Hath smaller f. . . . . SWIFT 6
fled: I f. Him, down, ... THOMPSON, F. 1
flee: They f. from me . . . . WYATT 1
flesh: f. is weak . . . . BIBLE: MATTHEW 31
pound of f. . . . . SHAKESPEARE: MERCHANT 6
thorn in the f. . . . . BIBLE: II CORINTHIANS 2
too, too solid f. . . . . SHAKESPEARE: HAMLET 2
Word was made f. . . . . BIBLE: LUKE 2
flies: as f. to wanton boys . . . SHAKESPEARE: KING LEAR 4
flowers: F. of the Forest are a' . . . . ELLIOT, J. 1
f. that bloom in the spring . . . . GILBERT 9
Say it with f. . . . . O'KEEFE 1
follies: f. which a man regrets . . . . ROWLAND 1
folly: a fool returneth to his f. . . . . . BIBLE: PROVERBS 5
'Tis f. to be wise . . . . GRAY 1
food: child is . . . wholesome f. . . . . SWIFT 5
fool: f. alone on a great mountain . . . . KILVERT 2
If the f. persist . . . . BLAKE 4
foolish: never said a f. thing . . . . ROCHESTER 2
fools: all the f. in town on our side . . . . TWAIN 2
F. rush in . . . . POPE 5
f., who came to scoff . . . . GOLDSMITH 3
what f. these mortals be . . . . SHAKESPEARE: MIDSUMMER 3
football: f. . . . life and death . . . . SHANKLY 1
force: f. that through the green fuse . . . . . . THOMAS, D. 1
May the F. be with you . . . . LUCAS 1
foreign: corner of a f. field . . . . BROOKE 2
forget: never f. a face but I'll . . . . MARX, G. 3
you should f. and smile . . . . ROSSETTI, C. 4
forgets: dies in pain and he f. to live . . . . LA BRUYERE 1

serve G. and mammon . . . . BIBLE: MATTHEW 9
the Cabots talk only to G. . . . . BOSSIDY 1
What G. hath wrought . . . . MORSE 1
gods: whether there are g., but . . . . . . DIOGENES 2
whom the g. love dies young . . . . MENANDER 1
gold: All that glisters is not g. . . SHAKESPEARE: MERCHANT 4
g., and frankincense, and . . . . BIBLE: MATTHEW 1
travell'd in the realms of g. . . . . KEATS 1
Water is best. But g. . . . . PINDAR 1
golden: g. age never was . . . . FRANKLIN 2
g. apples of the sun . . . . YEATS 3
g. rule is . . . no g. rules . . . . SHAW 8
G. slumbers kiss your eyes . . . . DEKKER 1
good: g. is the beautiful . . . . PLATO 2
greatest g. . . . . CICERO 1
I never saw any g. that . . . . DRYDEN 8
goodbye: G. to All That . . . . GRAVES 2
government: Conservative g. . . . hypocrisy . . DISRAELI 2
G. . . . necessary evil . . . . PAINE 1
the g. shall be upon his . . . . BIBLE: ISAIAH 4
grace: G. under pressure . . . . HEMINGWAY 2
grow old with a good g. . . . . STEELE 2
grammer: why care for g. . . . . WARD, A. 4
grammere: G., that grounde . . . . LANGLAND 2
grave: g.'s a fine and private place . . . . . MARVELL 2
g., where is thy victory . . . . BIBLE: I CORINTHIANS 4
greatest: g. happiness for the g. numbers . . . . HUTCHESON 1
greatness: g. thrust upon them . . . SHAKESPEARE: TWELFTH 5
greedy: G. for others' possessions . . . . SALLUST 1
Greek: G.: it stamps a man . . . . SHAW 12
it was G. to me . . . . SHAKESPEARE: JULIUS CAESAR 4
Greeks: fear the G. . . . bring gifts . . . . VIRGIL 3
The G. had a Word for It . . . . AKINS 1
grief: g. . . . develops . . . the mind . . . . . . PROUST 3
grin: ending with the g. which remained . . . . CARROLL 4
grind: mills of God g. slowly . . . . LOGAU 1
gruntled: far from being g. . . . . WODEHOUSE 4
guard: who will g. the guards . . . . JUVENAL 2
gude: There's a g. time coming . . . . SCOTT, W. 7
guilty: ten g. persons escape . . . . BLACKSTONE 1
guitar: You have a blue g. . . . . STEVENS 2
gunpowder: G., Printing and the . . . . CARLYLE 8
gutter: We are all in the g. . . . . WILDE 5

habit: H. . . . the test of truth . . . . CRABBE 2
hail: H. to the Chief who . . . . SCOTT, W. 5
half: I don't know which h. . . . . LEVERHULME 1
hand: h. that rocks the cradle . . . . WALLACE 1
   thy left h. know what . . . . BIBLE: MATTHEW 7
hanget: he was h. . . . . BRAXFIELD 2
hanging: be nane the waur o' a h. . . . . BRAXFIELD 1
   h. is too good for him . . . . BUNYAN 2
happiness: object . . . h. of the whole . . . . PLATO 5
happy: All h. families resemble one . . . . TOLSTOY 1
   Call no man h. . . . only lucky . . . . SOLON 1
harder: the h. they fall . . . . FITZSIMMONS 1
harp: h. that once through Tara's . . . . MOORE, T. 1
has beens: 'one of the *h.*' . . . . HONE 1
hasten: H. slowly . . . . SUETONIUS 1
hate: h. the man you have hurt . . . . TACITUS 2
   I h. and I love . . . . CATULLUS 5
head: anointest my h. with oil . . . . . . BIBLE: PSALMS 2
   Little Johnny-H.-In-Air! . . . . HOFFMANN, H. 2
   one small h. could carry all . . . . GOLDSMITH 4
   show my h. to the people . . . . DANTON 1
heads: H. I win, tails you lose . . . . CROKER 1
healthy: h. mind in a h. body . . . . JUVENAL 5
heard: You ain't h. nothin' yet . . . . JOLSON 1
heart: h. grown cold, a head grown gray . . . . SHELLEY 7
   h. has its reasons . . . . PASCAL 3
   h. is like a singing bird . . . . ROSSETTI, C. 1
   h. is through his stomach . . . . FERN 1
   My h.'s in the Highlands . . . . BURNS 10
   My h. is a lonely hunter . . . . MACLEOD 1
   my h. upon my sleeve . . . . SHAKESPEARE: OTHELLO 1
   What comes from the h., goes . . . . COLERIDGE 8
   Whatever your h. clings to . . . . LUTHER 1
   when the human h. is in the soup . . . . . . WODEHOUSE 5
hearts: Two h. that beat as one . . . . LOVELL 1
   wore at their h. the fire's centre . . . . SPENDER 1
heat: h., get out of the kitchen . . . . TRUMAN 1
heaven: All this and h. too . . . . HENRY, M. 1
   H. in a Wild Flower . . . . BLAKE 9
   more things in h. and earth . . . . . . SHAKESPEARE: HAMLET 7
   Puts all H. in a Rage . . . . BLAKE 9
heffalump: decided to catch a H. . . . . MILNE 5
help: gods h. those who help themselves . . . . AESOP 1

indifferent: nothing human i. to me . . . . TERENCE 2
  worst sin . . . to be i. . . . . SHAW 2
industry: Captains of i. CARLYLE 10
  I. without art is brutality . . . . RUSKIN 6
infant: I wish I'd been a mixed i. . . . . BEHAN 2
  i. phenomenon . . . . DICKENS 5
infinity: Hold I. in the palm . . . . BLAKE 9
Indian: only good I. is a dead I. . . . . SHERIDAN, P. 1
injury: i. is much sooner forgotten . . . . CHESTERFIELD 2
innocent: than one i. suffer . . . . BLACKSTONE 1
insult: adding i. to injuries . . . . MOORE, E. 1
intellect: feather to tickle the i. . . . . LAMB, C. 6
intellectuals: the treachery of the i. . . . . BENDA 1
intelligence: arresting the human i. . . . . LEACOCK 2
interpretation: I. . . . revenge . . . intellect . . . . SONTAG 1
invents: Everyone one i. is true . . . . FLAUBERT 1
invisible: no i. means of support . . . . BUCHAN 1
Ireland: I. is the old sow . . . . JOYCE 1
iron: i. hand in a velvet glove . . . . CHARLES V 1
Ishmael: Call me I. MELVILLE 1
island: Look stranger on this i. now . . . . AUDEN 2
  No man is an I. . . . . DONNE 6
isle: i. is full of noises . . . . SHAKESPEARE: TEMPEST 3
jacket: I could thresh his old j. . . . . COWPER 4
jailer: j. . . . one's self . . . . HAWTHORNE 1
jaw: j.-j. is better than to war-war . . . . CHURCHILL 8
Jesus: J. wept . . . . BIBLE: JOHN 8
jeux: *j. d'enfants ne sont pas j.* . . . . MONTAIGNE 2
Jew: Hath not a J. eyes? . . . . . SHAKESPEARE: MERCHANT 5
Jews: To choose / the J. EWER 1
jingo: by j. if we do . . . . HUNT, G. W. 1
joke: dirty j. . . . mental rebellion . . . . ORWELL 2
journey: Halfway through the j. . . . . DANTE 1
joy: J. shall be in heaven . . . . BIBLE: LUKE 7
  laugh with the voice of j. . . . . BLAKE 1
  not a j. the world can give . . . . BYRON 4
judge: J. not . . . . BIBLE: MATTHEW 12
justice: j. . . . be seen to be done . . . . HEWART 1
  'J.' was done . . . with Tess . . . . HARDY, T. 3
  J. with Mercy . . . . MILTON 13
justifies: end j. the means . . . . BUSENBAUM 1
keeper: Am I my brother's k.? . . . . BIBLE: GENESIS 5
kill: K. everyone . . . a god . . . . ROSTAND 2

Love . . . l. unto itself . . . . BOETHIUS 1
Wherever L. ends, Tyranny begins . . . . LOCKE 2
laws: L. . . . made to be broken . . . . NORTH 3
lean: l. and hungry look . . . . SHAKESPEARE: JULIUS CAESAR 3
learn: we l. by doing . . . . ARISTOTLE 3
learning: l. how to die . . . . DA VINCI 1
little l. is a dangerous . . . . POPE 1
leaves: L. on Trees the Race of Man . . . . HOMER 4
leaving: L. is dying a little . . . . HARAUCOURT 1
Legion: My name is L. . . . . BIBLE: MARK 1
legislator: people is the true l. . . . . BURKE 7
less: l. one has to do, the l. time . . . . CHESTERFIELD 6
l. is more . . . . MIES van der ROHE 1
letter: the l. killeth . . . . BIBLE: II CORINTH 1
levellers: Your l. wish to level *down* . . . . . . JOHNSON, S. 19
lexicographer: L. . . . a harmless drudge . . . . . . JOHNSON, S. 4
lexicography: lost in l. . . . . JOHNSON, S. 2
liberty: I a man and lackith l. . . . . JAMES I 1
L. . . . limited . . . . BURKE 3
l. . . . must be rationed . . . . LENIN 2
l. or give me death! . . . . HENRY, P. 1
l.! what crimes are committed . . . . ROLAND 1
L. . . . whatever the laws permit . . . . MONTESQUIEU 20
life, l. and the pursuit . . . . JEFFERSON 1
mountain nymph, sweet L. . . . . MILTON 4
tree of l. must be refreshed . . . . JEFFERSON 2
licence: freedom of poetic l. . . . . CICERO 3
lie: I cannot tell a l. . . . . WASHINGTON 1
l. for the good of the State . . . . PLATO 4
Take the saving l. IBSEN 3
lies: l., damned l. and statistics . . . . DISRAELI 7
life: if l. had a second edition . . . . CLARE 2
l. . . . opening a tin of sardines . . . . BENNETT 1
L. is short . . . . HIPPOCRATES 1
L. is too short to stuff . . . . CONRAN 1
l. may perfect be . . . . JONSON 5
l.'s rich pageant . . . . MARSHALL, A. 1
L. . . . to none freehold . . . . LUCRETIUS 4
L. . . . too short . . . German . . . . PORSON 1
L. without industry is guilt . . . . RUSKIN 6
a man lay down his l. . . . . BIBLE: JOHN 11
no one loses any other l. but this . . . . AURELIUS 1
light: dusk with a l. behind her . . . . GILBERT 1

let there be l. . . . . BIBLE: GENESIS 1
What l. through yonder window . . . SHAKESPEARE: ROMEO 2
like: L. cures like . . . . HAHNEMANN 1
lilies: Consider the l. . . . . BIBLE: MATTHEW 10
limelight: He's always backing into the l. . . . . BERNERS 1
lion: Early Christian gets the fattest l. . . . . SAKI 1
lions: l. led by donkeys . . . . HOFFMANN, M. 1
liquefaction: sweetly flowes/That l. . . . . HERRICK 3
literature: Bible is l., not dogma . . . . . . SANTAYANA 3
cultivate l. upon . . . oatmeal . . . . SMITH, SY. 1
L. is news that STAYS . . . . POUND 4
little: l. things . . . most important . . . . DOYLE 1
live: l. and learn but not . . . . POMFRET 1
l. with you – nor without . . . . MARTIAL 2
Lloyd George: L. knew my father . . . . . . ROBERTS 1
London: L. . . . the flower of cities . . . . . . DUNBAR 2
L. particular . . . a fog . . . . DICKENS 17
When a man is tired of L. . . . . JOHNSON, S. 28
lone: I am a l. lorn creetur . . . . DICKENS 10
lonesome: on a l. road /Doth walk . . . . . . COLERIDGE 3
look: L. on my works, ye Mighty . . . . . . SHELLEY 4
looking: Here's l. at you, kid . . . . BOGART 2
Lord: L. hath taken away . . . . BIBLE: JOB 1
Prepare ye the way of the L. . . . . . BIBLE: ISAIAH 7
lost: you see is l. let it be l. . . . . CATULLUS 3
love: be a-waggle with L. . . . . LAWRENCE 1
do not l. you Dr Fell . . . . BROWN 1
For l. that time was not . . . . MALORY 2
Greater l. hath no man . . . . BIBLE: JOHN 11
How do I l. thee? . . . . BROWNING, E. B. 2
I lo'e l./ wi' a scunner in't . . . . . . MACDIARMID 7
L. as it exists in society . . . . CHAMFORT 1
L. ceases to be a pleasure . . . . BEHN 1
L. conquers all . . . . VIRGIL 8
L. is ane fervent fire . . . . SCOTT, A.(C.1525) 1
L. is enough . . . . MORRIS 1
L. is like the measles . . . . JEROME, J. 2
L. . . . law unto itself . . . . BOETHIUS 1
L. means never . . . you're sorry . . . . . . SEGAL 1
L. that dare not speak . . . . DOUGLAS, LORD 1
l.'s the noblest frailty . . . . DRYDEN 11
l. thy neighbour . . . . BIBLE: LEVITICUS ▶
l.'s young dream . . . . MOORE, T. 2

mens: *m. sana in corpore sano* . . . . JUVENAL 5
messing: m. about in boats . . . . GRAHAME 1
mezzo: *Nel m. del cammin* . . . . DANTE 1
Michelangelo: Talking of M. . . . . ELIOT, T. S. 1
middle: m. way is the safest . . . . OVID 2
mighty: How are the m. fallen . . . . BIBLE: II SAMUEL 2
miles: m. to go before I sleep . . . . FROST 1
milk: m. of human kindness . . . . . SHAKESPEARE: MACBETH 4
millionaire: Who Wants to Be a M.? . . . . PORTER 3
mimsy: All m. were the borogroves . . . . CARROLL 12
mind: the human m. in ruins . . . . DAVIES, S. 1
  my m. to me a kingdom is . . . . DYER 1
  noble m. . . . o'erthrown . . . . . . SHAKESPEARE: HAMLET 16
mine: What's m. is yours . . . . SHAKESPEARE: MEASURE 2
minion: this morning morning's m. . . . . HOPKINS 2
minister: m. kiss't the fiddler's . . . . BURNS 11
ministers: actions are my m. . . . . CHARLES II 1
minute: Not a m. on the day . . . . COOK 1
mirror: The m. crack'd . . . . TENNYSON 1
mistakes: man who makes no m. . . . . PHELPS 1
mistress: O m. mine where . . . roaming? . . . . . . SHAKESPEARE:
                                                             TWELFTH 2
mists: m. and mellow fruitfulness . . . . KEATS 5
moanday: All m., tearsday, wailsday . . . . JOYCE 5
model: very m. of a modern Major- . . . . GILBERT 3
money: licence to print your own m. . . . . THOMSON, R. 1
  love of m. is . . . . BIBLE: TIMOTHY 3
  M. has no smell . . . . VESPASIAN 1
  M. . . . most important thing . . . . SHAW 11
  no art . . . draining m. from . . . . SMITH, A. 3
  time is m. FRANKLIN 1
  You pays your m. . . . . PUNCH 2
moonlight: Ill met by m. . . . . . SHAKESPEARE: MIDSUMMER 2
morality: Feeding . . . then m. . . . . BRECHT 1
  up agen middle class m. . . . . SHAW 15
morals: no m., man? Can't afford them . . . . SHAW 14
mordre: m. wol out . . . . CHAUCER 8
more: M. than somewhat . . . . RUNYON 1
  m. things change the m. they . . . . KARR 1
  Oh, the little m. . . . . BROWNING, R. 5
morituri: *m. te salutant* . . . . SUETONIUS 2
morning: M. in the Bowl of Night . . . . FITZGERALD, E. 1
morrow: m. shall take thought . . . . BIBLE: MATTHEW 11

mortal: all men M., but themselves . . . . YOUNG 1
mother: Dead! . . . never called me m. . . . . WOOD 1
mother-in-law: savage contemplates his m. . . . . FRAZER 1
mould: Nature . . . smashed the m. . . . . ARIOSTO 1
mountains: M. will be in labour . . . . HORACE 1
mouse: always leave room for the m. . . . . SAKI 5
    ridiculous m. will be born . . . . HORACE 1
movers: m. and the shakers . . . . O'SHAUGHNESSY 1
much: So little done, so m. to do . . . . RHODES 1
muck-rakes: men with the m. . . . . ROOSEVELT, T. 2
mud: M., m., glorious mud . . . . FLANDERS & SWANN 1
murder: M. . . . Fine Arts . . . . DEQUINCEY 1
    Sooner m. an infant . . . . BLAKE 5
music: how potent cheap m. is . . . . COWARD 1
    if m. be the food of love . . . . . . SHAKESPEARE: TWELFTH 1
    M. and women . . . give way to . . . . PEPYS 2
    M. begins to atrophy . . . . POUND 3
    m. . . . brandy of the damned . . . . SHAW 6
    M. hath charms to soothe . . . . CONGREVE 4
    M. is . . . useless, as life is . . . . SANTAYANA 2
    M. is your own experience . . . . PARKER, C. 1
    M., Maestro, Please . . . . MAGIDSON 1
    Wagner's m. is better . . . sounds . . . . TWAIN 6
must: M. it be? . . . . BEETHOVEN 1
mutton: Old was his m. . . . . HOME 1
myself: M. when young did . . . . FITZGERALD, E. 3
nail: hit the n. on the head . . . . PLAUTUS 1
naked: clothe my n. villainy . . . . SHAKESPEARE: RICHARD III 2
name: In the n. of God, go! . . . . CROMWELL 1
    What's in a n.? . . . a rose . . . . . . SHAKESPEARE: ROMEO 4
nameless: n., unremembered acts . . . . . . WORDSWORTH, W. 1
naming: we have the n. of parts . . . . REED 2
narrative: find a motive in this n. . . . . TWAIN 1
narrow: n.-souled people . . . . POPE 12
nasty: n., brutish and short . . . . HOBBES 2
    n. in the woodshed . . . . GIBBONS 1
nation: N. shall speak peace unto . . . . RENDALL 1
    n. talking to itself . . . . MILLER, A. 1
nationality: Other people have a n. . . . . BEHAN 3
natural: her colour is n. . . . come and go . . . . . SHERIDAN, R. 3
    N. Selection . . . . DARWIN 1
nature: drive out N. . . . pitchfork . . . . HORACE 6
    N. abhors a vacuum . . . . SPINOZA 1

N. is a temple . . . . BAUDELAIRE 1
N., red in tooth and claw . . . . TENNYSON 7
necessary: n. not to change . . . . FALKLAND 1
n. to invent him . . . . VOLTAIRE 4
necessitee: maken vertu of n. . . . . CHAUCER 7
necessity: N. . . . argument of tyrants . . . . PITT, W. 1
needs: each according to his n. . . . . MARX, K. 2
negative: N. *Capability* . . . . KEATS 6
neglect: devotes to the n. . . . duties . . . . . . THOMPSON, W. 1
little n. . . . mischief . . . . FRANKLIN 3
neighbour: love thy n. . . . . BIBLE: LEVITICUS 1
neurosis: N. . . . avoiding being . . . . TILLICH 1
never: n. had it so good . . . . MACMILLAN 1
N. in the field of human conflict . . . . CHURCHILL 6
n. the twain shall meet . . . . KIPLING 5
nevermore: Quoth the Raven, 'N.' . . . . POE 1
new: N. lamps for old . . . . ARABIAN NIGHTS 1
news: N. value . . . . RALPH 1
newspapers: n. . . . continuous form of fiction . . . . . . BEVAN 1
newspeak: N. . . . official language . . . . ORWELL 7
night: hard day's n. . . . . LENNON 1
no: The everlasting N. . . . . CARLYLE 4
Noah: two and two unto N. into the ark . . . BIBLE: GENESIS 7
noblesse: N. *oblige* . . . . LEVIS 1
nonconformity: N. and lust stalking . . . . WAUGH 1
nose: see further . . . n. . . . . FONTAINE 3
nothing: *behind them* . . . there is n. . . . . SARTRE 1
I owe much; I have n. . . . . RABELAIS 2
knowledge of n. . . . . DICKENS 1
N. can be created from n. . . . . LUCRETIUS 1
N. has yet been said . . . before . . . . TERENCE 1
N. in his life/Became him . . . . . . SHAKESPEARE: MACBETH 3
n. is constant . . . . HERACLITUS 1
N., like something, happens . . . . LARKIN 2
n. to lose but their chains . . . . MARX & ENGELS 3
N. will come of n. . . . . SHAKESPEARE: KING LEAR 1
When you have n. to say . . . . COLTON 1
nothingness: n. shows through . . . . VALERY 1
novel: n. . . . thrown with great force . . . . PARKER, D. 2
to read a n. I write . . . . DISRAELI 8
now: N. I'll have *eine* . . . . FERRIER 1
nunc: N. *est bibendum* . . . . HORACE 8
nunnery: Get thee to a n. . . . . SHAKESPEARE: HAMLET 15

nurse: always keep a-hold of N. . . . . BELLOC 2
oaks: Tall o. from little acorns . . . . EVERETT 1
obeyed: She-who-must-be-o. . . . . HAGGARD 1
objective: o. correlative . . . . ELIOT, T.S. 10
observe: He bid me o. it . . . . DEFOE 1
Odi: *O. et amo* . . . . CATULLUS 5
offer: o. he can't refuse . . . . PUZO 1
often: cannot avoid writing 'o.' . . . . KAFKA 3
old: no man would be o. . . . . SWIFT 2
   o. familiar faces . . . . LAMB, C. 8
   They shall not grow o. . . . . BINYON 1
   they think he is growing o. . . . . IRVING 1
   You are o. Father William . . . . CARROLL 3
older: She is o. than the rocks . . . . PATER 1
one: took care of number o. . . . . MARRYAT 1
   we are o./O. flesh . . . . MILTON 12
one up: How to be o. . . . . POTTER, S. 2
open: O. Sesame! . . . . ARABIAN NIGHTS 2
opinions: many men, so many o. . . . . TERENCE 3
order: Good o. is the foundation . . . . BURKE 5
origin: indelible stamp of his lowly o. . . . . DARWIN 4
originator: Next to the o. . . . . EMERSON 7
orthodoxy: o. . . . means being wrong . . . . . . CHESTERTON 1
Oscar: You will, O. you will . . . . WHISTLER 2
out: O., damned spot! o. . . . . . . SHAKESPEARE: MACBETH 14
outside: o. and may be some time . . . . OATES 1
ovo: *Ab o./Usque ad mala* . . . . HORACE 11
owl: O. and the Pussy-cat . . . . LEAR 6
Oxford: nice sort of place. O. . . . . SHAW 5
pain: No p., no palm . . . . PENN 1
painting: P. . . . blind man's profession . . . . PICASSO 1
pale: P. hands I loved . . . . HOPE 1
paper: Imperialism is a p. tiger . . . . MAO 1
paradises: true p. are . . . lost . . . . PROUST 2
parents: The joys of p. are secret . . . . BACON 5
   P. are the last people . . . . BUTLER 4
   what p. were created for . . . . NASH 2
Paris: P. is well worth a mass . . . . HENRI IV 1
   When P. sneezes, Europe . . . . METTERNICH 1
park: p., a policeman and a pretty girl . . . . CHAPLIN 1
parlour: walk into my p. . . . . HOWITT 1
pass: shall not p. this way again . . . . GRELLET 1
   They shall not p. . . . . NIVELLE 1

past: p. is a foreign country . . . . HARTLEY 1
pastures: Woods and P. new . . . . MILTON 2
pathetic: P. Fallacy . . . . RUSKIN 2
patience: *P*.: A minor form . . . . BIERCE 4
patria: *pro p. mori* . . . . HORACE 10
patriotism: p. is not enough . . . . CAVELL 1
   p. . . . refuge of a scoundrel . . . . JOHNSON, S. 24
pay: one can p. others to do . . . . MAUGHAM 1
peace: desolation . . . call it p. . . . . TACITUS 1
   Our p. betrayed us . . . . MUIR 1
   p. for our time . . . . CHAMBERLAIN 1
   p., good will toward men . . . . BIBLE: LUKE 3
   P. hath her victories . . . . MILTON 6
   P. is poor reading . . . . HARDY, T. 1
   The Prince of P. . . . . BIBLE: ISAIAH 4
pearls: p. before swine . . . . BIBLE: MATTHEW 13
peel: p. me a grape . . . . WEST 2
peep show: ticket for the p. . . . . MACNIECE 1
pelican: wonderful bird is the p. . . . . MERRITT 1
pen: p. is mightier than . . . . BULWER-LYTTON 1
penny: not a p. off the pay . . . . COOK 1
people: Be nice to p. . . . . MIZNER 1
   fool some of the p. all . . . . LINCOLN 4
   government of the p., by the p. . . . . LINCOLN 3
   P. don't do such things! . . . . IBSEN 2
   p. . . . legislator . . . . BURKE 7
   P. wish to be settled . . . . EMERSON 6
   Thy p. shall be my p. . . . . BIBLE: RUTH 1
   two kinds of p. in the world . . . . PAPPRILL 1
perception: doors of p. . . . . BLAKE 6
petals: P. on a wet, black bough . . . . POUND 1
Peter: Thou art P. . . . . BIBLE: MATTHEW 21
petticoat: Realm in my p. . . . . ELIZABETH I 1
Philadelphia: rather be in P. . . . . FIELDS, W.C. 1
photography: P. is truth . . . . GODARD 1
physician: p. can bury his mistakes . . . . WRIGHT 1
   P., heal thyself . . . . BIBLE: LUKE 4
pie: he was put in a p. . . . . POTTER, B. 2
   p. in the sky when you die . . . . HILL, J. 1
piffle: p. before the wind . . . . ASHFORD 1
pigs: whether p. have wings . . . . CARROLL 13
Pilate: P. saith unto him . . . . BIBLE: JOHN 12
pimple: remark all these roughnesses, p. . . . . CROMWELL 3

pine-apple: very p. of politeness . . . . SHERIDAN, R. 2
pissing: inside the tent p. out . . . . JOHNSON, L. B. 1
pitch: He that toucheth p. . . . . BIBLE: APOCRYPHA 1
plagiarism: steal from one . . . p. . . . . MIZNER 2
plaisir: *P. d'amour ne dure* . . . . DE FLORIAN 1
plashy: through the p. fen . . . . WAUGH 2
play: P. it, Sam . . . . BOGART 1
  p.'s the thing . . . . SHAKESPEARE: HAMLET 13
  P. up! p. up and p. . . . . NEWBOLT 1
played: but how you p. the game . . . . RICE, G. 1
  p. with both hands in the pocket . . . . SATIE 1
pleasant: How p. to know Mr Lear . . . . LEAR 2
please: P. sir I want some more . . . . DICKENS 3
pleasure: cannot understand the p. . . . . AUSTEN 2
  Love's p. only lasts . . . . FLORIAN 1
  P. . . . seldom found where . . . . JOHNSON, S. 7
pleasures: we will all the p. prove . . . . MARLOWE 6
plot: the p. thickens . . . . BUCKINGHAM 1
plus: *P. ça change, p.* . . . . KARR 1
poacher: p. a keeper turned inside out . . . . KINGSLEY 2
pocket: Is that a gun in your p. . . . . WEST 3
poet: A p.'s hope, to be . . . . AUDEN 6
  To a p. nothing can . . . . JOHNSON, S. 10
Poetarum: *P. licentiae liberiora* . . . . CICERO 3
poetic: freedom of p. licence . . . . CICERO 3
poetry: P. . . . exact a science . . . . FLAUBERT 1
  p. = the best words in the best . . . . COLERIDGE 7
  P. . . . lost in translation . . . . FROST 6
  P. is the record . . . happiest . . . . SHELLEY 9
  P. should surprise by . . . . KEATS 7
  quarrel with ourselves, p. . . . . YEATS 8
poets: P. . . . unacknowledged legislators . . . . SHELLEY 8
  P. utter great and wise things . . . . PLATO 3
  p. . . . write in words . . . . FOWLES 1
poison: food . . . to others bitter p. . . . . LUCRETIUS 5
police: He do the P. in different . . . . DICKENS 23
policeman: how young the p. look . . . . HICKS 1
  lying when one speaks to a p. . . . . PHILIPPE 1
  p.'s lot is not a happy . . . . GILBERT 4
politician: p. is an arse upon . . . . CUMMINGS 1
  statesman is a p. who's been dead . . . . TRUMAN 2
politicians: P. are the same everywhere . . . . . . KHRUSCHEV 1
political: healthy state of p. life . . . . MILL 1

property: give me a little snug p. . . . . EDGEWORTH 1
  'What is P.?' . . . 'Theft!' . . . . PIERRE-JOSEPH 1
prophet: p. is not without honour . . . . . BIBLE: MATTHEW 19
prose: p. = words in their best order . . . . COLERIDGE 7
prosperitie: troubill efter grit p. . . . . HENRYSON 2
Protestant: Gunpowder, Printing and the P. . . . . . CARLYLE 8
proved: Which was to be p. . . . . EUCLID 1
psychiatrist: man who goes to a p. . . . . GOLDWYN 1
public: p. is always right . . . . DE MILLE 1
public schools: P. are the nurseries . . . . FIELDING 3
publish: P. and be damned . . . . WELLINGTON 3
publisher: Barrabas was a p. . . . . CAMPBELL, T. 4
pun: who could make so vile a p. . . . . DENNIS 1
punishment: object of p. is . . . . MANN 1
pure: p. as the driven slush . . . . BANKHEAD 2
  Unto the p. all things . . . . BIBLE: TITUS 1
purer: To give a p. meaning . . . . MALLARME 1
purse: Stop looking like a p. . . . . MACCAIG 2
quality: q. of mercy is not . . . . . SHAKESPEARE: MERCHANT 7
quarrel: both . . . need for a q. . . . . RONSTAND 1
  takes . . . one to make a q. . . . . INGE 1
queen: I am your anointed Q. . . . . ELIZABETH I 1
  Yestreen the Q. had four maries . . . . BALLADS 1
queer: drink to the q. old Dean . . . . SPOONER 1
  what a q. thing Life is! . . . . WODEHOUSE 1
quiet: All Q. on the Western . . . . REMARQUE 1
  my scallop-shell of q. . . . . RALEIGH 2
quietly: stay q. in a room . . . . PASCAL 1
quod: Q. erat demonstrandum . . . . EUCLID 1
quotation: Every q. contributes . . . . JOHNSON, S. 3
quoting: Q.: the act of repeating . . . . BIERCE 3
radical: never dared be r. when young . . . . FROST 3
  r. chic, ... WOLFE, T. 1
rage: R., r. against the dying . . . . THOMAS, D. 3
rain: r. it raineth on the just . . . . BOWEN 1
  r. on the just . . . unjust . . . . BIBLE: MATTHEW 6
rainbow: Somewhere over the r. . . . . HARBURG 1
rampart: his corse to the r. we hurried . . . . WOLFE, C. 1
reach: did not miss . . . dared not r. . . . . SAPPHO 1
reader: R., I married him . . . . BRONTE, C. 1
  r. seldom peruses a book . . . . ADDISON 1
reading: art of r. is to skip . . . . HAMERTON 1
  r. is to the mind . . . . STEELE 3

r. . . . like a conversation . . . . DESCARTES 3
reap: r. the whirlwind . . . . BIBLE: HOSEA 1
reason: r. of this thusness . . . . WARD, A. 3
rejoice: r. with them that do . . . . BIBLE: ROMANS 3
relations: R. are made by fate . . . . DELILLE 1
religion: no reason to bring r. . . . . O'CASEY 2
   r. but a childish toy . . . . MARLOWE 1
   R. is an illusion . . . . FREUD 2
   R. is by no means a proper . . . . CHESTERFIELD 4
   R. is the opium . . . . MARX, K. 1
   r. without science is . . . . EINSTEIN 1
   We must have r. for r.'s sake . . . . COUSIN 1
religions: collector of r. . . . . SHAW 13
remedies: Our r. oft in ourselves . . SHAKESPEARE: ALL'S WELL 1
remember: R. me when I am gone . . . . ROSSETTI 3
   r. the past are condemned . . . . SANTAYANA 1
reminded: r. than informed . . . . JOHNSON, S. 1
render: R. therefore unto Caesar . . . . BIBLE: MATTHEW 27
repay: I will r., saith the Lord . . . . BIBLE: ROMANS 4
research: steal from many . . . r. . . . . MIZNER 2
respecter: God is no r. . . . . BIBLE: ACTS 2
responsibility: r. is to his art . . . . FAULKNER 1
result: r. happiness . . . r. misery . . . . DICKENS 13
retrograde: r. if it does not advance . . . . GIBBON, E. 3
return: I shall r. . . . . MCCARTHUR 1
returns: r. home to find it . . . . MOORE, G. 1
revenge: R. is a . . . wild justice . . . . BACON 6
rhetoric: quarrel with others, r. . . . . YEATS 8
rhyme: neither r. nor reason . . . . MORE, T. 1
rich: r. are different from us . . . . FITZGERALD, F.S. 2
   r. have no right . . . property . . . poor . . . . RUSKIN 4
   r. is better . . . . TUCKER 1
riches: R. are for spending . . . . BACON 3
right: not r. . . . but victory . . . . HITLER 2
righteousness: thirst after r. . . . . BIBLE: MATTHEW 3
ring: R. out the old, r. . . . . TENNYSON 8
river: Ol' man r. . . . . HAMMERSTEIN 2
   step twice into the same r. . . . . HERACLITUS 2
riverrun: r., past Eve and Adam's . . . . JOYCE 4
road: right on to the end of the r. . . . . LAUDER 3
   rolling English r. . . . . CHESTERTON 6
robbed: We was r.! . . . . JACOBS 1
rock: upon this r. . . . . BIBLE: MATTHEW 21

silent: s. majority of Americans . . . . NIXON 1
  thereon one must remain s. . . . . WITTGENSTEIN 1
silver: s. apples of the moon . . . . YEATS 3
  S. threads among the gold . . . . REXFORD 1
similia: *S. similibus curantur* . . . . HAHNEMANN 1
sin: He that is without s. . . . . BIBLE: JOHN 6
  wages of s. is death . . . . BIBLE: ROMANS 1
  your s. will find you . . . . BIBLE: NUMBERS 1
since: S. there's no help . . . . DRAYTON 1
single: s. . . . talked of population . . . . GOLDSMITH 6
sinner: over one s. that repenteth . . . . BIBLE: LUKE 7
sinning: sinn'd against than s. . . . SHAKESPEARE: KING LEAR 3
sins: your s. be as scarlet . . . . BIBLE: ISAIAH 1
  s. were scarlet . . . books were read . . . . BELLOC 3
sisters: s. and his cousins and . . . . GILBERT 2
  s. under their skins . . . . KIPLING 8
six: s. honest serving-men . . . . KIPLING 10
  s. of one and half-a-dozen . . . . MARRYAT 2
skating: s. over thin ice, our . . . . EMERSON 5
skin: Got You Under My S. . . . . PORTER 2
skull: the s. beneath the skin . . . . ELIOT, T. S. 3
sky: Who aimeth at the s. . . . . HERBERT, G. 1
slaughter: ox goeth to the s. . . . . . . BIBLE: PROBERBS 1
slavery: S. they can have . . . . BURKE 8
sleep: S. . . . ravell'd sleeve of care . . . SHAKESPEARE: MACBETH 6
sleeping: Lay your s. head my love . . . . AUDEN 3
sleeps: Now s. the crimson petal . . . . TENNYSON 5
slouches: S. towards Bethlehem . . . . YEATS 2
slough: name of the s. was Despond . . . . BUNYAN 1
slowly: twist s., s. in the wind . . . . EHRLICHMAN 1
sluggard: 'Tis the voice of the s. . . . . WATTS 1
small: In s. proportions, we . . . . JONSON 5
  S. is Beautiful . . . . SCHUMACHER 1
smiles: Venus when she s. . . . . JONSON 4
smoke: good cigar is a S. . . . . KIPLING 4
  horrible Stygian s. . . . . JAMES VI 1
  turn s. into gold . . . . ELIZABETH I 2
smylere: s. with the knyf . . . . CHAUCER 6
snake: s. came to my water-trough . . . . LAWRENCE 5
snapper-up: s. of unconsidered trifles . SHAKESPEARE: WINTER'S 3
Snark: S. *was* a Boojum . . . . CARROLL 17
so: s. much owed . . . to s. few . . . . CHURCHILL 6
sober: s. as a judge . . . . FIELDING 2

socialism: S. with a human face . . . . DUBCEK 1
society: No s. can . . . be flourishing . . . . SMITH, A. 1
  no such thing as s. . . . . THATCHER 3
soldier: Ben Battle was a s. bold . . . . HOOD 1
something: now for s. completely different . . . . CHAPMAN, GRA. 1
  time for a little s. . . . . MILNE 6
son: gave his only begotten S. . . . . BIBLE: JOHN 4
  s. of his old age . . . . BIBLE: GENESIS 9
song: What s. the Sirens sang . . . . BROWNE 3
sorrow: Love's s. lasts . . . . DE FLORIAN 1
soul: dark night of the s. . . . . FITZGERALD, F. S. 1
  Death . . . migration of the s. . . . . SOCRATES 1
  nature of the s. . . . mortal . . . . LUCRETIUS 3
  Never mind about my s., just . . . . JOYCE 6
sound: full of s. and fury . . . . . . SHAKESPEARE: MACBETH 16
  s. . . . echo . . . sense . . . . POPE 3
sounds: s. will take care of themselves . . . . CARROLL 7
space: S. may produce new Worlds . . . . MILTON 10
  S. – the final frontier . . . . RODDENBERRY 1
spaceship: passenger on s. Earth . . . . FULLER 1
sparrow: swift flight of a lone s. . . . . BEDE 1
Spartans: Go, tell the S. . . . . SIMONIDES 1
speech: true use of s. is not . . . . GOLDSMITH 5
  where s. is not, there . . . . HOBBES 1
speed: safety is in our s. . . . . EMERSON 5
  s. the parting guest . . . . POPE 7
speranza: *Lasciate ogni s.* . . . . DANTE 2
spider: said a s. to a fly . . . . HOWITT 1
spirit: Hail to thee, blithe S.! . . . . SHELLEY 5
  s. giveth life . . . . BIBLE: II CORINTH 1
  s. indeed is willing . . . . BIBLE: MATTHEW 31
spoke: s. among your wheels . . . . BEAUMONT 2
  s. among your wheels . . . . FLETCHER 1
sport: frogs do not die in s. . . . . BION 1
stair: As I was going up the s. . . . . MEARNS 1
star-cross'd: pair of s. lovers . . . . . . SHAKESPEARE: ROMEO 1
stars: mud and one the s. . . . . LANGBRIDGE 1
  s.' tennis balls . . . . WEBSTER 1
start: If I'm late, s. without me . . . . BANKHEAD 1
state: I am the S. . . . . LOUIS XIV 1
  s. without the means . . . . BURKE 4
statistics: lies, damned lies and s. . . . . DISRAELI 7
  s. . . . look up and . . . make up . . . . STOUT 1

uses s. as a drunken man, ... LANG, A. 1
steady: S. the Buffs! . . . . KIPLING 2
steals: good composer . . . s. . . . . STRAVINSKY 1
Who s. my purse. trash   SHAKESPEARE: OTHELLO 3
stealth: do a good action by s. . . . . LAMB, C. 7
stick: carry a big s. . . . . ROOSEVELT, T. 1
stiff: Keep a s. upper lip . . . . CARY 1
still: at the s. point . . . . ELIOT, T. S. 7
stir: s. things up seemed . . . reward . . . . SALLUST 2
stomach: army marches on its s. . . . . NAPOLEON I 3
stone: let him first cast a s. . . . . BIBLE: JOHN 6
s. . . . rolling . . . no moss . . . . TUSSER 1
stones: Never throw s. at your mother . . . . BEHAN 1
storm: let the s. wash the plates . . . . MORGAN 1
story: old s. . . . forever new . . . . HEINE 1
That's another s. . . . . STERNE 3
This is the saddest s. . . . . FORD, F. M. 1
strain: s. at a gnat . . . . BIBLE: MATTHEW 28
stranger: I was a s. and ye . . . . BIBLE: MATTHEW 30
s. than fiction . . . . BYRON 9
straw: Oft stumbles at a s. . . . . SPENSER 1
streets: Down these mean s. . . . . CHANDLER 1
strength: S. through joy . . . . LEY 1
stretching: S. and Fainting in Coils . . . . CARROLL 8
strike: If you s. a child, take care . . . . SHAW 10
particularly fine, s. it out . . . . JOHNSON, S. 23
strings: two s. to my bow . . . . FIELDING 1
struggle: history of class s. . . . . MARX & ENGELS 2
perpetual s. for room . . . . MALTHUS 2
sturm: S. und Drang . . . . KLINGER 1
sublime: s. and the ridiculous . . . . PAINE 3
subordination: legal s. of one sex . . . . MILL 3
subtopia: S. . . . . NAIRN 1
succeed: If at first you don't s. . . . . HICKSON 1
To s. in the world . . . . ROCHEFOUCAULD 2
success: bitch-goddess s. . . . . JAMES, W. 2
s. . . . before work . . . dictionary . . . . SASSOON 1
true s. is to labour . . . . STEVENSON, R. L. 2
sucker: There's a s. born every minute . . . . BARNUM 1
suffering: man who fears s. . . . . MONTAIGNE 5
summer: one swallow does not make a s. . . . . ARISTOTLE 2
Summum: S. bonum . . . . CICERO 1
sun: dominions . . . s. never sets . . . . NORTH 2

going down of the s. . . . . BINYON 1
s./came peeping in at morn . . . . HOOD 2
Sunday: a rainy S. in London . . . . DE QUINCEY 2
superman: doctrine of the s. . . . . NIETZSCHE 1
support: s. rather than illumination . . . . LANG, A. 1
survival: S. of the Fittest . . . . DARWIN 2
suspects: Round up the usual s. . . . . EPSTEIN 1
suspension: willing s. of disbelief . . . . COLERIDGE 6
swallow: s. a camel . . . . BIBLE: MATTHEW 28
swans: S. sing before they die . . . . COLERIDGE 4
swindles: simple . . . truly great s. . . . . HENRY, O. 1
sword: pen is mightier than the s. . . . . BULWER-LYTTON 1
perish with the s. . . . . BIBLE: MATTHEW 32
this s. of this stone . . . . MALORY 1
swords: s. into plowshares . . . . BIBLE: ISAIAH 3
Sylvia: Who is S.? . . . . SHAKESPEARE: 2 GENTLEMEN 1
symbols: among forests of s. . . . . BAUDELAIRE 1
symmetry: frame thy fearful s. . . . . BLAKE 8
T: description . . . to a . . . . T FARQUHAR 1
tails: Heads I win, t. you lose . . . . CROKER 1
talent: T. does what it can . . . . MEREDITH, O. 1
talked: not being t. about . . . . WILDE 3
Tao: method of T. . . . . LAO-TZE 1
Tar-Baby: T. ain't sayin' . . . . HARRIS 1
tarts: Hearts, she made some t. . . . . CARROLL 10
taste: t. and fancy of the speller . . . . DICKENS 2
t. was . . . of madeleine . . . . PROUST 1
taxation: T. without representation . . . . OTIS 1
taxes: death and t. . . . . FRANKLIN 6
Tay: Bridge of the Silv'ry T.! . . . . MCGONAGALL 1
tea: T. for two and two for t. . . . . HARBACH 1
tea-drinker: hardened and shameless t. . . . . . . JOHNSON, S. 6
teach: T. me, my God and King, ... HERBERT, G. 2
while they t., men learn . . . . SENECA 1
teaches: He who cannot t. . . . . SHAW 9
tears: no t. in the writer, no t. . . . . FROST 4
teatray: Like a t. in the sky . . . . CARROLL 6
telescope: God . . . wrong end of a t. . . . . MACDIARMID 6
telling: t. of which we all wait . . . . JACKSON 1
tellt: I t. ye, I t. ye . . . . SCOTT, A. 1
tempera: *O t.! O mores!* . . . . CICERO 4
temperament: artistic t. is a disease . . . . CHESTERTON 3
tempus: *fugit inreparabile t.* . . . . VIRGIL 10

terrible: t. state o' chassis . . . . O'CASEY 1
terrorist: t. and the policeman both . . . . CONRAD 2
terrorists: t. . . . end up with drinks . . . . GAITSKELL 1
Thames: Sweet T., run softly . . . . SPENSER 3
thin: t. man inside every fat . . . . ORWELL 1
things: T. fall apart . . . . YEATS 6
think: I t., therefore I am . . . . DESCARTES 1
    Ye are not paid to t. KIPLING 7
thinking: good or bad but t. . . . . . . SHAKESPEARE: HAMLET 11
thistle: then in t. days . . . . MORGAN 3
thorn: t. in the flesh . . . . BIBLE: II CORINTH 2
thought: Only the T. Police mattered . . . . ORWELL 6
threescore: t. years and ten . . . . BIBLE: PSALMS 3
thus: I refute it t. JOHNSON, S. 21
tidings: good t. of great joy . . . . BIBLE: LUKE 2
tiger: T.! burning bright . . . . BLAKE 8
time: age, but for all t.! . . . . JONSON 3
    half as old as T. . . . . BURGON 1
    t. . . . flies . . . . VIRGIL 10
    T. held me green and dying . . . . THOMAS, D. 2
    T. is a great teacher . . . . BERLIOZ 1
    t. is money . . . . FRANKLIN 1
    T. is on our side . . . . GLADSTONE 1
    t. is out of joint . . . . SHAKESPEARE: HAMLET 8
    T., the devourer . . . . OVID 4
    t. to stand and stare . . . . DAVIES, W. 1
    T.'s wingèd chariot . . . . MARVELL 2
timor: T. Mortis conturbat me . . . . DUNBAR 1
toads: imaginary gardens with real t. . . . . MOORE, M. 1
tobacco: T. . . . remedy to all diseases . . . . BURTON 1
today: pluck the fruits of t. . . . . HORACE 7
toil: Horny-handed sons of t. . . . . KEARNEY 1
tomorrow: T. and t. and t. . . . . . SHAKESPEARE: MACBETH 16
    t. is another day . . . . MITCHELL 1
    t. we shall die . . . . BIBLE: ISAIAH 6
    what you can put off till t. . . . . PUNCH 3
tongues: t. of men and of angels . . . . BIBLE: I CORINTHIANS 2
tonight: Not t., Josephine! . . . . NAPOLEON I 4
tools: Give us the t. and . . . . CHURCHILL 7
tooth: eye for eye, t. for t. . . . . BIBLE: EXODUS 2
torch: relay the t. of life . . . . LUCRETIUS 2
tough: When the going gets t. . . . . KENNEDY, J. P. 1
tourist: loathsome is the British t. . . . . KILVERT 1

COLLINS POCKET REFERENCE

Other titles in the Pocket Reference series:

Etiquette
A practical guide to what is and what is not acceptable and expected in modern society

Speaking in Public
A guide to speaking with confidence, whatever the occasion

Ready Reference
A fascinating source of information on measurements, symbols, codes and abbreviations

Weddings
An invaluable guide to all wedding arrangements, from the engagement to the honeymoon

Letter Writing
A practical guide for anyone who needs to write letters, whether for business or pleasure

What Happened When?
Thousands of dates and events in one handy volume

(All titles £4.99)

COLLINS POCKET REFERENCE

Dictionary of Quotations

Edited by
A. Norman Jeffares & Martin Gray

A new and authoritative compilation of over 20,000 quotations drawn from familiar and not-so-familiar sources. From classical to modern times, from poets to politicians, from philophers to philanderers, from saints to alternative comedians – this is a book to browse through for enjoyment as well as a reference work that will be indispensable for home or office use.

£25.00